Expert Advice on

Gun

Dog

Training

To:
Terry Shermoe and
his fine grouse dog Setter
David Michael Duffey
June 1977

Expert Advice on

Gun Dog Training

David Michael Duffey

WINCHESTER PRESS

Library of Congress Cataloging in Publication Data
Duffey, David Michael.
  Expert advice on gun dog training.
  Includes index.
  1. Hunting dogs. 2. Dogs—Training.
I. Title. II. Title: Gun dog training.
SF428.5.D79   636.7'52   76-30596
ISBN 0-87691-195-5

Published by Winchester Press
205 East 42nd Street, New York, N.Y. 10017
Printed in the United States of America
WINCHESTER is a Trademark of Olin Corporation used by
Winchester Press, Inc., under authority and control of the
Trademark Proprietor.

DEDICATION

To a brace of darlin' daughters, Deborah Medb and Kathleen Patricia Duffey, who never complained about having to share their dad with old Twist, old Briar, old Flirt, Kraut, Poncho, and a host of others in the house and kennel, knowing that, deep down, they outranked even the best of dogs in their "old man's" heart.

ACKNOWLEDGMENTS

Professionals can be relied on. Besides the professional dog trainers who so willingly contributed their know-how for the benefit of *Expert Advice on Gun Dog Training*, some other "old pros" deserve recognition for their contributions.

To improve on and back up my own camera work, I leaned heavily on some talented photographers, as the credit lines with various illustrations indicate, and I owe some special thanks to several top-notch dog photographer friends. Among them were: Larry Mueller, Belleville, Illinois, an author and dog authority in his own right; George R. Quigley, Cincinnati, Ohio, editor and publisher of *Hunting Dog* magazine; John Friend, Columbus, Ohio; Andy Shoaff, Santa Ana Heights, California; Hugh P. (Mickey) McLinden, Madison, Wisconsin; Alan Hill, Regina, Saskatchewan; David Hasinger, Philadelphia, Pennsylvania, and Bernie Donahue, DeSoto, Missouri.

My gratitude to other professionals, whose contributions to a book are too often taken for granted, is expressed here. It was a pleasure to work for and with them. Thanks to the staff of Winchester Press for granting a time extension when personal matters interfered with the interviewing and writing that went into *Expert Advice on Gun Dog Training*. In addition, I am particularly grateful for their assigning a skillful and meticulously careful editor, Barbara Harkins, to the task of making the text read better than the original manuscript.

David Michael Duffey
Scotland Neck, North Carolina
March 1977

Contents

Introduction

Life and learning would be greatly simplified if there were only one way to skin a cat . . . or to train a gun dog . . . or to write a book. But, fortunately, there are numerous ways and means to accomplish a fixed goal and the world is full of a variety of ideas and methods. Some are good, some indifferent, and some bad.

As far as training dogs is concerned, regardless of the technique, the most important question is a pragmatic one: *does it work?* But there is also a secondary consideration when one recognizes that there is no never-fail, know-it-all, single system of doing anything. What works best for one man or for one dog may not work as well with other individuals. A somewhat different approach, a tip here and there, a unique technique might be the key to a better trained gun dog. Variety, they say, is the spice of life. It may also provide solutions for the sportsman with dog-training problems.

In the nearly two decades that I have been hunting dogs editor for *Outdoor Life* magazine, and for years before that, I have been training, hunting with, and writing about dogs. In monthly articles in *Outdoor Life*, contributions to numerous other periodicals and encyclopedias, a series of cassette tapes for Woodstream Audiolibrary, and half-a-dozen books including *Hunting Dog Know-How* for Winchester Press and *Dave Duffey Trains Gun Dogs* for Sporting Dog Specialties, I've tried to help other sportsmen attain dog-training success with a minimum amount of effort.

Reader response has indicated my personal methods have aided in the training of many thousands of hunting dogs, so another book based on what has worked for me would be both practical and useful. But such a book would also be a rehash, tilling ground already plowed. The need is for something different—new, yet tried, proven, and practical—not just some harebrained theories arrived at by someone with a flair for writing and a fortunate but limited experience with dogs and dog training.

What, or who, would provide the most reliable source of factual information and methods employed in gun-dog training? The answer is obvious —the professional trainers. What's more, the pros, the men who make their living turning out useful hunting and field trial dogs for sportsmen who haven't the talent or time to properly train their own dogs, are a largely untapped source of information, stemming from the fact that there are a number of cogent obstacles in the path of putting pros into print.

A good professional dog trainer is a busy man, doing what he does best—training dogs. He is not only short of the time required to offer instruction but he may also feel that writing about dogs is not his thing. Based on wide experience he recognizes the danger of making flat, no alternative claims, the existence of exceptions to all general rules, and that the know-how possessed by others practicing his craft may be equal or superior to his own. So the pro may be hesitant about expressing himself and reluctant to impose his methods upon a man who is undertaking to train his own dog.

Finally, while respecting hard-won, practical knowledge possessed by others, professional trainers more than anyone else hold in contempt much of the inconsequential and erroneous blather that has been written about dogs and dog training. As a result, they are often chary about being interviewed and quoted. Based on misconstrued facts, misquotes, and fanciful theories expounded by clever writers with a superficial understanding of their subject matter, men who make their living training dogs are often suspicious of men who make their living writing.

To overcome such obstacles in bringing to the reader the benefit of the best brains in the dog-training field requires careful selection of respected experts who know what they are about as well as trust and rapport between the interviewer and the expert being interviewed. I am deeply gratified by the wholehearted cooperation I was accorded by the professionals who contributed to this book, voluntarily and without recompense, for the benefit of the reader.

It was, of course, impossible to interview every proficient professional known or unknown to me. But selection was made from the best in the business, not on the basis of personal friendships, which do exist, but because I've watched them train and handle dogs in the field. They are the ones I would select to start and finish a field dog of my own for pleasure or competition, or if I encountered a specific problem difficult to cope with.

How and why professional trainers succeed in starting a gun dog properly or overcoming faults and errors committed by amateurs, or what prompts them to "wash out" a poor quality animal and recommend the owner start over with something more talented, has remained a mystery to many. This book gives the amateur trainer or the owner of a hunting dog, who cannot undertake the training himself or who has tried and made mistakes in training, an insight into and acquaintance with just how and why the experts do as they do in turning out hunting dogs that will perform up to the potential bred into all good gun dogs, be they pointing, flushing, or fetching game afield. But it also helps to achieve a better understanding between a dog's owner and the man who trains the dog, as well as providing proven methods endorsed by top professionals in the nation for the benefit and edification of "do-it-yourselvers" undertaking the training of their own dogs from start to finish.

The book is divided into three major sections, each devoted to the training of one of the three different types of "bird dogs"—pointing, flushing, and retrieving—used in North America. Within a single book's covers are detailed proper and practical means of getting the most out of your hunting dog, whether you have a spaniel, a retriever, or one of the pointing breeds. Many hunters settle on one type or one breed of dog. Others change from time to time. The proper approaches to training breeds within the three general classifications are seldom identical and frequently dissimilar. But if you switch from one type of dog to another, you needn't buy another book—just turn to the appropriate section in this one. If you need answers to specific questions, feel free to skip around as your needs dictate; or read the entire book to broaden your overall know-how and for a solid background in the training of any style of bird dog.

Each section is made up of questions and answers. It is hoped that this will make for quick and interesting reading. The questions asked of the experts and the answers each offers at varying lengths are organized in such a manner as to take the reader through a step-by-step training of gun dogs, with each expert offering in sequence his personal advice and opinions.

Thus, the methods of each expert are dealt with in the same section, making readily available for comparison and selection the advice the reader decides is most compatible with his individual personality, dog, and situation. As a reader, you are not locked in by this book; in fact, you have several choices in dealing with each training procedure. There may be suggestions from one expert that are not applicable to what you know about yourself and your dog. But in all likelihood another expert's answer to the same question will strike you as something you can undertake and succeed with if you apply it, and you may find yourself saying, "Now that makes sense to me. I ought to be able to train my dog doing that." But careful reading of all opinions will provide you with insights into how to get the job done and why it's done a particular way by each professional trainer interviewed.

As the training progresses, there will be things you will want to review or specific questions you want answered, or a certain technique you want to try on your dog. The format of the book makes it quick and easy for you to find the question that pertains to your immediate problem or concern.

Following the experts' answers to the specific questions that arise in dealing with dogs you will find a commentary by me, which constitutes a minor contribution to this book by the editor-author. The major contributions are from the professional trainers whose reputations and expertise in their fields exceed mine.

I've tried to refrain from personal opinion and advocacy of one method over the other and hope the commentary is not an intrusion or second guessing. Its purpose is to clarify or enlarge when necessary, by acting as a go-between. It's as if I were a country doctor who had referred you, the patient, to top specialists in their field of practice. And just as medical gobbledygook may go over your head, it's the general practitioner's job to interpret, if necessary, things you might find lacking in clarity.

A good book should inform in a highly readable manner. So I hope that the conversational style of this book makes it pleasant and easy to glean the information you seek about dog training. The information comes to you as it came to me off the tapes. The only thing you will be deprived of is the rich variety of accents—midwestern, southern, north of England, and German—which called for attentive listening of the tapes, as the experts tell you and me how to train dogs. There was the temptation to try to reproduce the dialects on paper, but this is impossible and could lend itself to ridicule.

Except for that and the elimination of repetitive statements, pauses, and the fumbling for the right words, with a little compromise between conversational and written English, you are getting verbatim answers to the basic questions regarding how to train a "bird dog." It is hoped that the professionals and experts offered in this book are successful in passing on to you the information you've long sought and that their individual phraseology, tempo, and expressions relieve any monotony that might crop up in one man's writing style.

This is an unusual and different book, drawn from the resources and knowledge of a group of experts who were willing to freely share their secrets with other dog devotees. It is meant to be used. Don't let it gather dust on the shelf. Take it with you when you embark on a training session or a hunting trip. Have in on hand for a ready reference. Most important, get out with your dog and do it like they tell you. Learning the right way to do it is only half the battle. Putting what you have learned into practice will determine how good your dog becomes and the rewards you'll reap from going afield with a good gun dog.

The experts you will meet in text and photos as you read the book are Epp, Gates, Smith, Kegel, Carey, Delaney, Benson, Lorenz, Isaacs, Hurst. It is *their* book! I turn you over to those who can do and have done, answering questions for the benefit of those who want to train a dog right and who appreciate some assistance in attaining that goal. Best wishes in successful training and better hunting.

PART 1

Pointers

Freddie Epp

A wide-going Gordon setter that laid down when pointing got Freddie Epp, a soft-spoken, quietly competent professional handler who has been "public training" for the past fifteen years, interested in bird dogs.

As a boy, a market hunting neighbor mounted Epp on a horse so he could spot the belly-flopping dog when it "pointed" a covey of birds. Until his father's death, Epp worked with him in his machine shop, bird dogging only as a hobby and then started his professional career by charging neighbors for training their dogs.

He spent two summers working for the John Gates organization on the Canadian prairies and a year as a private trainer for Magnolia Plantation near Albany, Georgia, before deciding he wanted to operate as a public trainer with his own kennel. (Public trainers are independent operators free to take in dogs from anyone they choose, while private trainers work for one owner or one corporation.)

As in most dog-training operations, the Epps family is an integral cog. This "unhired help" includes wife, Mary, and three teen-agers, daughter Ruth Ann and sons Ed and Roy. Epp still fondly remembers Tecumseh, a Pointer shooting dog that was his first trial winner. Rated among the top dogs he's trained and handled in the intervening years are Ch. Fabricator, Ch. Chickaboom, Ch. Just A Nip, Ch. Blackbelt, and Ch. Gail Possessed.

Epp can be reached at Route 1, Box 24-A, Marion Junction, Alabama 36759 (Phone: 205—874-7814).

Freddie Epp with Sugar Baby.

John Rex Gates

A list of the field trial champions John Rex Gates has trained and handled would fill a page. At age thirty-two he topped the record of seventy championships established by his father, the late John Gates, a Field Trial Hall of Fame member. Now at age thirty-six he has won eighty championships, more than any other past or present pro, and with a trainer's top years ahead of him will probably establish a never-to-be-broken record.

John Rex has handled two National Champions, Safari in 1966 when she was nine and Gates was in his mid-twenties, and The Texas Squire in 1972. In both those years, the Gates-handled National Champions also won the Purina Dog of the Year award, with Squire amassing the largest point total of any winner of that honor, given to the highest scoring dog and handler competing in the major trials each season.

Safari and Oklahoma Flush, another Gates dog, with ten championship wins each, are tied for the all-time high of titles acquired by dogs competing in open events. Both John Gates and John Rex Gates handled Safari to five titles each, illness forcing John Gates to retire from training. Taking over Safari from his dad for the first time, John Rex Gates guided her to the National Championship. John Gates also handled two National winners during his long career, Lester's Enjoy Wahoo in 1940 and War Storm in 1964.

Maintaining a string of brood bitches, Gloria Gates manages the puppy end of the Gates organization, which encompasses all phases of pointing

John Rex Gates poses one of his champions after winning the Quail Invitational Championship.

dog training, breeding, and development. She and John Rex have two daughters, Deborah Carol and Sheri Rex. Gates' younger brother, Robin, a college student, is training on a part-time basis. Gates can be reached at P.O. Box 72, Leesburg, Georgia 31763 (Phone: 912—759-6838).

Collier Smith

Into full-time training since 1968, Collier Smith started out assisting his Field Trial Hall of Fame father, Herman, when he was fifteen years old, growing up in the "bird dog business."

Not yet thirty, the youthful trainer has established a record as being one of the most consistent winning handlers of major stake trials in the nation. Some of the outstanding dogs Smith has trained and handled include such Pointer champions as White Knight's Button, the 1975 top-point dog in the Purina Dog of the Year competition, Warhoop Dapper Jack and Warhoop's Last Stand, and English setter champions Mr. Thor and Jimbo's Mr. Thor. Smith also conducts a twice-a-year training seminar in cooperation with *Hunting Dog* magazine instructing amateur owners in the proper care, training, and handling of bird dogs at the Smith Kennels and training grounds. The Smith operation encompasses breeding, training, and selling gun dogs as well as field trial campaigning.

Smith's father, who won the 1957 National Championship with Wayriel's Allegheny Sport, is semiretired but available for consultation, and his younger brother, Rod, is an active assistant in the training and scouting during trial competition. Smith and his wife, Suzanne, have two small children, Reid and Marietta.

Smith can be reached at Smith Kennels, Star Route, Box 177, Hatchechubbee, Alabama 36858 (Phone: 205—667-7847 or 667-7946).

Collier Smith fondles a young bird dog, Rex's Herman, right after announcement was made that he had won the 1976 Dixie Puppy Classic.

What were your reasons or what influenced you to decide to specialize in training Pointers and Setters primarily, rather than other breeds of gun dogs?

Epp: I decided to train bird dogs because I like to hunt and like to work with bird dogs. My dad told me when I was a boy that nothing was really work unless there was something else you'd rather be doing, and there's nothing else I'd rather do than work a bird dog.

Gates: My reason, simply, is I grew up in it and liked it. There is a different challenge every day. I like the running-type dog and I believe we get more of that with Pointers and Setters. There's just more challenge in breaking that type of dog.

Smith: I just more or less inherited it. Pointers and Setters were what my father trained all the time and having grown up in it, it just came natural. This gets in your blood. I don't believe anyone in the dog business ever gets out completely. They may leave for a year or two but they always come back. There wasn't as much money in it as working in the business world or something like that but being your own boss, being outdoors, breathing fresh air, being in a different place every week and doing something different all the time is worth a great deal.

Do you look for any physical traits that might give an individual dog an edge in his training and work? Are there traits of temperament or disposition that indicate to you that the dog you are dealing with may be relatively easy to train or be difficult? In effect, describe your kind of dog.

Epp: I'm not an authority on picking out a dog's build, what that build makes him capable of. I just don't want any abnormalities about his structure. Of course, I like a high-tailed dog, one that uses his tail when he's running, as well as a dog that has a reasonably long stride so he doesn't overwork himself running.

As far as temperament, naturally I like a dog that seems somewhat responsive. I don't like a dog that shows too much cowardice, especially working him in the yard on a check cord. I try to avoid dogs that lay down, don't want to be caught, the shy sort of dog.

Gates: The ideal prospect? There's no such thing. I like a dog with brains, one that displays boldness, good temperament, and character. Of course, he also has to have a good nose. I look for a classy-type dog that has a good high tail, that carries himself well and stands up on his feet, with enough legs to carry him over the cover instead of through it. His finishing-out weight should be from 45 to 55 pounds, possibly to 60. A dog that's too big usually won't make the distance, won't carry himself too well.

Smith: I like a dog that looks good when you walk down the kennel, one that has a good square head, stands up on his toes, carries his tail in a lively manner. The way competition is now in field trials, by the third day the judge has been looking at dog after dog and he's sore and he's aching. The dog must have a little extra something that catches the judge's eye in order for him to be a winning dog.

19

Backed by judges and reporters, two winning handlers, John Rex Gates, left, and George Moreland, right, pose the winner and runner-up in a championship event. Note the lean, hard-muscled condition of the dogs.

Each dog has a different personality, just like people, and I prefer a dog that wants to be around people, likes people, likes to be petted. The days of cold-blooded, runaway dogs are gone. There's just no place, and not enough time, to run dogs like that any more.

The same criteria apply to the shooting dog. Whether you want him for field trials or hunting, you want a dog that's got good conformation, especially if you're going to breed him, since anything that's bad, like an undershot jaw, will be passed on. It's just as important for a hunting dog to have stamina, and all that, as a field trial dog because actually people hunt a whole lot longer than the hour that makes up a field trial heat. And, somehow, a bird just seems to taste better if it's killed over a dog with a little class, a good gait and everything.

At approximately what age, recognizing variations in individual dogs, do you prefer to have a dog brought to you for training? For what reasons?

Epp: I don't like to have a dog brought in under a year old. I would like to get them younger but I don't feel I can justify my normal charging rate on a dog that young, for what I can do to him. But if the dog has had reasonable care at home and some handling, I think a year old is about right for starting training on him so you can teach him something and give a man some constructive work for his money.

Gates: Normally, one year to eighteen months, because the dog is mentally and physically developed enough to work with at this time. If a trainer could get a puppy and fool with it, that would be real good. But it's just not economical for an owner to put a puppy with a handler, considering what he can accomplish. But fooling with a puppy is a great thing for an individual who can take the puppy along himself.

Smith: I like to get dogs at about nine months old if they've had any experience at all at home, if their owners have taken them out, played with them, had them in the field a little bit so they know how to run in cover, and stuff like that. If the owner doesn't have time to do this, then I like to raise the pup myself. I have several customers who don't have the time but like a good dog. So I keep the pup from the time he's eight weeks old, and in the spring we start fooling with these January puppies in the field, teaching them to pattern.

Too many people make the mistake of going to the field with the pups in the truck. They open the door and just sit there and watch the pups run all around. When they send pups like that to a trainer, it's like taking a box of rabbits out in the field and turning them loose to run them. They just go every which way.

Knight's Battle Button—probably the best dog I ever trained—was a good example of starting a pup right. But when he was brought to us, about 50 to 75 yards was all he'd run. He was busy as he could be, but he'd stop, look at you as if to see where you were going. We were just walking along with the horse and he was always running in that pocket, that 45 pocket, in front. The more birds he got in and the stronger he got, the more he widened out. But he was always in the front, and he maintained that ground pattern from the very first.

I had another customer and the first fifteen dogs he brought to us just ran everywhere under the sun, no pattern, and yet they probably had had two hundred hours in the field before being brought to us. But the owner didn't know that it is important from the time the pup is five, six, or seven months old to start him, develop those basic things, let the dog develop a gait, try to get him in as many birds as you can and not punish him for anything, unless he's been chasing cars or something like that.

What steps can a dog's owner take to help ensure that the pup will be trainable and the formal training job made easier when he brings the dog to you?

Epp: First, regarding the care of the dog, I think it's wrong for the dog to have a self-feeder. This generally causes the owner to do a lazy job and he doesn't look at the dog much, doesn't handle him as much. The dog that is fed manually is naturally going to get more contact. Of course, the owner should also add some handling, get the dog out, walk with him, go fishing with him, get him out in the field. From a little puppy on, the dog should be in constant contact with the owner. I don't think he has to give him any formal training, any discipline. Mostly he's making the dog's life happy, and that's good. Really, just giving a lot of time to his dog, making the dog like him, that's the main thing an owner can do.

Gates: Maintain the pup in good physical condition and keep him in a pleasant environment. I would suggest taking the pup out for daily walks in the field as much as possible and not putting any demands on him, since the pup needs his freedom to obtain aggressiveness and boldness, to develop mentally in the correct way. Then at about a year of age, the pup should be ready to start with some training.

If the owner has a litter, or picks a pup from the litter, he should start fooling with them when they are three, four, five weeks old, about the time he usually starts to feed them along with the bitch's feeding. When out there feeding, back off and start shooting a cap pistol over them and get into something a little heavier when they get a bit older. And when they're old enough to go out in the field, take them out, walk with them, don't put any pressure on them or make any demands. Just walk them. Let them do their own thing.

Smith: The main thing is if a pup is obtained from someone else, *don't* just put him in the kennel until he's seven, eight, or nine months old, old enough to take in the field. Instead play with the pup every day, have the pup in the house with the family. If you're figuring on a major circuit dog, have him around horses and other dogs. This may not be necessary with a gun dog.

If a dog knows that every time you put your hands on him you're not going to punish him, it makes him easier to train. Don't teach him to heel on a rope. That interferes with a trainer's check cording him in the summer. We've had dogs come in that were taught to heel perfectly but when we put them in the field with that rope attached to their collars they just wanted to walk alongside us and didn't hunt like they ought to.

Most anything owners can do to save the trainer time—teach the pup to come, to lead, fool with them—is good. If owners have the time to fool with the pup, take him out two or three times a week, walk with him in the field, get him started, they're doing the same thing I'm going to do with him up until he gets old enough to break. If the guy has the time, I'd just as soon he keep the pup and run him in the field until he starts flash-pointing, then bring him in.

If an owner chooses to train his own dog, are there ages or stages a puppy or young dog goes through when he will learn certain things more readily than at any other time?

Epp: There are times when a dog can learn some things better than others. Ordinarily we yard-break dogs before we really break them in the field. With the dogs that don't yard-break well we skip this and give them field training first and then sort of mix the yard training in as they get used to it. Ordinarily a dog can take this at a year old but a particular dog might vary.

As to pointing, I think you have to watch the dog hunting. When he begins to flash-point or hold briefly, that's the time to steady the dog. This would show up at a certain time in his development. A dog will generally give you a sign of whether he's capable of standing or not standing, and if you watch maybe you can catch that sign.

Gates: As I mentioned in answer to a previous question, I would put no training on the pup until he is a year old. But, again, a very important factor in the development of a young dog is getting him out of the kennel and walking with him in the field until he is old enough to start his formal training. If you've brought him along pretty well in the field as a pup, from a year to two years is the time to get all the basic things done with him. If you don't, he's going to develop habits and traits of his own and it's going to be hell breaking him.

Smith: If the owner is going to train his own dog he has to understand that it's got to be constant repetition. He can't go out on Saturday and Sunday and break his dog while leaving him in the kennel Monday through Friday.

The dog has to do basic things himself. For example, you can't make a dog point. That's got to be bred into him. You run the dog until he starts pointing. Then you can break him. The main thing is don't try to break him too early. The first time he points is not the time to break him.

Just don't try to carry him too fast. Different dogs learn at different paces. If you've got the birds and you're working more than one or two dogs, you can tell which dogs learn quick and which don't. But don't try to rush it and take it too fast. That's the main thing.

Assuming that for different people there are different choices, under what circumstances will someone buying a dog be best satisfied with a puppy, a started dog, or a trained dog?

Epp: I think a bird hunter who hasn't hunted a lot and is beginning to get interested in it might like a puppy, maybe a small, weaned puppy to start with, rather than an older dog. No doubt he's hunted with somebody's trained dog and got the idea he'd like to train one himself. It would be good for him to go through this. A person who lives in town and doesn't have a place to keep puppies or develop them probably would do better to buy a trained dog. Or a person who just doesn't have the knack, the patience, to develop a dog should get a trained dog.

People who like field trial dogs but may want to develop them themselves should consider a started dog, say a pup that's old enough to show whether he *will* run, maybe fit the description that they like.

Gates: Choosing a pup is a rather difficult task. I'd look for a pup with a good tail, boldness, independence, and above all with proven breeding. I'd consider the markings but not let it be a deciding factor. In the started dog, I'd look for the same factors as in the pup, but at this stage the dog's ability to handle his nose should be considered. For a trained dog, I would get the dog that would suit my situation, the type of game and the type of country I planned to do most of my hunting in, at all times staying with a class dog.

If you've got the time and everything, you'll probably be best satisfied starting with a puppy. But, of course, there's a long way to go from puppy to a trained dog. And you might go through several puppies before you get a trained dog. The cheapest and quickest way to get a good dog is to buy a trained dog, but you don't get the self-satisfaction of bringing him along from a puppy.

Style and intensity frost the cake when a good gun dog Pointer is working. Seairup Twist, shown here on Missouri quail, virtually trained herself hunting with her owner, Dave Duffey.

Smith: The cheapest way to get a dog that's trainable, if you want just a hunting dog, rather than going to the trouble of breeding a puppy and raising him, is to buy a dog already trained. Anyone who has only a day or two a week to hunt would be better off buying a dog already broke. Someone retired or in business for himself, who has leisure time, will get a lot of enjoyment and a lot of exercise, too, out of fooling with a young dog. It just depends on how much leisure time you've got to train a young dog. If you're in a hurry and want a dog ready for hunting season, the best way is to buy a trained dog. If you have the time, want the satisfaction of breeding and raising something out of your own bloodlines, training the dog yourself, stuff like that, then you're the type of person who should buy a puppy or start off with a young dog.

Describe a started dog in terms of what the buyer of such a dog might expect with regard to obedience and hunting ability. In other words, what has a started dog learned and what can he do?

Epp: With a started dog I think most people are expecting a dog that's been taken afield, that knows what birds are, has probably started to point, and is yard-broke at least to the degree that he knows his name and knows what "Whoa!" means. It doesn't mean the dog will hold his game or be finished but he should have a reasonable amount of experience. I'd compare it to a kid in the sixth grade, who you'd call a started one, and another in the twelfth grade, who you'd call a trained one.

Gates: A started dog is a dog that is thoroughly yard-worked. He should know his fundamental commands, should have been introduced to game in the fields, and should be demonstrating an ability to hunt. He should be liking birds, chasing birds, maybe beginning to point some.

24

Smith: The definition of a started dog would probably be a little different with each dog trainer. But in our case a started dog would point and hold until you got there, and if everything went fine would be steady to wing and shot. But, if not, the dog would probably break when the birds got up. Most people who hunt don't care if the dog is steady to wing and shot. It's just simpler for us to break him steady to wing and shot and then if the hunter wants to let him go ahead and become unbroke, that doesn't take very long, especially if other dogs he hunts with aren't steady.

If a guy called me up and wanted a started dog, it would be a dog that handled to the front, that knew "Whoa!," "Come Here!," "Heel!" and would point maybe 90 percent of his birds, might get a little reckless once in a while, and would have had probably three months' work. We don't do a whole lot of work on force-retrieving or retrieving. We just kill birds over every dog in training and by the time they're trained, unless there's something wrong and they don't like dead birds, they'll usually retrieve.

What tips would you offer for the selection and purchase of a puppy to help assure the buyer that he will be getting a sound, healthy pup that should be potentially trainable?

Epp: Provided the pups are in good health, you should look for conformation to the point of not selecting a dog with an undershot jaw. We're

When a dog does right he can be called to you and praised as Freddie Epp does with a young Pointer.

Top

Mrs. David Hasinger, Philadelphia, Pa., moves in to flush a planted quail in front of the Pointer while a field-type Irish setter backs during a training session in the Northeast. (David Hasinger photo)

Bottom

The strong-flying quail flushes and will be shot by Mrs. Hasinger, while the Pointer stays steady to wing and shot. (David Hasinger photo) getting a lot of dogs bred this way now, and it's been my experience that a dog with an undershot jaw is a little bit off in the brain. I'd look at that right off and wouldn't want a pup that had that fault.

The dog should have a decent looking head, not deformed, and he should have a good tail set on him. By a good tail I mean one that comes high up out of the back. If it comes out too low, there's no way that a dog can point with a high tail or run with one. You might say you're not interested in style, but if a dog's got a low tail, you're generally going to have trouble with a sore, bloody tail. There's a little bit about disposition, too. If the pup doesn't want you to get your hands on him, you ought to shy away from him yourself.

Gates: Obtain a pup from proven bloodlines and purchase from a reliable source.

Smith: The best thing to do is buy from reputable people any time you're buying over the telephone or through the mail. If you select the pup in person, you can pick the one from the litter that suits you best. Pick one that has a tail and markings and conformation that you like. I'd ask whether the pup has had his distemper shots and been wormed. Most reputable breeders, if the pup turns up with hip dysplasia, deaf, or something serious like that, will replace the puppy and won't object to you having the pup checked by a veterinarian. Or the breeder may already have done so.

Do you have any particular guidelines or rules of thumb in your approach to training pointers that govern your actions around dogs and make training efforts easier, quicker, better? Some do and don't suggestions?

Epp: One of the most important things to watch in a dog when you're training is his eyes. When you administer even mild discipline in the form of training, you may jerk on the rope to teach him to stop, or you may upset a dog hard when teaching him to stand shot. A dog's eyes show fear or enjoyment. If his eyes show fear when you give him that jerk, then you're giving him too much. If he shows fear or cowardice without sufficient pressure to cause that, you generally want to quit that dog pretty quick.

There are other rules I use as a professional trainer. I've got a rule that when I'm working a dog, if he ever leaves me to go back to the truck or the kennel, if he goes back three times I quit that dog. It's a sure sign he's a quitter and you never will make anything out of him.

Gates: Never rush your training. Never try to go through too many steps at one time; when you start with a dog teach him one thing at a time before you leave it. This is done by repetition. But be careful not to overdo it and stop with your training each day when the dog is still enthusiastic and interested.

Remember never to lose your temper. If you do, both you and the dog will suffer from it. If you do lose your temper, put your dog back in the kennel that day. By your next training session your emotions will have cooled, your dog will be fresh, and you'll probably be surprised at how much better he will do.

Never go out to train your dog thinking that punishment is the only way to success. When he does right, reward him with a good pat on the head.

Smith: The main thing is to learn to control your temper. If you get mad, the best thing to do is just pick the dog up and put him on the wagon, sit down and smoke a cigarette or drink a cola until you get hold of yourself. No one can control an animal of any kind—horses, dogs, or what have you—until they can control themselves.

You can undo more in a fit of anger in five seconds than you can do for a dog in five years of patient work. For some reason dogs know the difference between discipline dealt evenhandedly and discipline dished out in a fit of rage. When you've reached the point where you're screaming at the dog, you're not doing any good. You're better off just to hush for a minute or so and then speak to him in a lower tone of voice.

Also, training animals is basically repetition. Try to do a little bit every day, instead of all in one day.

What, if anything, must a field trial dog possess to a greater degree, regarding natural ability, than a reasonably good hunting dog? Or is it primarily the type and quality of training that makes the difference?

Epp: A field trial dog really has to be a more superior animal than the ordinary hunting dog. He's got to have more determination, more ability, more brains, more stamina. By ability I mean ability to take training and possibly think for himself. In a gun dog we can accept faults. A dog that can locate birds, even if he roots them up, if you're close enough to shoot you can get by. A field trial dog can't do that. A gun dog can point with a low tail, lay down even, and you can shoot birds over him. But a field trial dog can't win with that.

A hunting dog can run a reasonable amount and find birds but a field trial dog has to measure up to a certain standard of distance, particularly an all-age dog. So while they both have to want to point birds, after that there's a whole lot of difference in the dogs.

Gates: In my judgment field trials play a great role in improving the breed. Hence we look for the highest standards in quality in the individual dog—style, nose, and so forth. A dog that doesn't quite measure up in all these qualities might still be a good gun dog.

It takes more time and training for a field trial dog, because basically this dog is a showman and should show and display his training in the best form.

Smith: Field trial dogs have to have more class than a gun dog. Whether a gun dog points with a level tail, a 45-degree tail, or a tail hanging straight down doesn't affect how many birds you kill. But a field trial dog has to have class, he has to run with class—something to catch the judge's eye. That's the main difference.

The trainer basically polishes the field trial dog more than anything else, besides teaching him to be steady to wing and shot. What separates the trainers is the degree of polish a top trainer can put on the dog, the class, the style, and leave everything in him. His handler also knows the dog's faults and handles him to cover up the defects in the dog. What he's doing is acting, really, trying to present an even performance for the judge.

A gun dog might not be real classy, but if he's got the best nose in the world you might be able to kill ten times the birds over him than over the one that's got a nice tail and everything. But the field trial dog needs that class and a little faster gait to get the judge looking at him. A dog that's hunted all day long is not going to have the speed that a field trial dog has. And nobody would run a field trial dog all day long.

Of the many dogs you have trained to be reasonably good hunting dogs and field trial competitors, what percentage of all dogs that were successfully trained had the potential to be field trial winners?

Epp: Possibly 10 percent of the dogs brought to me have the capability of being field trial dogs. Of course, I don't mean that all those will be great dogs, but I believe that many could be winners, although some wouldn't go past puppy and some not past derby. By and large, the biggest percent of dogs that are trained are good dogs to hunt with but they lack perfection in certain qualities, which prevents them from becoming field trial dogs.

Gates: Somewhere in the neighborhood of 10 to 15 percent of our dogs have potential field trial breeding, in other words top breeding, behind them.

Smith: Everybody's got a different idea about that. On a yearly average, I'd say we pick twenty to thirty young dogs in the spring. First we pick dogs we think are trainable. Then we try to pick out those we think have field trial potential. Say we start training thirty young dogs in July, by August 15 there are probably ten to fifteen that are still in the field trial category. By the time the quail Futurity comes along, there's probably six or seven of them that go on through the derby year. Then of those six or seven that complete the derby year, there's going to be only one or two that makes a real all-age dog.

Field trial standards have been established, but what constitutes a good hunting dog is largely a matter of personal opinion. What are the minimum requirements, what should a bird dog be able to do, to be considered a reasonably good hunting dog?

Epp: A good bird dog's main purpose in life is to find and point birds for the gun. To do this, a dog has to have a good nose. He's got to have desire to find those birds. He has to have a good enough physical makeup to carry his nose and brains around to point the birds. So he can't be crippled or deformed. But the main things are nose and desire and the willingness to hunt, not run off.

As to the degree of training on the hunting dog, it's not really necessary that he be steady to wing and shot. But I do think a good hunting dog, one I like to hunt over, should be able to retrieve, and he definitely ought to hold point and let the hunter flush the birds. Generally, you should be able to call a hunting dog in and put him where you want him. A lot of hunting is on single birds, where you'll have to help him, and if he's not

Retrieving two birds at once is quite a stunt for any dog to pull off, but a staid old momma Pointer does it with aplomb here.

biddable he's not going to find them. So handling response is an important facet.

Gates: I would want a dog to be bold and eager in what he does. He must have a good nose, class, cover the ground good, and hunt with a purpose.

Smith: Everybody likes different things. Personally, I think it'd be easier to find a man a wife than a dog that suits him. To be reasonably good, a gun dog would first of all have to point, he'd have to have a good nose and find a lot of birds. If you hunt from horseback, you want a little wider dog than if you hunt from foot.

A lot of people who don't want any of our good stuff come into the kennel. They just want a dog that won't run off and leave them and one that will point, back, and retrieve. Our good dogs don't run off, and they point, back, and retrieve. But they range too wide for most hunters.

In the past five or six years, the range that's wanted for a hunting dog has gotten closer and closer. For a while everyone wanted a horseback dog in range. Now they want a real close dog. A large number of people we work dogs for have gone to Brittanys [Brittany spaniels]. They're close working dogs. The hunting grounds are gone. People load up in a jeep and go to this place, hunt a little while, get back in the jeep and drive down the road to the next field, and so on. It's obviously a matter of individual taste.

The first question buyers ask is "Does he point, back, and retrieve?" The second question is "How much does he cost?" Then the third question is "How wide does he run?"

Can one dog be both hunter and field trialer? How often does this actually occur? If it is usually impractical for an owner to expect to have a "two-in-one" dog, what factors prevent this from occurring much more frequently?

Epp: I think a dog can double as a hunting dog and as a field trial dog, but this has to be within bounds. It doesn't happen very often because the people who want to hunt the dog will probably hunt him too long, too ardently. Hunt him too long and it's going to make the dog slow up; then when you get him in a field trial, he's not going to give you a good snappy lick and the judges are not going to look at him.

Also, when you're hunting it's easy to get into single birds and hack that dog around, not let him go, make him hunt in close, handle or hunt dead birds. Of course, this is just the opposite of what is needed in a field trial dog. So in doubling a dog as a shooting dog and a field trial dog, you need to remember not to hunt him too long so that he gives you that "all-day" lick. Don't hold him in too long against his will, stopping him from

A big-boned, big-going Pointer, Warhoop Eagle Rip, owned by a Montgomery, Ala., veterinarian, Dr. L. C. Cardinal, shows proper pointing form.

Extreme intensity and style is displayed by this well-bred young Pointer. (George Quigley photo)

reaching out. The dog is liable to be confused if one day you expect him to point a covey of birds, then turn him loose and make him hunt around, hunt singles for twenty minutes, then pull out; but then the next day you have a find at a field trial and expect him to pull out immediately.

It can be done but it has to be done with judgment. Think what you're doing to the dog and conditioning him for.

Gates: Yes, a dog can be both hunter and field trialer, but the owner has to be well tutored and at all times, while hunting, keep in mind that he is going to compete with his dog in trials. For example, going out and shooting over him with an automatic shotgun, letting him break shot and doing things that would be against his formal training, would be absolutely disastrous if you want to continue running him in trials. But it is good to kill birds for your dog while you are working him.

Smith: There's a lot of cases where people trial the dog they hunt over. But at the all-age level there's very few—maybe one in a hundred, even two hundred, maybe a few more if the hunting was from horseback—that a man could run in an all-age stake and then go bird hunting with the next day.

A lot of dogs in the amateur stakes are hunted and then they're brought to us to ready for amateur trials. If a man has a dog that's got the class, got the gait, and everything to win field trials, and he wants to hunt him, he can do it if he'll not get gun-happy and bird-greedy—instead of shooting six times on a rise, shoot one or two times and keep the dog steady.

That's how I train my dogs. Take White Knight's Button [1975 Purina Bird Dog of the Year]. We took him out from the kennel, turned him loose, kept him out there about 150 to 500 yards in range, hunted and killed birds over him, maybe on every other rise, every third rise, something like that.

Clyde Morton [recognized as one of the all-time top trainers, now deceased] always said he never went to work a dog, he always went hunting. That's the name of the game, killing birds over them.

If the owner will take a dog that's steady to wing and shot, one that's capable of winning trials, he can go kill all the birds in the world over him if he'll make sure he keeps him steady. Then he can hunt him today and go win a field trial with him tomorrow.

If there are variations in your approach to training a hunting dog and a field trial dog, other than more intensive and longer training for the competition dog, what procedures do you emphasize, add, or eliminate in training the hunting dog?

Epp: The main difference that I find with hunting dogs and field trial dogs is probably just range. I try to break them all the same way on game. I steady my hunting dogs just like I do the field trial dogs, teach them to back one another. But I don't encourage the hunting dogs to run any. I make them mind better, turn quicker. If your field trial dog is too biddable, when your opposing handler has to get pretty rough in calling his dog, he's going to turn yours, too. A hunting dog won't have this problem; you only have to call him two or three times where you know the dead birds are to call him in.

The only real difference in training hunting dogs and field trial dogs is that the hunting dog must be trained to be more biddable and keep his range closer.

Gates: It is a longer and more intense program for the field trial dog. The field trial dog is going to compete and has to show a quality of training in the highest standards.

Smith: We basically try to start out the same way, training the gun dog steady to wing and shot just like the field trial dog unless the owner doesn't care about it. We might even train some gun dogs longer than we would field trial dogs. The problem is, if you take the field trial prospect and grind him two or three hours, three days a week, you cut down on his speed, give him an all-day gait.

A young Pointer remains steady as his trainer flushes a bird during a training session. (Larry Mueller photo)

We might take some meat dogs out and hunt half a day, particularly if the dog's a little wide, because that's the way the guy is going to hunt him when he takes him home—he's going to hunt him half a day. Basically we train the same but we would often work a gun dog a longer heat than we would a field trial dog.

Explain the term "yard breaking" or "yard training." Do you yard-break a bird dog before you take him afield or do you allow a dog to do what comes naturally for some time before you start disciplining him? Why?

Epp: If a dog's old enough to take training when he comes to me, has been handled a reasonable amount and hunted some, the first thing I do is to yard-train the dog. I might take him out and run him two or three times just to get him familiar with me so his first encounter with me is not unpleasant.

As soon as that's over I like to yard-train—come when I call his name, stay there when I say "Whoa!" Some dogs just can't take this training all at once, and this has to be done at a later date. But most can. If they can't, take them hunting and sort of sneak it in while you're training the dog in the field. For instance, when you've got the dog in the field trailing a check cord, just step on that rope and the instant you step on it say "Whoa!" Then get to him and pet him up. It comes so quick to him it surprises him and he doesn't know just when you can whoa him. A little of this while he's hunting doesn't make him want to quit, and yet he's learning right along.

Gates: The term yard breaking means to get the dog ready for his training. Simply get him used to the check cord, the basic command of "Whoa!" and to come when called. This starts developing his mind and associates him with his trainer. This procedure should be first done after your puppy routine.

Smith: We allow a dog to do what comes naturally for a certain period of time as long as it's the right thing. The first morning that we take him out, if the pup goes with the horses, stays in front, and can be picked up easily, we won't yard-break him until he's ready to break on game, to steady to wing and shot. If the pup's behind, gone all the time, we'll go to yard breaking, teaching him to come when we call and lead and all that kind of stuff.

The term yard breaking means teaching him to stand at the command of "Whoa!" while you walk around in front of him and make like you're flushing birds. Or when you're running him in the field, if you want him to stop and get a direction, you tell him "Whoa!" and he's supposed to stop.

We do a great deal of our yard work in the spring. We give our dogs considerable experience in the field, where they're running loose and pointing birds and we're getting to them. And then we don't turn them loose again until we've got them steady to wing and shot on the rope. After that, we drop the rope and lope right along behind them until they're steady to wing and shot without the rope and then we back off a little bit, let them stand there a little longer on point. We gradually work down to where they don't have anything on them, no hobbles, no ropes, nothing.

A dog's eyes and expression will tell his handler a lot and while locked up here, Jeb, a litter brother to Stupido, shown on page 47, indicates he's not at all sure he should have established point.

Dogs should be stroked and their tails teased, as Dave Duffey does here with a young Pointer bitch, early in their training when they lock up on birds.

If a dog is biddable, handles good, handles easy, keeps in touch—whatever description you want to use—describe his actions and what he is doing while out hunting. How do you train to instill this behavior?

Epp: A biddable hunting dog wants to hunt, he wants to find the game but at the same time he doesn't want to forget his handler. He's almost going to want to be within sight, or at least within hearing, of that handler. He's going to make casts to objectives when he hunts the area out. If he's lost contact with the handler, if within sight he should stop, look, and see which way the handler's going and go to the next objective in that direction. He wants to please the handler and find birds in front of him.

It's important for the dog to hunt with the handler because a lot of times you'll be hunting small places where you don't have permission to hunt on the adjoining land, or there may be roads around. So this biddable dog would watch the handler and hunt to the front, but still have that desire to find game. In training a dog to do this, you have to be careful not to give it to him too quick, otherwise you get his mind completely on minding the handler and he'll forget about finding birds. So it's a sort of touch and go thing. Just don't get in too big a hurry.

To teach a dog a turn signal if he gets to going too far, we give him a "Huh! Huh!" command, which is a sharp sound that a dog's ear can pick up and which isn't likely to be confused with the softer "Whoa!" that means stop. When we start a dog he's dragging a check cord, and if he doesn't turn when we holler we just ride our horse up there and step on that line, and the second the horse steps on that line we give him the call. A few times of that and the dog will generally begin to respond and turn to the call.

We release the dog on two toots on the whistle, and after constant releasing he learns that's the "go" signal. When you're teaching the turn signal, if he doesn't turn enough turn him a little more and when he's started in the right direction give him the go signal—toot, toot—on the whistle. It gets to be sort of a sign language for the dog.

Gates: A biddable dog should handle with ease and be a good hunting companion. A lot of this must be born in a dog if he is ever to have it to any great extent. Of course, there are training methods, repetition, that can help to develop this.

Smith: A dog that is handling good, to me, is one that stays in front in that 45-degree pocket and quarters if the objectives are such that the dog can go to them in that pattern. A dog that handles good is going to stop and look every once in a while to see which way you're going, or catch your direction from your horse if he doesn't stop. But he's not going to have any extended periods of absence, when he's not listening. When you holler at him two or three times, if he's handling well, he's going to turn.

My dad's theory on training dogs is that you can't expect a dog to do out there half a mile away what he won't do right in front of you. Train them right when you've got them under absolute control and then gradually work them out.

If you have a true running dog, nothing you do is going to stop him from running. But if you've worked him in tight country, when you take him to the field trial he's going to run, but he'll handle better, be more biddable, than a dog that's just running big.

We spend a great deal of time in the summer with the dog in a harness on a long rope, teaching him to hunt in front of the horse. We call it check cording. This goes on until the dog is broke in that roading harness, until he's steady to wing and shot.

A dog has to learn to "Heel!" not behind but in front of the horse. When a scout goes over there and gets the dog, if the dog's heeling behind the horse he's not going to point the birds. If he's hunting 20 to 25 yards in front of the horse, he's going to smell the birds in time so the scout can stop before he rides them up. It'll look like he came up on the dog on point.

With a hunting dog the range would be a lot shorter, but you do basically the same thing on a rope—get him into birds when you have control of him, then direct him out to the next place where there are birds or where you've put some out.

Describe how you teach a dog his name and to come to you when called.

Epp: With most dogs it can be done with the check cord, and the biggest part can be done in the yard. A little reward will help with some dogs. If you've got the dog out on the end of the cord, walk away from him, call his name; if he doesn't come, give him a light jerk. When he comes to you, praise him, pet him up. Some dogs, one of those rough dogs, for example, may take a harder jerk, some might even require a spike collar. When they get so they'll do this good on a check cord in the enclosed yard where they can't get away, then take the check cord off and call them in.

A lot of them aren't going to come even though they know that their name means come. They are willfully disobeying. So you can go there, pinch his ear, slip your spike collar on and give it a jerk, take it off, step back and call him again. Then when he does learn to come in the yard, you take him to the field. You may have to go all over the same thing. If he doesn't come, you've got to run him down, switch him, give him another jerk, etc., anything to tell him he's doing wrong and to make him come to you. He's got to find out that if he doesn't come to you he's going to get caught and punished. But you don't want to punish him too much. Just enough to let him know he's done wrong, not to the point where he doesn't want to come to you.

Gates: Teaching a dog his name and to come to you is mostly repetition, using the dog's name over and over until he responds to it, calling him to you, making him come by using a check cord to pull him in if you have to.

Smith: When I'm working a dog I teach him to come on his name. I don't say "Come!," I say "Jake!" This is done in the yard on a rope. Remember that each dog has a different pain threshold, degree of discipline he can absorb, whatever you want to call it. One dog you might just snap the rope on his collar, snatch him about twice while you call his name until he comes to you. If he's tough, you put a spike collar on him, do the same thing. Haul him to you, hand over hand on the rope.

We also use the pulley on a stake in the ground and rope a dog around the waist in teaching him to stand while we flush, after we've taught him to come with the 25-foot rope and the spike collar. We run the rope through the pulley, call him to us and say "Whoa!" Then we snatch against that pulley and he stops. He can't go anywhere, he's right there on the rope. We do it again. It's just repetition. A lot of dogs can be weeded out by the attitude they take toward yard training. Some that won't take, that are practically worthless, won't stand up under any training.

Describe your method of teaching a dog to "Whoa!" What's your release command, allowing the dog to move up to relocate or to move out when no birds are produced?

Epp: I use two methods to teach a dog to "Whoa!" My favorite one is to use a check cord or what is called a drag rope with a snap on the end of it. Just add another snap to that snap so it's two snaps long and fasten that on the collar. Let it hang under the dog's jaw. Step away from the dog, tell him "Whoa!" Naturally he's going to step toward you. Just sort of flip your wrist and pop him under the jaw with that snap. Some dogs will stop with the first pop.

You may also have to hold the dog with your hands and stand by him, saying "Whoa!" a few times when he starts to move so he begins to understand that "Whoa!" means to stand still. Then apply the method I've just mentioned with the snap.

After he's first learned to stop, you don't want to make him stay there too long. You want to anticipate his move. Before he does it, you let him move. At first, the signal for this is two toots on the whistle and a pat on your leg. Coax him to come on to you. Then, as he gets to standing better, don't bring him on with the whistle but make him stand there until you walk back to him, touch him on the head, tell him "All right!" or toot the whistle. He should learn to stay there until you touch him.

Another way of teaching them to "Whoa!," since some dogs don't like

At a training seminar sponsored by *Hunting Dog* magazine, Collier Smith demonstrates the use of a post, pulley, and rope to teach a dog to "Whoa!" or to come when called. (George Quigley photo)

this tapping under the chin and it cowers them, is to take a long switch or something like a buggy whip. Get in front of the dog and when he goes to you, you can reach out, low, not over the dog, reach under his head and just tap his front legs and tell him "Whoa!" so he won't want to come to you. Some dogs respond to this better than the snap. Watch his eyes. If you get him scared, better stop and pet him a while.

Gates: Teaching a dog to "Whoa!" is done by yard work. For a dog to relocate after you have started to flush birds, come back and touch him on the head and say something like "Okay, boy!" or maybe give a short blast on the whistle.

Smith: We use two methods. If the dog is on the timid side we use the pulley because it's not as hard on the dog. It takes a little longer, but if you've got a soft dog it works out a lot better. Put the dog on the pulley, as described previously, and go through that a hundred million times until he does it.

The quickest way is to take a rope, tie a knot in it about 8 or 10 inches from the snap, run it around the dog's waist and snap the snap in the knot so the rope doesn't slip. Take the dog out and let him go through all the flipping and contortions until he gets used to the rope being around his waist.

Then tie the rope to a post and set him up, tell him "Whoa!" and walk out in front of him. When you start out he'll also start, until he hits the end of that rope. Pretty soon he'll get the idea that the rope is going to snatch him in two, so when you walk out, he'll stop. When he moves out to the end of the rope, take him back, stand him up, leave a little slack in the rope. Walk back in front of him, tell him "Whoa!" and make out like you're flushing, until you get him so he'll stand there.

You get occasional cases where the dog's real tough and you don't believe he's going to "Whoa!" So get a spike collar, take it apart, then buckle

Pointing dogs in training drag a check cord that aids the trainer in controlling and training a bird dog.

In teaching a dog to "Whoa!" a check cord is cinched around his middle, the other end tied to a tree or stake while a trainer like Collier Smith, shown here, backs off and cautions the dog to stay put. (George Quigley photo)

it around the dog's waist, snap the snap in that, and tell him "Whoa!" If he breaks off, he won't hit that spike collar but about twice, no matter how tough he is. We've never hurt a dog doing this.

When you get the dog so he'll stand tied to the tree, take him loose on the rope, tell him "Whoa!" and give a little snatch on the rope and stop him right there.

When you get him so he'll stand to "Whoa!" while you're flushing, when you go back to him, always whoa the dog up while you're petting and rubbing him up for standing there. I tap him on the side and say "All Right!" and whistle through my teeth, to send him to relocate. As the dog gets older, if he's in a place difficult to get to, just whistle to him and tell him it's all right to move up. But with a dog in training, to release him, always go back to him, pet him up, tap him, take him by the collar and start him off and tell him "All Right!" and let him go ahead.

At what age do you prefer to start a young dog in the field and what do you do and look for while out training, hunting, running, or working a dog?

Once he points, you get to your dog, get your hands on him, restrain him and stroke and praise him as Collier Smith does with this young Pointer. (George Quigley photo)

Epp: My preference for starting a dog in the field is really younger than what I've mentioned for training. I like to start them when they're three months old. Of course, most dogs don't get to you that young, so a year old is the maximum age at which you'd want to start.

I look for a dog's desire to move out and hunt. Dogs that really don't want to get away from me, just mope around, don't show much interest in anything but following with me, I don't keep them too long before I send them back. I like a dog that shows interest in something besides me, especially cover, little birds, or anything that's there. I want the dog to be moving. I don't like a dog that stops and potters too much. Even a young dog should show some desire to go to something and hunt.

Gates: Serious field work starts at approximately one year. I've pretty much covered what I look for in a dog in answer to previous questions.

Smith: We try to start our pups at about nine months old, if they've got any field experience at all. Basically we check out how they look running, how they handle, and whether they find any birds. Usually you categorize your dog either as a field trial prospect or a shooting dog, by the range alone. Then you go on from there, weeding out the dogs in the field trial category that don't have enough class and you put them back in the gun dog category. In the gun dog category you look for the dogs that have the most jump and find the most birds and then you grade them according to their stamina and stuff like that.

You look for independence in these young dogs and eliminate the dogs that just trail all the time. One that "rats" all the time, with no desire to hunt, you weed him out. Those are obvious things that show up in first workouts.

If a dog shows real class but is a trailer, you might decide to try to break him of that but usually you don't ever stop a dog completely from trailing. If he's hunting all the time he wouldn't be a trailer, so you're really better off to start over with one of those independent puppies.

Describe your procedure for encouraging a dog to run big, "hunt to the limits." What's your procedure for developing a dog to restrict his range?

Epp: To encourage the field trial prospect to run more, I don't run a pup too long. I might give him two or three workouts, maybe from twenty to thirty minutes each. I'm talking about a pretty young pup not over a year old. He gets used to pulling in the harness and this keeps him strong, and if you road him behind other dogs it will give him a little more desire to go.

Then after working him this way two or three days, I turn him loose out of the harness to run free. Even though the roading has built up interest, I don't let him run long, maybe just five minutes. If he runs good, makes a good tear or two and then looks like he's going to stop, I'll pick him up, put him back in the harness or up in the truck or kennel. If a dog doesn't run enough, road him more and run him less. But you have to use common sense.

As to training the hunting dog to restrict his range, I don't make much noise, I don't ride fast if I'm on horseback. With the running dog I make more noise, sing to the dog, so he'll know where I am and doesn't have to worry about finding me. If you want to keep the hunting dog in, don't make any noise. Then he doesn't know exactly where you are and must look for you all the time. You might even trick him by turning him into a place, then turning around and riding the other way so he doesn't know just where you are going to be. Make too much noise singing to him and he knows where you are and doesn't worry about you. If you're quiet, he'll generally stay closer and will keep his mind on watching and listening.

If a dog deliberately runs off, use the training system with the turn signal. If he goes too far and won't turn back, catch him, give him a jerk with your cord, call him. Run him down with the horse. I don't mean step on the dog; step on the cord so he gets a jerk while he's going away when

Smokepole, possibly the greatest shooting dog champion to date, of Gunsmoke Kennels, in a solid stand on game.

you call him. Enforcing the turn command when you want him and being quiet the rest of the time, teaching him to look for you, is the way to work the close dog.

Gates: Simply encourage the dog with a blast of the whistle when he starts back to you, running him in open range so that he'll have to reach farther for objectives. If I wanted a dog to come in and hunt closer, I would run him in tighter country. I might use a harness and let him drag a check cord or a rubber hose, possibly, in order to slow him down, hoping this would restrict his range in the future. But, basically, a dog's range is a natural thing with him.

Smith: To encourage a dog to run bigger, try to widen him out, try to encourage him with the whistle. Ride the dog a little harder with the horses, take him to wide open country where the objectives are far apart and drive the dog from one objective to the other, trying to get the dog to hunt bigger. It doesn't pay to whip the dog out, stuff like that. When you whip-run a dog you make him manshy and mess him up in other ways. It just doesn't pay off usually.

Facing page
A deadeye assistant to kill birds your dog has pointed in training is a big help in teaching a bird dog his manners. (George Quigley photo)

When you work a dog in order to bring him in, make him quarter. When you get him out as far as you want him to range, call him all the way back to you, and let him start out again. If you work at making him quarter, but can't get anywhere without some help, put a set of chains, hobbles, electronic trainer, or what have you on him so when he gets to a certain outer limit you can call him back. Work him like that long hours and you'll usually bring him in.

Are there natural "big-going" dogs and "close-working" dogs? If there are, except for unusual circumstances, is it worthwhile to try to go against the grain and convert the dog's natural style to a different pattern?

Epp: Yes, I believe some dogs are born to run big and some dogs are born to hunt close. I don't think it's wise to try to change the nature of a dog. If you take a big-running dog he can be made to hunt in, but he can't be happy about it so he won't do a good job. Likewise, by nature, a dog that is a close-hunting dog, by conditioning him and by pushing him, you might get him to run more. But he generally won't find any birds. All he'll be doing is running. So it's best to try to figure out what your dog's nature is and sort of work around to it. You possibly can bend one a little, maybe pull a big-running dog in some or push a shorter dog out, but basically you can't change his nature at all.

Gates: There are natural big-going dogs and close-working dogs. Under certain situations a dog's pattern can be changed, but this should be attempted only by a well-qualified individual. You do not want to try to change one thing to suit your needs and create a problem that is harder to deal with.

Smith: There are a lot of dogs that naturally run big and others that just naturally don't. A good rule of thumb in training any dog is what we tell all our owners who come in and say, "I want a field trial dog out of this nine-month-old puppy."

We say, "We'll take him and we'll work with him and we'll let him be what he's going to be. If he makes a field trial dog fine, if he makes an amateur dog fine, if he makes a gun dog fine. We'll train him, and if that's not what you want we'll sell him and get another dog."

You put so much on a dog just training him to be steady to wing and shot. Then if you try to alter his range and make him something that he's not, chances are you're going to ruin him before you get through.

Generally, what is the difference, if there is any, between a "covey dog" and a "singles dog"? Are there indications or other ways to spot how a young dog is likely to turn out?

Epp: The basic difference between the covey dog and the singles dog

---

Facing page
Dave Duffey and his Pointer, Cannonade's Stupido, exchange confidences in front of the kennel before going into the field. Praise and confidence instilled in a dog make for close rapport between hunter and gun dog.

Professional handlers literally have a "string of dogs" and they stake them out on breaks during long trips or while the dogs aren't being run at field trials. (Ken Hawkins photo)

is that the covey dog covers more ground. Of course, there can be variations in ability to handle birds. Some dogs seem to be confused by a lot of scent given out by a lot of birds in a covey scattered out over an area. Some just never know when to point in a situation like this. But the same dogs smelling only one bird can point real well.

The covey dog has the ability to know where the whole bunch of birds is and establishes point immediately. I think this is born in a dog. A lot of dogs can find game and tell you there's birds around, but it's hard for them to decide when to point. These dogs probably make the best singles dogs because the one bird is their easiest thing to do. But the covey dog has a knack of when to point at the right time, when he first smells those native birds.

The long-range dog would more or less be suitable as a covey dog because he has to cover more country to find the coveys. The singles dog can be short range because you can generally tell him about where the birds are and he can stay with you and point these.

In a young dog, when you're trying to discern what he's going to be, you can get by with a low head in a singles dog. In fact, sometimes this is an advantage. In thick cover the high-headed dog might run on by and miss the bird. A dog with a lower head, that slows down, will probably point it. By the same nature, the high-headed dog will generally make the best covey dog.

Gates: There really should be no difference, not if a dog is trained and broken well. Although there are indications sometimes as to how a young dog should turn out, there is really no way a person can be 100 percent sure. About 60 percent would hit it closer.

Smith: The covey dog would be the wider ranging of the two, the singles dog the closer. Singles usually fly to a thicket and a singles dog would get in there and work in the heavy cover and point singles. If my trial dogs find a covey of birds and I want to kill them a bird and then get an opportunity on that covey, I go down to where the singles are, get off my horse and walk with them. They point just as many singles as they do coveys. Some trainers don't fool with single birds with their field trial dogs. I don't understand why, unless maybe the dog might get in a habit of rooting around a little after he's had a find if you work him on singles every time. I don't do it every time, just when I want to kill a bird for the dog or have some other specific purpose for working on singles.

You hear hunters all the time talking, "He's a good covey dog" or "He's a good singles dog," and I'd like to go with them sometime and find out what the difference is. Mostly the terms have to do with whether the dog is naturally wide or close. But if that wide dog was trained to come in close, and walk, hunt careful, he'd be just as good a singles dog as the dog that's slow and close anyway. If you train your dogs to do what you tell them to do, come in and hunt close, to range out, there wouldn't be any difference in the two as such. But everybody's ideas can be different.

How do you introduce a young dog to birds? In the yard? On planted birds? On wild birds? Starting from puppyhood do you fool with a bird wing on a string with little pups? Do you prefer to wait until they are old enough to encounter birds in the field?

Epp: I like to introduce my pups on wild birds. Then they learn to find game on their own. They don't feel like you're showing it to them. If you start young pups on liberated birds, the pups hunt with you and they pick up the idea they'll find the birds in close, and that's where they'll look for them. Also, when pups are young and you have liberated birds in thick cover the birds don't flush readily and the pups will begin to play with them, maybe run around them when they can't bust the covey and this is a bad habit. They might even catch some, which makes it hard to train them. So I like to start with wild birds, get the pups to where they're beginning to find them, possibly flash-point them. Then they can be shifted to liberated birds. But I don't like to stay with liberated birds. I shift them back and forth so they don't get set in one way.

The time to start a young dog on birds could vary from five or six months to over a year. If I get them later I still like to start them on wild birds. Of course, if a dog is older than a year and is a really bold dog, some liberated birds could be used, particularly if it's hard to find wild birds to get him in.

As to using a bird wing on a fish pole, I don't use it at all. I think it's a detriment to dogs, teaching them to sight point and not use their nose. I can't see that it accomplishes anything good. Maybe if you want to let somebody see how your puppy looks pointing, you might do it just that one time.

Gates: I first introduce a dog on planted birds. I like to do this along about the time I am yard working, being careful not to overdo it—say about ten minutes, stopping while the dog is still excited about the whole affair.

I think fooling with a bird wing on a string with little pups is fine. Anything you can do with a little pup to get him out of the pen is good. While I am going through the tame bird work with a dog, I also like to run him in the fields and let him chase wild birds before I start any serious training in the field.

Smith: We introduce our dogs to wild birds in the field during the spring, or whenever we get a young dog to start out. We try to get him into some birds in a workout, root them out, chase them out. While he's chasing birds we shoot the gun, no matter where we are. Introduce birds and gun at the same time and pretty soon the dog will begin to associate that gunfire with having a good time. Then you can get closer and closer with the gun until he actually points a bird and you kill it for him. Then you're off and running.

We try to start our dogs with native birds. We fool around with pigeons and liberated birds to get the dog pointing, but he's usually knocked a lot of wild birds before we start that. Fooling around with a quail wing on a pole to get the little pup to sight point it looks good, but too much of it is a bad thing. A pup then doesn't use his nose; he gets to looking for everything instead of trying to point.

Once a dog starts pointing game, when do you start staunching him and how do you go about doing this?

Epp: Start staunching him after he's pointed enough times so you know he's definitely establishing a point. It could be maybe the second or third time you see him point game, or maybe even the first if you know he's a bold dog and you've got the means of getting to him. I start all my dogs dragging a check cord, about a 25-foot rope. That way, if a dog points and I can get close to him, I can get hold of that check cord and hold him steady. If you have a helper, one of you can hold the cord while the other flushes the birds. I don't like to jerk the dog down. Just hold him there and don't let him chase the birds off or knock them. The first few times that I flush I like to kill the dog a bird. Kill him a bird and take him out there, let him pick up the bird so he gets to liking them and knows there's nothing unpleasant.

After he gets to liking the birds and doesn't mind holding, then you can begin to steady him by catching a short hold on that rope when he points, maybe 3 or 4 feet back from the collar. Either you or the assistant can do this while the other one flushes. When you're flushing, that dog's going to want to move and you can use that short hold to keep him in pointing position watching you. The second the birds flush you turn that short hold loose and let the dog start to chase after the birds. When he gets to the end of the rope, jerk him down and set him back up.

When he hits the end of the rope, the man flushing the birds says "Whoa!" and the one holding the rope doesn't say anything. The dog gets the feeling that the man out in front is the one stopping him. That way, he'll learn not to break when there's no man behind him. He begins to think it's the "Whoa!" that's stopping him, which is just what you want to ingrain in him.

Gates: Generally speaking, after the pup has been thoroughly yard worked, has been introduced to birds and has had his fling in the field chasing wild birds and is really interested in the whole affair, I start with the staunching process by getting my hands on him after he has chased a bird, bringing him back to where he got the bird up, standing him there and whoaing him—this is where your yard work comes in—keeping him under the command of "Whoa!" Walking out in front of him, I make a good flushing effort, keeping him standing in position until I get back to him, then I give him a pat and rub him up. When going through this breaking stage, I always let the dog drag a check cord when I run him in the field. This makes it a lot easier to get your hands on him.

Smith: When the dog is running out there, without anything holding him, and he starts finding and pointing birds, and holding them until you get there, then you put the rope on him to drag. If you have a helper, one man grabs the rope, one man flushes the birds. You hold the dog steady until the birds get up and, of course, the dog breaks. The guy with the rope jerks the dog back and stands him up. That's where the whoa training you taught him in the yard comes in.

Then you stand him there and you say "Whoa!" You walk in there and make like you're flushing in front of him. If he's excited he's going to jump around so you go back and get him by the ears and shake him a little bit and tell him "Whoa!" Then go back in front of him, flushing like, until he calms down enough to where he'll stand there for you to do that. With a scattered covey you might get a bird up every time you go out there and flush. What you're doing is making him stand there to command, and with repetition, covey after covey, you bring him back.

If the birds are wild and he takes them off, ride him down with a horse, get him, lead him back, stand him up in the right spot and tell him "Whoa!," walk in front of him and flush. You're teaching him steady to wing and shot and stop to flush all at the same time. You keep trying and trying and you think you aren't getting anything done and then one day he runs over a bird, he just styles up. Then you know you're getting somewhere. When he's pointing birds, you flush and he's ready but doesn't go, you should go back and reward him by petting and stroking while he's standing there on point. Then the next covey he does right and you kill him a bird for his reward.

Describe your procedure in introducing a dog to gunfire, assuring that the dog will not be gunshy.

Epp: I like to fire the first shot over pups when they're afield well away from me. I generally just shoot off horseback while the dogs are running, having a good time. If they don't notice that, I gradually shorten the distance, shooting nearer but not right over them.

Something I think you definitely should not do ever—and I used to do it—is to shoot a bird in front of the dog when he first starts chasing the birds. This being the first time he hears a shot, if he doesn't happen to like it he generally associates it with the birds. Then he's going to be both gunshy and birdshy. If he doesn't like just the shot, it's possible to get him to like the birds and get him over it. But if he gets afraid and doesn't know whether it's the shot or the birds that bothers him, he's almost washed up for life. So I shoot in the field without birds, while the dog's running and hunting and then as he gets used to it I shoot when he's chasing birds, but not right over him.

Gates: If I have a dog as a pup, three months or older, I'll start by shooting a cap pistol at feed time, at least 75 to 100 feet away from him, while's he's eating and then move in a little closer as time goes by. Next, I use a .22, following the same procedure.

When I start shooting live birds over him, I use a .410 bore, being careful to shoot just one time, several feet away from the dog, trying my damndest to kill the bird. Never go out and unload an automatic or pump shotgun in rapid fire over a young dog before he is well versed about the gun.

Smith: When they find birds and they're chasing birds, we shoot the blank pistol, the .410, or what have you. Too many people make the mistake of buying a young puppy, about ten weeks old, and then take him out in the yard to "see if he's gunshy." They load up an automatic, tie the dog to the car bumper, and "bam, bam, bam." Naturally the dog goes under the car. "That dirty son of a gun sold me a gunshy dog," the guy says. Well, he is gunshy *then*. You shouldn't just shoot over a dog. You should have a reason, should have the dog in birds, when you shoot.

Some people shoot a blank pistol on their way up to the puppy pen every time they go to feed. The pups get the idea that when they hear a gunshot something good's going to happen. This doesn't *always* keep dogs from being gunshy. Some bad experience in "early childhood" may still cause them to be gunshy.

Describe your procedure in teaching a dog to retrieve. Do you start in the yard or afield? Do you force-break or take advantage of a natural inclination to pick up and carry?

Epp: I like to encourage the natural retrieving in a dog if I can. To do this I always have a check cord on the dog when I kill the first bird for him. I try for a situation where the dog can see the bird fall and immediately take him right on to the bird while he's looking at it, let him pick it up, encourage him. If he chews it too hard, you may have to squeeze a front foot until he releases it. If he doesn't chew it too hard, try to walk back away from the dog and coax him to bring it on to you. If he's got some natural ability, he'll generally begin to retrieve the bird this way.

It is important to have the rope on the dog, because if you let him free on that first bird very likely he's going to run out there, grab it up, and run off with it. You aren't going to want him to chew that bird up so you're going to start chasing him and he's going to get nervous and sure enough chew it up. It will just make a bad situation worse. But if you've got that check cord on, you have control to start with to prevent this bad habit from developing.

Of course, some dogs just won't pick a bird up. If they don't, then you have to force-break them to retrieve. I use the method I suppose most do, teach them to take the retrieving dummy by squeezing their foot or pinching their ear. It's just a long routine to go through. Retriever trainers could teach a lot more about this than I could.

Gates: There are several ways to teach a dog to force-retrieve. I won't go into this in detail since various means are explained in several good books.

To teach a dog to retrieve natural, I would put a check cord on the dog and kill a bird over him, keeping him steady to wing and shot through the procedure. This is the easiest way to break him around game, regardless of whether you plan to keep him steady to shot after you start to hunt birds over him. Then holding on to the check cord, go with the dog to the bird and encourage him to pick up the bird. As he gets to the end of the check cord, I pull him toward me with the bird in his mouth. After he brings the bird, I give him a pat on the head, usually giving him the twisted-off head of the bird as part of his reward. Most dogs will get the idea after several of these lessons.

Smith: We mainly take advantage of the natural inclination to pick up and carry. In training the dog, we're killing birds. Getting his mouth on a bird is the dog's only reward for the briars, the mud, and everything else.

We take one dog, kill him a bird, snap the check cord on him, take him out there to where the bird fell, let him hunt around and find the bird. He

If spooky birds try to sneak out on a dog, an experienced gun dog, or even a smart youngster like this Pointer, will cautiously stalk them, keeping track of them but not crowding and flushing.

mouths it a little bit and while he's doing that you pull him to you and say "Fetch, boy!" Let him hold it in his mouth, pet him a little, remove the bird from his mouth, throw it out again, let him go out and get it until he's disinterested in it.

My father used to teach all his dogs to force-retrieve; that was just part of the training. But we've gotten away from it through the years. He thought that it made for a better trained dog, and he was right. You always had the dog under control when you taught him force-retrieving. There have been times when people had a force-trained dog, they took him hunting, he took to knocking birds, they'd call him in and have a little session with him, make him go out and pick up a beer can or a glove, something like that, and start out again. This seemed to be what it took to calm the dog down and get him back in the slot.

All our field trial dogs will retrieve. They haven't been force-broken to retrieve. But when I kill a bird I go back to them, tap them on the head, and tell them "All Right" and they go to where the bird is, run around until they find it, pick it up and bring it to me. They might mash it quite a bit, but that's okay. The main thing is I want them to get their mouth on a bird.

Describe your procedure for steadying a dog to wing and shot.

Epp: Most of the work of steadying a dog to wing and shot can be done with the check cord. Some dogs might require a spike collar but I hardly ever use it. The procedure is similar to steadying the dog on game. The main thing is to get to the dog before he flushes. If he'll just hold the

Top
Once the dog staunches up, the trainer should get to him, stroke him, tease his tail, as Dave Duffey is doing here. The shooting should be left to a hunting buddy.

Bottom
Once the bird is knocked down the dog is sent to claim his reward—getting his mouth on the bird—and he should be coaxed back to deliver to hand as this well-bred youngster is doing here. Pet and praise but don't snatch the bird away. (Three photos in series by Mickey McLinden)

birds and you can get to him, then you can break him to wing and shot by jerking him down with the cord, as Mr. Shelley [Er M. Shelley, old-time trainer and author of a treatise on bird-dog training] told us how to do years ago. Mr. Shelley recommended a 40-foot cord to jerk him down with, but since cover's thicker now I generally use a 20- to 25-foot cord. It's important to have a short hold and a long hold on the rope, like I described in staunching the dog. The short hold is to keep him from flushing the birds. Keep him standing there. Don't let him move in to help flush. If he goes to move a little, give a sharp jerk, not enough to pick the dog up, just enough to pop his collar and keep him standing there while the birds flush.

When the birds flush don't tell him "Whoa!" or anything. Just drop that short hold but hold onto the end of the rope. Let the dog race out after the birds and when he gets to the end upset him, real hard. You may tell him "Whoa!" or you may not say anything. After he's been jerked down, take him back where he should have stayed to start with, set him up and pet him. Repetition of this is what is needed.

One day when you've got him standing good, you've got to take the rope off. This is when he's probably going to break on you. You'll have to chase him down and either slip a spike collar on him and give a little jerk or sort of pick him up and choke him slightly with the regular collar and take him back to where he should have stood. Then slip the collar off and pet him. Give him the discipline where you catch him, give him a lot of petting where he should have stayed pointed.

Gates: I always run the unsteady dog with a check cord on him. After he breaks when the birds get up and you shoot, either have someone else on the check cord or, if this is not possible, try to be in position so you can catch the end of the check cord when the dog breaking shot comes by you.

If the dog is bold enough, give him a good snatch and roll him over when he hits the end of the check cord. Take him back to where he was originally pointing. Stand him up. Give him the command "Whoa!" Walk back out in front of him and fire over him. Usually he will stand at this time, since the birds have already gone before. By repeating this procedure several times he should soon get the idea.

Smith: Basically, you use a two-man team. One man holds the rope while the other flushes. You steady the dog without a lot of pressure. You can steady him quickly by just whaling the tar out of him every time he breaks with the birds, but you'll have a dog that looks like he's had the tar flailed out of him all the time. The thing that separates the trainers is being able to leave everything in the dog and still have him trained. You'll leave the class in him if you just restrict him with that rope each time. Through repetition he'll get so he'll point those birds, you'll walk in there and he'll stand proud as he can be.

We try to teach staunchness and steady to wing and shot at the same time. To me, staunch means he's pointing those birds with high intensity and tight until they get up. When the birds get up, you want him steady to flush, or steady to wing. You can't train him to be staunch by letting him chase the birds for a while and all of a sudden cracking down. Likewise, if you get him staunch and steady to wing, you can't let him break shot, then crack down for that.

Train the dog gradually all the way through to be staunch, steady to wing and shot. This way you've got a trained dog and you don't have to go back somewhere and redo it. If you do it gradually there'll be less whippings, every one of which takes a little bit out of him in style or something else. With the competition today you can't *break* a dog. You have to teach or train a dog.

If a guy has a dog that's been trained steady to wing and shot and wants to keep him that way, he'll shoot in front of the dog one or two times as long as the dog is steady. If the dog breaks after he shoots one time, he should go get the dog and bring him back by the ears to the same place it happened, stand him up and walk around in front of him and shoot again until the dog stays. Then he should go on to the next covey but not kill a bird, just shoot. This will straighten out the dog. But he'll have to work to keep him steady. You can't expect to go out there and just start slaying birds and expect your dog to stay steady.

There can't be any accidents. A dog that's not steady to wing is going to run over some birds accidentally. If he's steady to wing and shot, he would normally stop to flush. If not, he's going to chase those birds and pretty soon he's not going to be as careful about running over them. There won't be any hesitation between the time he smells the bird and chasing. "If it's all right for me to chase it, why isn't it all right for me to get it up, too?" is the way he'll think.

If you've got a completely trained dog, it's easier to let him come back some than it is if he's just half-way trained; he's going to come all the way unbroke then, unless he's an old dog that's hunted a hundred years like that.

How do you assure that your dog will stop to flush?

Epp: This can be helped a lot by a good session of yard training. That's getting him so he'll whoa almost anywhere around you. After your formal sessions in the yard, when you're working the dog in the field, especially on foot, any time he unsuspectingly runs by close, step on the check cord and just as it stops him tell him "Whoa!" This way he'll learn whoa almost anywhere in the field.

When he runs over a bird and you say "Whoa!" he's supposed to stop. He's probably not going to do it the first few times so you've got to catch him and discipline him by pinching the ear a little bit, or giving him a moderate whipping. Just anything to let him know that he's done wrong. But you need to catch him quick, while he's chasing. Tell him he's done wrong, take him back to where he flushed the bird, tell him "Whoa!" While he stands there, go out and go through the flushing motions, shoot, and make him stand there. After repetition of this, one day he'll start doing it. Some dogs don't like to do it, but eventually most of them will.

Gates: If you have done the steadying to wing and shot procedure and have done it well, stopping to flush should not be a big problem. But when a dog does not stop to flush and takes out after birds, you need to get to him as quickly as possible, giving the type of punishment that is in keeping with his disposition, not too severe if he is soft, harsh if he is tough. Take him back to where the flush occurred. Stand him up and again walk out in front of him, making the flushing effort, keeping him there until you get back to him.

I'd like to make an important point here, which will save anyone training his own dog a lot of wasted time and trouble. After a dog has finished his bird work, he should always be led out of the area where the birds got up and took off. The dog should not be allowed to pussyfoot around in the area where the birds have left from. This will eliminate a fault before it gets started.

Smith: We teach our dogs to stop at flush at the same time we teach them to be steady to wing and shot. If a young dog runs over a bird and he chases it, we go get him, bring him back, stand him up at that spot, tell him "Whoa!" and flush in front of him.

It serves two purposes: it gives the dog practice at being brought back, and having birds flushed in front of him. Your natural instinct when the bird gets up is to holler "Whoa!" "Whoa!" Then if you go get him and bring him back a few times, punish him a little bit, stand him up there, pretty soon when the bird gets up you'll holler "Whoa!" and he'll stop. Soon he'll be stopping when he sees the bird in the air, he'll be stopping at flush.

Describe your procedure for training a dog to back.

Epp: This can be relatively easy with most dogs if you have another good steady dog that can point a lot of birds. We like to road our young dogs behind a pointing dog, bring them up to watch that dog point, make them stand there. When they see the dog and recognize that he's pointing, give them a little jerk until they stand. But make them stand with a slack line, like they're standing on their own. Don't ever hold them there. Of course, you'll have to give a jerk from time to time to keep them there. Try not to be too long flushing the birds. To start, kill a bird and then let the

An experienced, staunch pointing dog is an aid to teaching young bird dogs to back, as they can be brought in on the check cord while the experienced dog or dogs are locked up as is being done here.

Under Collier Smith's supervision, this Weimaraner is restrained and styled up on a bird while the owners of a setter and pointer bring their dogs up to back. (George Quigley photo)

dog that you're training get his mouth on the bird so he realizes that when that other dog is pointing there's birds up there, and if he stays back and stops them he's going to get to pick the bird up.

If he's reasonably intelligent with some instinct to back, he's going to be backing automatically before he knows it. A mixture of this and teaching him to "Whoa!" will teach him to back when you take him off the check cord. If he doesn't back, catch him and do him just like you would when you steady him. Give him a little punishment, take him back to where he should stand, make him stand again.

Gates: To train a dog to back, with the check cord on him, I bring the dog up to another dog on point, let him get into view of the dog and "Whoa!" him. Usually a dog will back before he really begins to point birds, but there are some exceptions to this.

Smith: When we're training young dogs, we road one in the harness behind another dog, or when we're working a dog just on backing we put him in the harness to give him backing opportunities. We bring him in every time another dog points, try to teach him to back by just stopping him in the harness, hoping he'll pick it up naturally.

If he doesn't, the quickest way is to put an electric collar on him. When he comes in, sees the other dog and you say "Whoa!," shock him with the collar and make him stop. Do this if you've tried bringing him in a number of times and couldn't get him to stop. But you have to watch it, because sometimes they get so they just blink the other dog when they see him on point. It's a gamble, but it's better to have him blinking the dog than running in and knocking birds all the time.

When a dog displays serious faults—self-hunting, blinking, hard mouth, gunshyness—is there much point in an amateur trainer working to try to correct these faults?

Epp: As many young dogs as are available and at a reasonable price, it's really not practical to try and correct these faults. If a person just wants to prove to himself that he can do it, that's a different thing. But it's always more trouble to get a dog over a fault than to start on another dog. Working with a dog with these faults is about like trying to start with a business in debt. It's pretty hard to make a go of it.

Gates: No, in most cases.

Smith: The cheapest way to correct these faults is to send the dog to a professional. Often the reason a dog has these faults is that he wasn't trained properly to start with. Sometimes a guy doesn't want to spend the money to have training done, wants to do it himself but doesn't know what's going on, and a dog just runs around doing what he wants, the dog is maybe training him.

So the cheapest way is to let the trainer look at him a couple of weeks to see if he thinks he can break the dog of whatever fault he has. If he can't, then get another dog.

Do you have any tips or suggestions to help avoid serious faults before they become established?

Epp: Tips to avoid these faults can be obtained from various books on dog training. Watch a dog's eyes every time you administer punishment. If that dog shows much fear, don't go any further. Don't lose your temper with that dog. Take a little time. Always figure you can add another lick, but you can't take one back.

Gates: Follow the procedures that have been outlined in answer to previous questions to get a dog started right and trained properly.

Smith: If you're an amateur trainer and you've trained your own dog, but your dog starts getting away from you and you lose him every time, or if you shoot your gun and you see your dog flinch—well, don't do it again. Take the dog to a professional and get some help before you completely ruin him. If you see a dog going sour, don't just keep on until he's gone. Even if you don't want the trainer to train him, he'll at least tell you what to do to try and stop it.

Aside from the necessity of using good judgment, is there generally a time to punish and a time to praise? What forms should punishment and praise take, and when are they used to discipline and reward a dog?

Epp: There definitely is a time to punish and to praise a dog. Punishment should not be given a dog unless he understands what he's getting it for. So, as illustrated in steadying a dog to wing and shot, after he's taught to "Whoa!" he's supposed to stay there with the check cord on till you release him. If he deliberately breaks shot when you're telling him "Whoa!" and he knows it, catch him right in the act, pretty quick. He should be punished then because he knows he's doing wrong. When you bring him back and stand him where he should have stayed pointed, while he's standing there give him praise. That way he'll always associate good with staying where the birds were and bad with chasing them. As to forms of punishment, I don't think a young dog should be whipped. Any action or motion with your hands to punish the dog may make a dog afraid of you even if you reach a hand out to pet him. So this shouldn't be too severe. You might punish a dog by slipping a spike collar on him, stepping back and giving it a jerk. Even if he associates this with you, it's not enough to make him afraid of you. Sometimes I might bite or pinch the ear a little bit. I don't think it hurts to whip an old dog that knows better and deliberately does something wrong, especially a gun dog. You have to be awfully careful about a field trial dog because you definitely don't want to put him on the ground. I never have won anything with one down.

Gates: Using good judgment is the key. Remember that all dogs are different and can take different amounts of punishment. But all of them love praise.

Smith: There's always a time to praise, and to punish, too. But you get more with sugar than salt a lot of times when you're training a dog. I praise for whatever the dog does right. For punishment, start out with a mild degree and build up until you find the degree that gets through to your particular dog. Punishment has to be dealt out evenly. If you're going to punish for a mistake, you have to do it every time, not let it slide now and then because it just wasn't an opportune time to do it.

Probably the most innovative and well-publicized training device to appear in recent years is the electronic shock collar. Based on your experience, can the electronic shock collar be of much aid to an amateur training his own dog? If it has drawbacks, how should the person using it exercise caution to achieve the most from this device?

Epp: I don't think an amateur should use a shock collar on a dog, unless he's been training dogs for several years or has worked with a professional trainer who uses the collar. The amateur must definitely understand the reason he is punishing the dog.

An amateur dog trainer who doesn't have much time to work his dog can lose his temper pretty quick knowing he's got to accomplish something in a short time. Because he doesn't have to catch the dog when using the electric shock collar, he can get mad quick, shock him quick, and ruin him. Whereas if he didn't have the collar on and he got mad at him and wanted to whip him, he'd at least have to catch him first and that might give the

The use of an electric shock collar can be an aid in meting out punishment at the instant the dog commits an offense. Pointer is shown with shock collar and receiver on neck and handler holds the transmitting unit which, at the push of a button, will deliver a shock to a disobedient dog up to one-quarter of a mile away. (Larry Mueller photo)

guy time to think about it and change his mind. So I wouldn't really recommend the shock collar unless you have some guidance from a professional or are an experienced amateur.

Gates: The electric collar, in the right hands, is the best tool available. But it can absolutely destroy a dog if not used at the right time for the right thing. Excessive use of it is never good. The dog should be tested with it, very lightly, in the beginning. I think a dog should be thoroughly versed in the "don'ts" by other means before you attempt to use the shock collar.

Smith: I only know one or two amateurs who are capable of using a shock collar the correct way. To a professional it's the greatest training aid since the check cord. You can do so much with it and the dog doesn't associate the pain and the punishment with you.

But too many dogs have been running on an electric collar before the professional trainer gets them. Their owners buy a collar and they buy a book and they go out there on weekends and try to train their dog. Instead they screw him up. Then they send him to us and we start training and if we get to a point where we need to use it we can't use it to advantage because the dog's already buggered on the collar.

What are the advantages and disadvantages of a sportsman keeping his bird dog as a house dog and companion, as opposed to kenneling him strictly as a hunter?

Epp: There are many more advantages to making the dog a house dog than there are disadvantages. The dog is with you more, understands you more, you're closer to him and you understand him better.

There are some disadvantages, possibly, in the fact that the dog gets used to warmer temperatures and better care. He's not as hardy in the field and may be more subject to taking colds if he stays in a nice heated house.

If you do make a house dog of him, do it on a limited basis. Bring him in for a while in the evenings, then ease him out, because in severe weather changing from a warm house to an outside cold house could be hard on him. For these physical reasons, you have to use some judgment. But as far as the close association and the petting that some say is bad, I don't think there's anything to that at all. The more petting and the closer you get to him, the better dog you'll have.

Gates: I see no reason in the world why your dog can't be your companion and your hunting partner at the same time.

Smith: I don't see any particular disadvantages in keeping a dog as a housepet unless you just let him run loose. As long as he's contained in the house or the kennel, that's okay. But don't let him run around and be common.

Most of the good trial dogs are housebroken and stay in the house. It develops a companionship between the hunter and his dog or the trainer and his dog. In a lot of field trial dogs, it can mean the difference between a dog that runs off and a dog that thinks enough about you to come back. A dog that tends to be a little cold blooded on the birds or doesn't care about people, sometimes making a house dog out of him is what it takes. Setters seem to be more that way than Pointers.

Based upon your extensive experience, would you give some off-the-cuff advice, odds and ends of information, pet peeves, tips, remarks on conditioning, etc., that weren't touched upon in previous questions?

Epp: Even though they don't want it professionally trained, all amateurs would benefit greatly if they'd have a professional take a look at the dog they're going to buy. They should take time to go afield with the pro, sort of find out what they want out of a dog and let him look at the dog and advise them if the dog is suitable for them. If so, they could have the pro outline a program for them to follow. I think almost all professional trainers would be glad to do this for a small charge. Some, like myself, would do it for nothing. This way, if a dog isn't suitable at all or has some fault that will never be cured, the pro could see it immediately and tell you about it, give you a little advice, and even from time to time help you with it.

Trust your professional trainer. Most of them started out training dogs as amateurs and know what you're likely to run up against. Talk to him a bit, tell him what kind of dog you want, ask him to look at it and tell you something about it.

If you're an amateur wanting to compete in field trials, where the handlers are on horseback, in your training you'll have to get your dog acclimated to running from horseback. Otherwise, when you get to the trials, it's going to be a different world for this dog and he might not know where you are when you're on a horse. If you don't have a horse, very likely you can find a professional who will be glad for you to work out with him a few times from horseback and this might make the difference between winning a trial and looking silly.

Conditioning a dog has several facets. The first one is keeping your dog free of parasites. That's very important. Also important is your feeding program. Naturally you want to feed a good quality commercial feed at the same time every day. I don't think it's necessary to add things like meat to your dog's feed for any ordinary heats of up to an hour, which all amateur stakes would include. Watch his weight. If he's getting too fat, you need to cut his feed down. But if you're working him hard, you can't cut too much but will have to work his weight down. You have to experiment some to find the weight at which your dog seems to run best. When he seems in the condition he runs the best, weigh him every now and then. Work toward that weight and try to keep him there.

He's got to have a certain amount of exercise. If you don't have time to work your dog once or twice a week and you're going to a field trial, you should take time to road him. Roading a dog will help keep him in condition. If you're going to condition a dog for a thirty-minute stake, you probably would need to road him an hour or better, maybe two or three times a week, if you are going to run him on a weekend for that long. An hour of roading is not equal to even half an hour of running.

So combining the feeding, the weight, and the roading, you can condition the dog and keep him like you want. If you hunt regularly or your hunting days are long, you may need more than one dog, so that you can alternate. If you hunt, say, half a day at a time, three to five hours, it takes a very strong dog to do this every day. If you notice the dog weakening, slowing up, getting too many false points, anything showing you've overworked him, don't hunt him so often or get more dogs to hunt with. A tired dog generally can't point many birds.

There's an old saying, "If he's tired enough he'll point." But if he's that tired he can't look for the birds and his mind is sort of out of gear, too. So don't overwork your dog.

Most people feed their dogs at night and do their hunting in the afternoon. If you start hunting around two o'clock, your dog's about twenty hours away from when he's been fed. Some dogs will work better if you give them a light feeding before you hunt, not enough to make them sick, but just a little extra something, maybe a chunk of hamburger. A little snack will stretch your dog's endurance and keep him perked up.

Gates: To be in top condition a dog has to be completely free of all parasites. A good balanced diet is also required. Two or three workouts a week in the field, starting off with short heats and working up to longer ones, should get him in condition.

Never work or hunt a dog until he is completely given out. This is done too many times and has shortened many a dog's life. I personally believe that if a dog is in good condition, covers the ground well and really applies himself, one and a half to two hours is long enough to hunt him if you want your dog to live to a normal age.

Smith: I think the more an amateur can learn about the dog and training of him, whether he's a gun dog or field trial dog, before bringing him to a trainer the better. But he doesn't have to try to do the training himself. In fact, I'd rather get a dog the owner hadn't yard-broke—or taught to sit! That's one of the main things. They teach their dogs to sit and you're out there yard training and you move your hand and the dog sits down. But I like to work dogs for people who are *really* interested in their dogs, not some guy who just sends his check every month but no letter or concern about how the dog is doing. I like to have people come to see their dogs, show interest in the dog.

The guy who thinks he's interested in field trials should go to a few field trials, see what it takes to win, learn as much as he can, then get a dog and start out with the objective in mind that he's going to have the best there is. He must try and maintain objectivity, not fall in love with a certain dog and thus not be able to see that there's anything wrong with the dog. If there's something bad wrong and you don't want to face up to it, you're wasting the trainer's time and your money. All trainers get customers that just can't believe "ol' Joe" isn't going to make it. In fact, they get mad at you. You send the dog home and they say, "This just can't be, I'll send Joe over to so and so."

The other trainer tells them the same thing but the owner figures "those two guys must be in cahoots" and sends the dog to still another trainer. Well, that kind of guy winds up spending about $15,000 and he hasn't got anything more than he started out with.

The dog owner who wants to train his own should read books, talk to dog trainers, learn as much about the fundamental process as he can. It's just like playing golf or anything else—the more he knows about it the more enjoyment he'll get out of it.

There are several books that are very good. One technique might not work on a certain dog, but maybe something can be picked up from another book or trainer that works perfect for that dog.

If you're a bird hunter and you have the time to do it yourself, figure to take your dog out three or four times a week starting two months before hunting season. If you've got a place to work him, turn him loose, run him until he starts to get tired. Then pick him up. Keep running him until you get him in shape to go the period of time you want to hunt him, two hours, half a day, whatever it is.

If you aren't situated where you can run your dog, you can use a road harness to get him in shape. If you can't work him or road him, send him to a trainer. That's usually about the best money you can spend. Let the trainer have him for two or three weeks, get him in shape, touch him up on his minding and around his birds and have him ready to go when hunting season opens up.

You just can't take a dog that's not in top shape out in October to hunt pheasants, turn him out and hunt him all day long, three to five hours, and figure to hunt him three to five hours the next day. He'll be so damn sore he can't walk.

If you're going on a hunting trip where you'll be gone several days, take enough dogs so you don't have to hunt one dog all day, every day. The first day that dog will do pretty good, but every day thereafter he'll probably do worse. He'll be too sore and beat up to dig in and find the birds. It's better to hunt a day, then skip a day and give the dog a rest. A rested dog will just naturally find more birds than one that's tired.

If you work a dog down to a point where he's completely exhausted, that's where he'll pick up a lot of his bad habits. Just rooting around, a dog that's tired, he gets hardheaded, doesn't listen, then stumbles into something, makes a mistake and one thing just leads to another.

If you've got a dog that's in good shape, I'd think you could hunt him an hour a day for three or maybe four days. The more hours the fewer the days. A lot would depend on the terrain; with a lot of briars and stuff like that it might be just a day out of every three or four. By not overhunting a dog, you get the most out of him. The dog gets some rest, but he doesn't have enough rest that he's wild and he doesn't get so beat up that he's not any good.

PART 2

Versatiles

John Kegel

John Kegel manages a private hunting club near Goodwood, Ontario, Canada, and has been training dogs professionally for over ten years.

The forty-three-year-old Canadian was the original secretary-treasurer of both the North American Versatile Hunting Dog Association and the Pudelpointer Club of North America when those two organizations were founded. Along with Bodo Winterhelt, Kegel is one of two major breeders of Pudelpointers in North America. He has qualified more than fifteen dogs of that breed in NAVHDA tests, but has trained spaniels, retrievers, and pointing breeds as well. Born in Hamburg, Germany, and fluent in both German and English, Kegel frequently visits the Continent to keep up on the development of German dogs and the field trials held in that country. He is in demand as a judge of NAVHDA trials in the United States and Canada.

He is an avid chess player, a director of the North American Game Breeders and Shooting Preserve Association, and has written training articles for breed and specialty magazines, one of which on the preparation of a young dog for NAVHDA testing is included in this book. His business background is in cost accounting.

His wife, Margaret, is a native of Scotland and they have two children, a son, Jason and a daughter, Sonja. Kegel can be reached at: Goodwood Club, Route 1, Goodwood, Ontario, Canada (Phone: 416—294-5227).

Training the versatile or Continental-type pointing dog requires many of the techniques of both pointer and retriever training, usually modified and melded to achieve the goal of a multipurpose gun dog that will work both fur and feather on land or in water.

The Versatile breeds, which include German shorthaired pointer, German wirehaired pointer, Pudelpointer, Weimaraner, Pointing griffon, and Brittany spaniel, can be taught their field work by the customary pointing dog training methods and their water work by retriever training procedures. But because of minor variations, differences in approach, and the growing importance of these breeds in North America, I felt it was vital to include a chapter by a competent trainer who specializes in the training of versatile hunting dogs. Thus, in this chapter, the questions I felt were appropriate to ask such a trainer are answered by one man and the chapter is laid out in that manner. Then, to make sure the reader would know exactly how to get a young Versatile started as a hunting dog, my commentary following the question and answer sections relates how to prepare a pup for testing in the nation's newest and increasingly popular type of field trial, the natural ability test for versatile hunting dogs as conducted by the North American Versatile Hunting Dog Association.

What were your reasons or what influenced you to decide to specialize in training gun dogs of the versatile type primarily, rather than other breeds?

The reason was mainly due to my hunting activities. I'm what you would call an all-around hunter. I hunt upland game as well as waterfowl.

John Kegel with a Pudelpointer in training.

I feel if you have only one dog, a combination dog like one of the Versatiles is an ideal choice.

I was introduced to Pudelpointers by a friend and took a liking to the breed and its all-weather, all-terrain coat, a low-shedding coat so the dog can be an excellent house dog. I decided on the Pudelpointer because it's fairly easy to train and has lots of desire. Also because it's an excellent water dog and retriever.

Do you look for any physical traits that might give an individual dog an edge in his training and work? Are there traits of temperament or disposition that indicate to you that the dog you are dealing with may be relatively easy to train or be difficult? In effect, describe your kind of dog.

If I have a choice I prefer at least an average or larger dog, a strong dog with a smooth gait. I feel the larger dog has an edge in high cover or in working a difficult marsh or in reeds. In my opinion he will last longer and have more stamina.

I would prefer a calm dog as opposed to a high-geared or high-strung dog which is, in my opinion, much more difficult to train. A high-strung dog takes almost twice as long to train as a calm, even-tempered, good-natured dog with a sound temperament. I try to avoid dogs that constantly bark and pace in their kennels as they also usually give the greatest difficulty in training.

At approximately what age, recognizing variations in individual dogs, do you prefer to have a dog brought to you for training? For what reasons?

The ideal age to start the dog would be at about three months. I'd want to keep the dog until he is approximately twelve months old. That would give the greatest scope to work with the dog. But that is impossible for economical reasons, so we have to settle on the next best. By taking the dog in for a three-month period of training, I would specify that the dog not be much younger than eight months.

What steps can a dog's owner take to help ensure that the pup will be trainable and the formal training job made easier when he brings the dog to you?

The owner can help a great deal by instilling some discipline in his dog. Take him out in the fields and in water as much as possible so I don't start out with a completely green dog. The training is much simplified if the dog has some basic obedience, understands the word "No!," not a staid, but an all-around mannerly dog.

If an owner chooses to train his own dog, are there ages or stages a puppy or young dog goes through when he will learn certain things more readily than at any other time?

The training can really commence from the time the pup is weaned. But discretion has to be used, timing is of utmost importance. It would be futile to start the dog on, say, scent pointing at the age of four months. The dog is just not ready, the pointing instinct has not developed properly and may not come through until the dog has reached more maturity and has actual bird contacts, which may be six to eight months, depending upon breed and actual field experience.

On the other hand, sight pointing, if not overdone, is very helpful and could be practiced at a much earlier age, say eight weeks. Another example would be searching. Young puppies often are reluctant to leave the handler's heels. It takes a certain maturity and confidence until the dog goes out to explore cover and display some initiative. This is a matter of time and can't be expected in a very young dog.

Assuming that for different people there are different choices, under what circumstances will someone buying a dog be best satisfied with a puppy, a started dog, or a trained dog?

The best relationship would be developed if a puppy was trained by his owner. However, this is not always possible. Some people don't have the time or facilities to train their own dogs, and in that case it would be a wiser choice to start with a trained dog or even a started dog.

Some people like to train dogs, undertake the challenge, but don't seem to have the right temperament, lack the aptitude, or just do not have any dog sense. These people also would be better off acquiring a trained or started dog.

Another very useful alternative would be if the dog owner would work at times with the professional or, as is done in some NAVHDA chapters, have working groups, clinics, supervised by somebody knowledgeable in dog training. Excellent results have been achieved that way and expenses can be kept down with birds purchased on the pool system and land use shared by a group.

Describe a started dog in terms of what the buyer of such a dog might expect with regard to obedience and hunting ability. In other words, what has a started dog learned and what can he do?

If I were selling a started dog, the dog probably would be between the ages of eight and sixteen months. He would range well. He would point, although he would not necessarily be staunch on point and would not be steady to wing and shot. He would be mannerly. You would be able to call him in. He would enter water without hesitation. A started dog would, of course, have been introduced to the gun and a number of birds shot over him, but he would not be force-trained to retrieve.

What tips would you offer for the selection and purchase of a puppy to help assure the buyer that he will be getting a sound, healthy pup that should be potentially trainable?

Picking a good prospect at an early age, say seven or eight weeks, is in my opinion a great gamble. There's very little to go by or indications of what will make a good hunting dog. I would make sure that the pup is alert, bold in manner, and is not sensitive. I would clap my hands a few times or make some noise and watch his reactions carefully. I would avoid the puppy that backs up immediately or tries to hide. The one that stays out and has an outgoing personality, that would be my pick.

Dogs of the Versatile hunting breeds start early, as demonstrated by this five-month old Pudelpointer just doing what comes naturally.

Do you have any particular guidelines or rules of thumb in your approach to training Versatiles that govern your actions around dogs and make training efforts easier, quicker, better? Some do and don't suggestions?

In training dogs I've found it of much importance that both trainer and dog are in the proper frame of mind. I've had excellent results in confining a dog to an isolated spot, a holding kennel, for approximately one hour before training time. I have found that the dog's attention span was much greater and the training generally easier.

If I reach a stalemate in my training, rather than losing my temper or overstressing the dog, I break off the training session and perhaps try again several hours later. If the problem can't be worked out then, sometimes laying the dog up for two or three days shows a completely different attitude in the dog.

Explain the term "yard breaking" or "yard training." Do you yard-break a dog before you take him afield or do you allow a dog to do what comes naturally for some time before you start disciplining him? Why?

In my opinion, it's beneficial to see if the dog is worth training. If the dog shows natural tendencies such as ranging, finding birds, and flash pointing, once his natural abilities have been properly evaluated or located, that is the proper time to start with obedience, or as it is sometimes called, yard training or yard breaking.

Once the dog searches well, finds birds, is birdy in general and flash points as well as enters water readily, I don't hunt the dog at all or run him in the field but concentrate for approximately six weeks on obedience. The proper sequence in my particular case is: leash training, then "Stay!" and then "Come!" Once the dog is obedience trained and force-trained to retrieve, I switch back to field work.

If a dog is biddable, handles good, handles easy, keeps in touch—whatever description you want to use—describe his actions and what he is doing while out hunting. How do you train to instill this behavior?

A well-bred Versatile hunting dog should show great independence in the field and hunt with great desire. He should work the cover accurately and systematically, depending upon the type of cover you hunt in. One must take into consideration great regional differences in bird population and cover. In some areas a dog that hunts the hedgerows where birds in this particular locale would be is desirable. In other woodcock or eastern cover that is more dense, I'd expect a dog to quarter more than just run fence rows.

A mannerly dog that is easy to handle in the field should respond well to the whistle, preferably check back once in a while with the handler. It's very difficult to state what a dog's range should be. I prefer a medium-ranging dog, 75 to 150 yards from me, depending upon the cover. In dense cover, perhaps a dog should work only 30 yards from the gunner. A dog of good breeding may shorten his range according to the cover. Others won't do this naturally and would have to be controlled with the whistle.

Whistle training is a very important part of my yard breaking. I use only two whistle signals. One is the "Whoa!" whistle, one long blast. The

A pair of champion German wirehaired pointers (Drahthaars) belonging to Cliff Faestel, Brookfield, Wis., are shown in pointing and backing postures.

"Come!" whistle is two short blasts. That's all that's really needed in the field to control a dog's pattern. If you want to work your dog in a direct quartering pattern, bring him to a stop with a "Whoa!" whistle and then call him in and wave to the opposite side. The dog will soon catch on that a double blast means that he has to turn.

When hunting on a shooting preserve, it is very important that the dog work the cover thoroughly and quarter well without passing too much ground or missing birds. So I concentrate a great deal on having a dog quarter properly. Once a dog is whistle trained, to get the same performance in the field, he will carry a shock collar after being introduced to the dummy collar for several days. If he does not respond to the whistle signal, that signal is backed up by the shock collar.

The electronic shock collar is much more effective than any check cord system I have used in the past. It is just a matter of a few days to have a well-quartering dog on hand.

Describe how you teach a dog his name and to come to you when called.

The dog gets introduced to his name at feeding time. When I put down his feed dish, I call his name and say "Here!" or "Come!" In the more formal training the "Here!" or "Come!" is enforced by teaching the dog to

Heeling is taught on collar and leash by pulling a dog up to the side of the train-er's leg if he forges ahead, lags behind, or pulls away and commanding "Heel!" until the dog learns to walk in the proper position. John Kegel demonstrates.

"Whoa!" first. From a stationary position, he is called with the double-blast "Come!" whistle and the verbal command "Here!," and a slight tug on the check cord fastened to his collar controls his direction.

Describe your method of teaching a dog to "Whoa!" What's your re-lease command, allowing the dog to move up to relocate or to move out when no birds are produced?

The command "Whoa!" or "Stay!" is taught in the following manner: Place a spike or force collar on the dog, with 6-foot training lead attached. Alternately walk and stop with the dog at heel on the left side. I walk ap-proximately 25 or 30 feet, stop abruptly, keep his head high, and command in a sharp voice, "Stay!"

I try to restrain the dog in that position for several seconds and then resume walking another 25 or 30 feet, stop, again with the command "Stay!" On the first day this would be repeated perhaps a hundred times, taking up about ten or fifteen minutes. The second day would be pretty much a repeat of the first day, just walking and stopping until the dog has the idea of stopping and remaining perfectly still. Since he usually will fol-low you if you resume walking, the next step is to have the dog remain on the spot.

This is most easily done by restraining the dog with the left hand and then taking one step to the right. There is less tendency for the dog to follow you than if you make a step ahead of him. If the dog stays in this position, you might increase the distance by two steps. When he holds under the continued restraint of the leash held by your outstretched arm, take one step ahead of him, still restraining him. This is followed by circling the dog, walking behind him. Each hold in this position would not take more than three or four seconds. The dog is then released by the "Heel!" command, walked 25 or 30 feet as the exercise is repeated. By the end of a week, the dog should remain in a "Stay!" position without too much difficulty. You should be able to walk 25 or 30 feet away from the dog and he'll stay. If he breaks, just carry him back to the spot, command "Stay!" in a sharp voice, and give a little tug on the force collar. That's all that is needed at this stage to correct the dog.

The dog is released by "Heel!" or "Come!," which is really the fundamental way of teaching the dog to come. Once the dog responds fairly well to the verbal command "Stay!," I introduce the whistle.

I usually use a Roy Gonia whistle, giving one blast. It would work something like this: walk 25 feet, stop abruptly, say "Stay!," and immediately blow the whistle. This transition usually takes very little time; dogs catch on quite easily. It is much more difficult to stop the dog some distance away from you.

I usually do this with a check cord and force collar and some type of light livestock or buggy whip. Walk the dog, make him stay, call him to you and, when he's halfway in, either command "Stay!" or blow the "Stay!"

One method of teaching a dog to "Whoa!" on command is demonstrated by John Kegel. Trainer tells the dog to "Whoa!" and backs away holding cautioning hand upright; he flicks the dog's front legs with whip if the dog moves forward.

Once the retrieving lessons are instilled, a force-trained retriever will hold game just as he did the training dummy, as Zeno, a Kegel-trained Pudelpointer does here with a mallard hen.

whistle. Of course, at this stage, he will not obey. So I stretch one hand out as a stopping signal and then administer a slight slap across the front legs with the buggy whip. It doesn't take long and the dog will stop to just the swishing sound of the whip.

In the field, under actual hunting conditions, the dog is released from the "Stay!" position by either the command "Hie On!," which indicates to the dog he's to go out and hunt; or in the case of relocating, let's say, a running pheasant, just the command "Easy!," which is a cautionary command. Easy just means to keep in scent touch with the bird or to try to relocate with caution; I don't want the dog to go full steam ahead and accidentally flush a bird.

Another way of teaching the dog to "Whoa!" when he is some distance from you is to plant a stake in the yard or field, loop a long check cord around it, command the dog to "Stay!" and just tighten the check cord attached to his collar to restrain him in a position some distance from you. This is a very effective method and should be used to supplement the buggy-whip and stretched-out-hand method described earlier.

This is one particular obedience drill where a shock collar should *not* be used. If you command "Stay!" or "Whoa!" and the dog does not obey you and you press the shock button, invariably the dog will come to you for protection. I have not yet seen a dog that would stop dead and not come to you when the shock collar is used in such a manner.

Using the shock collar out in the field when the dog is not obeying the "Whoa!" command and is chasing the bird is another matter. That is an instance where the shock collar *can* be used. But during the yard exercise, the shock collar is a No-No!

At what age do you prefer to start a young dog in the field and what do you do and look for while out training, hunting, running, or working a dog?

Prior to formal training I like to take the young prospect out in the field as early as possible. If it is a client's dog, that probably would be about eight months of age. I take my own dogs out at four or five months and watch their progress in the field. The one thing I value more than any other trait in a gun dog is independent and intelligent search, which sometimes just comes with experience.

Describe your procedure for encouraging a dog to run big, "hunt to the limits." What's your procedure for developing a dog whose range is more restrictive?

Most Versatile gun dog owners seem to prefer a short- or medium-ranging dog. Far-ranging dogs are very seldom desired. But there are times when dogs just do not have an adequate range. A dog that ranges no more than 25 to 30 yards out from you does not have practical value in the field when hunting wild game birds.

In order to hunt out farther, a dog must possess an instinct to hunt. If he does not have that inbred desire, there is very little you can do to make a big-running dog out of a short-running dog. However, you can improve his range somewhat by giving him more confidence and hunting him with a big running dog, hunting him in low cover, walking fast and urging the dog on, trying to control him as little as possible, and overlooking such things as chasing birds. You must obedience train at a later stage than with the dog that has shown sufficient desire in the first place.

Are there natural "big-going" dogs and "close-working" dogs? If there are, except for unusual circumstances, is it worthwhile to try to go against the grain and convert the dog's natural style to a different pattern?

There is a great difference in range among Versatile hunting dogs, not only in the various breeds, but within the breeds. You might have a Brittany that searches out there 200 yards and some strains of Brittanys are extremely close-working dogs, which work within 30 to 50 yards. In my opinion it is difficult to make a far-ranging dog of a natural close worker.

If someone is not happy with a dog whose natural range is 30 to 50 yards and desires one whose range is 150 to 250 yards, my advice would be to discard the dog and look for one of another breed.

On the other hand, I don't think it is too difficult with Versatile dogs to bring a dog in. One of the most effective devices in controlling the range is the electric shock collar. If the dog gets out too far, I just whistle him to turn. If he does not turn, I back up the whistle command with an electric jolt. This is most effective and I've had great success with all breeds of dogs in the Versatile category.

The range of the Versatile dogs is perhaps not as great as with Pointers and Setters where reference is often in terms of half a mile or more. Far-reaching Versatile dogs may have a range of 200 yards; anything over that is really exceptional.

Generally, what is the difference, if there is any, between a "covey dog" and a "singles dog"? Are there indications or other ways to spot how a young dog is likely to turn out?

I've had only limited experience quail hunting. I would say that most Versatile dogs would make better singles dogs than covey dogs. Most Versatile dogs that I have hunted with, particularly Pudelpointers, seem adequate to be covey dogs, although their range may not be sufficient in big wide-open country. However, where I have hunted the range was good enough to find coveys and then do some very good work on the follow-up singles.

How do you introduce a young dog to birds? In the yard? On planted birds? On wild birds? Starting from puppyhood do you fool with a bird wing on a string with little pups? Do you prefer to wait until they are old enough to encounter birds in the field?

I try to tease a seven- to eight-week-old puppy with the bird wing and get some sight points out of the dog. I'm not convinced it has a great effect on developing his pointing instinct, but it does show some reaction and you sometimes can detect pointing style that the dog may possess. Dogs that point the bird wing with a fairly high tail will later on point the live birds in the same manner. But because a pup shows no desire to point a bird wing does not mean a total lack of pointing instinct. I've had several cases where a dog that never pointed a wing in puppyhood developed into an extremely staunch, intense pointer.

From there my next step would be to take the puppy out in the field in fairly low cover and let him chase birds, butterflies, or anything he desires. I also might tempt him by planting an occasional quail in his path to see how he reacts and to develop his birdiness. When the dog has reached five or six months and we start with the training program, my first step is to teach the dog to sight point.

Usually I anchor a bird with a cola bottle tied by a string to its leg, bring the dog up on leash and as soon as he sights the pheasant, I just restrain the dog, don't give any commands at all, just sweet-talk him while restraining him. After three or four lessons the dog develops into a fairly staunch sight pointer of live birds.

From the low cover where he can see the bird I would move into slightly higher cover where the dog has the additional chance of scent pointing the pheasant or getting scent before he sight points. With this transposition I find it much easier to staunch the dog later on.

I simulate a flush by picking the pheasant up and tossing it over a fence, stone wall, some place out of sight, and perhaps repeat the procedure by allowing one or two relocations. I don't think it should be overdone. One training session would consist of three sight points. From there I would go to quail or chukar. Quail is the ideal game bird if the cover is low and there's sufficient scent for the young dog.

Once a dog starts pointing game, when do you start staunching him and how do you go about doing this?

Once a pup shows birdiness and flash points with some intensity and chases the birds, this is usually the time for me to start working on his staunchness. I don't see anything to be gained by letting the Versatile dog chase for a period of time before staunching him.

Once the dog starts to point I usually work him on planted quail in strategic locations. I make every effort to get to the dog before he has a chance to jump in. This is done by either letting the dog drag a check cord or placing myself, or an assistant, in such a location that as soon as the dog gets into a flash point he can be restrained. At this point I do not use "Stay!" or any other command. I just try to staunch him by sweet-talking and perhaps lifting him up slightly by the tail, pressing him toward the bird and making him very comfortable in the process of pointing. I would let him maintain the point for a few seconds, then flush the bird and restrain the dog at the same time.

I feel it is much easier to get the dog steady to wing and shot by not letting him develop the habit of chasing the bird. So every time I have a chance to restrain the dog at the flush, I just keep him back and praise him. When the bird is out of sight, I order him on to hunt.

Describe your procedure in introducing a dog to gunfire, assuring that the dog will not be gunshy.

I usually do not introduce a dog to gunfire until he is sufficiently birdy and hunting well and chasing birds. While the dog is in the process of chasing a bird, I wait until he gets approximately 50 yards away from me and fire a shot with a 20-gauge shotgun. In his excitement he usually does not pay any attention to this. I don't recall any instance where I had a sound dog that turned gunshy with this method. I do not go through the complicated process of starting with a cap pistol and working up through a .410 and so on.

Describe your procedure in teaching a dog to retrieve. Do you start in the yard or afield? Do you force-break or take advantage of a natural inclination to pick up and carry?

I'm a great believer in force-training a dog to retrieve. At no time will

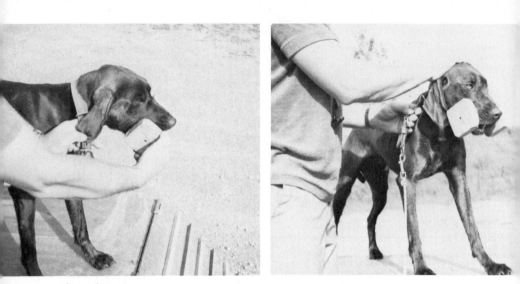

Above left
John Kegel demonstrates a force-training procedure in teaching a dog to fetch. The dog is induced to take a dumbbell-shaped dummy by pinching ear between thumbnail and force collar. When the dog opens mouth in protest, the dummy is inserted.

Above right
The dog is praised and petted as he stands and holds the dummy, which is placed in a comfortable position in his mouth.

I rely on a dog's natural ability to pick things up or bring a bird in. It's fine if a dog does that but it is not the basis upon which a reliable retriever is made.

My method of training a dog to retrieve is strictly a step-by-step, force-training method, consisting of eight different steps. It is taught at the same time the dog is taught to "Stay!" or "Whoa!" The end product is a much better dog. The force-training seems to show up in other phases of the training. He learns to adjust to discipline better and becomes a more mannerly dog all around.

To describe the method in a nutshell, I have a 6-foot training table, the dog is led up a ramp onto the training table, put in a stay position and a wooden dumbbell is placed very gently in the dog's mouth, which is opened by pressing the lip against the upper teeth. No great force is really needed to open the dog's mouth. When the dumbbell is placed in the dog's mouth, it is held there for a few seconds. The dog will be more inclined to hold the dumbbell if you just grasp the loose skin at the throat and tighten it, so the dog will give up the attempt to spit the dumbbell out.

While I usually have the dog hold for two or three seconds, I do not place any great emphasis on the holding. At this stage I just want the dog to get used to the dummy. The introduction should be a pleasant experiment. I praise lavishly and stroke the dog gently over his back, rub his ears

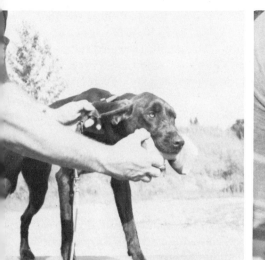 

Above left
Once he will hold reasonably well, the dog is encouraged to make the "1-inch" reach to take the dummy on command. The distance the dog must reach to take hold of the dummy is gradually increased.

Above right
The dog continues to "key" off the hand holding the dummy, gradually moving forward to get the dummy and eventually bending down to pick it up off the ground, until he will pick up on command even though the hand is taken away.

Below
Once the dog will pick up and hold satisfactorily he may be left in possession of the dummy as the trainer moves back, calls him in to him to deliver the dummy.

while the dummy is in his mouth. I have two or three of these dummy-insertion sessions, then walk the dog around the table for a few times to get his mind off it. Then I bring him back up on the table and repeat the procedure. In total I would not exceed fifteen minutes training time. If fast progress is desired, this should be repeated later on the same day for another fifteen minutes. I would spend altogether six training sessions just getting the dog used to holding the dummy in his mouth, or tolerating the dummy in his mouth. That is step one.

Step two is for right-handed people to hold the dog's J.A.S.A. force collar with the left hand (whether you use this spike collar that I prefer or a choke chain collar doesn't make much difference) and with the other hand just press the dumbbell against the dog's lips and command "Fetch!"

The dog will twist and turn his head and you just follow it constantly, bearing pressure with the dumbbell against his lips and eventually he will open his mouth. Some will take it immediately, others it might take half a minute to three minutes. The important thing is to persevere and place the dumbbell in the dog's mouth. Care should be taken not to place it so deeply in his mouth that you cause discomfort. Again, as a matter of routine, I repeat the grasping of his throat skin to make him hold for two or three seconds, rubbing his ears, rubbing his back, and praising while he holds, giving the dog a very favorable impression of this training aspect. This should be repeated until the dog opens his mouth willingly when the dummy is pressed lightly against his lips and teeth, usually requiring two or three days, and should not take longer than four or five days with the most stubborn dog.

Step three is what I call the "1-inch reach." By now the dog should know what "Fetch!" means. You hold the dummy approximately 1 inch in front of his muzzle, grasp the collar with the left hand and also place the left hand thumb on the dog's ear, using the collar as a backing or base under the ear.

Tell the dog to "Fetch!" His initial reaction will probably be to do nothing. Pull the dog's head forward with the collar, making sure you do not pull him by the ear, and when the dog's teeth reach the dummy, pinch into the dog's ear with the thumb, pressing the ear flap against the collar under it, until the dog lets out a little yelp. That is the time you place the dumbbell in the dog's mouth. Ideally the dog's muzzle closes over the dummy. It may take some practice on your part, but it should go very smoothly without pain to the dog except for the ear pinch.

To the trainer's amazement, some dogs will show no reaction to the initial ear pinch, pretending there is no discomfort. But if you increase the pressure for a few seconds, every dog will respond sooner or later, and give out a little yelp. He will then open his mouth and you can gently pull his head toward the dumbbell so he receives it in his mouth. Immediately the dog should be praised lavishly and be made very comfortable. When you take it out of his mouth, you should command "Out!" or, as some prefer, "Give!" Once the dog starts to reach for the dummy willingly, it is time to go to the next step.

This consists of a 6-inch reach. Again about two or three days will be required before the dog makes the longer reach. It is accomplished by a repetition of the procedure that established the 1-inch reach. Once the dog does the 6-inch reach willingly, I concentrate on the "Hold!" technique.

Make the dog keep the dummy in his mouth while commanding "Hold!" Or if you don't want to teach an additional command, just order him to "Fetch!" while making him hold onto the dummy. Most dogs have a tendency to spit out the dummy. I restrain the dog gently, raising his chin or holding that loose skin at the throat for a short period of time, and then let go and if the dog spits it out, I give a short bump against his nose with the back of my hand. Dogs find this annoying and soon associate this nose bump with dropping the dummy. If he holds for any extended period, fine. Praise him and try to make gradual progress rather than trying to have him keep the dummy for several minutes on his first lesson.

Once the dog keeps the dumbbell in his mouth reliably, this is the time to walk around with the dog carrying the dumbbell. Sometimes dogs lacking confidence will stubbornly stand still and refuse to move around carrying the forced object in their mouths. However, they can be enticed to come or move by bending down to the dog's level and gently coaxing. Very little can be accomplished by using raw force at this particular stage.

When the dog carries the dumbbell reliably, go back and gradually increase the distance of the reach until the dog reaches down to the floor, or to the training table if you use one, while you still keep your hand on the dummy.

No matter how well or far he reaches, he will not take up the dumbbell unless your hand is present. To get him to do so must be done very gently, from holding the dumbbell slightly above floor or table level, to holding it actually right on the surface, to moving the hand back a few inches free of the dummy and gradually accomplishing getting the hand out of the dog's vision.

Dogs that go through the routine with no difficulty at all will sooner or later rebel. No trainer should think he can skip the gradual increase of the distance because the dog is doing so well. That will backfire sooner or later. There will always be setbacks in this training method. For no known reason, the dog will refuse to reach out for a certain distance. What you do then is just return to the previous level of a shorter reach, pick it up from there and gradually increase it.

All training sessions should be started with a repeat of the previous session. This will save you time in the end. Once a dog picks up the dumbbell off the floor, then on the leash he can be asked to pick it up if you put the dog in a stay-sitting position. Place the wooden dumbbell between you and the dog, and point to it. Make sure he stops there. In case he ignores it, bring him back. Always have your hand ready if he does not get the sight picture; that will remind him there is no fooling around.

Once he brings the wooden dumbbell reliably from a distance of about 20 yards, a heavier object or a canvas training dummy with feathers wrapped around it can be substituted. Then you can go to a small frozen bird such as quail, chukar, or pigeon; then to a pheasant, preferably with the wings removed or wrapped to the body with string to make the pickup easier. Then on the check cord he should be asked to bring it a little distance, gradually increased to longer distances, and then finally the object is placed in cover.

No game should be made of this—by that I mean tossing the dummy or game bird into the cover and urging the dog to "Get it, Rover, get it!" The dog should remain very calm and the retrieve should be very deliberate. This is the only way you will get a finished retriever as the end product.

Describe your procedure for steadying a dog to wing and shot.

Steadying to wing and shot is really just an extension of making the dog staunch. I never allow the dog to chase the bird after the dog has been made staunch, hence the dog will remain steady automatically, at least through the training period. I just restrain the dog in his original position by not giving any slack on the check cord at all. I don't use the method where the dog runs into the collar and then gets toppled over. I prefer that the dog remains steady at the point.

How do you assure that a dog will stop to flush?

If the dog makes any attempt to chase an accidentally bumped or flushed bird, he is immediately whistled to the stay position or commanded verbally to stay. If the dog ignores the command for some reason, then I place the electric collar around his neck and back up the command.

Describe your procedure for training a dog to back.

Backing is not one of the strong suits of Versatile dogs. Their eagerness to retrieve quite often makes them poor backers. However, a dog trained well to the command "Whoa!" or "Stay!" can be backed mechanically.

An extension of that mechanical process will make a fairly reliable backer in the field. Versatile hunting dogs, in contrast to many instances with Pointers and Setters, are hunted singly rather than in braces. So being an individual hunting dog there is not as much need for a backing dog. However, if you hunt with a friend who also hunts with a pointing dog, the situation may arise where you don't want your dog to interfere with a friend's dog and you command your dog to stay by either whistle or voice.

When a dog displays serious faults—self-hunting, blinking, hard mouth, gunshyness—is there much point in an amateur trainer working to try to correct these faults?

On a percentage basis the amateur trainer probably does not have a good track record when it comes to solving serious problems—and sometimes these cases are very difficult for a professional. Patience is required, as well as an understanding of why the problem developed in the first place. Some problems may be incurable for even the best professional.

Do you have any tips or suggestions to help avoid serious faults before they become established?

Many serious faults can be avoided by following the proper training methods. Rushing the training often leads to serious problems. Hard mouth is almost always avoided if the dog is properly force-trained to retrieve. Most hard mouth is caused by the so-called natural retrieving methods where the dog is teased into bringing a bird, dummy, or object and bad habits start to develop and are left unchecked in early stages. Severe harshness or discipline at an early age might lead to problems such as blinking.

Improper introduction to gunshot can also cause that problem. But timing is one of the most important aspects of dog training; also understanding the nature of your dog. If he's a soft dog, very submissive, a different timing schedule must be applied than to a hard-nosed dog that can take quite a bit more pressure.

Probably the most difficult thing for the amateur trainer is to evaluate the training potential and the speed at which a dog can be trained. Most first dog owners are overly eager and rush their training too much, and invariably some of those faults will occur.

Aside from the necessity of using good judgment, is there generally a time to punish and a time to praise? What forms should punishment and praise take, and when are they used to discipline and reward a dog?

I do not believe you can train a dog without any physical punishment. However, the judgment as to when to punish a dog is very important. You must ascertain that the dog can fully understand your commands and only punish him when he is obviously defying them, trying to revolt or rebel against your wishes. The basic fundamental for successful training, however, is really praising. You never can praise enough, especially if you are certain the dog has done whatever he is asked to do in the required fashion.

Based on your experience, can the electronic shock collar be of much aid to an amateur training his own dog? If it has drawbacks, how should a person using it exercise caution to achieve the most from it?

The electronic shock collar seems to have a great appeal to the amateur trainer, judging from numerous ads appearing in magazines and the like. However, amateurs should be cautioned to use the electric shock collar very sparingly. There is great danger that irreparable harm can be inflicted on the dog by improper use. When used properly and with discretion, the electric shock collar is a marvelous tool, a great time saver for the professional. But good judgment as to the proper time to use it is very important.

The electronic shock collar cannot be used to teach a dog a command. It can only be used to enforce a command that the dog has fully understood but refuses to obey once he realizes he's out of the reach of his handler or trainer. It is almost like an invisible check cord or leash. The dog can be reached out at 100 or 200 yards and great time can be saved by not having to run down the dog or go over multiple repetition of certain training aspects.

It is probably best used in obedience training, preventing chasing cars, killing chickens, or even chasing birds and restricting range. But it should never be used when the dog is on point or in the process of retrieving.

An amateur partial to its use should seek the advice of a professional or someone greatly experienced in the use of a shock collar. When a dog owner does seriously consider buying a shock collar, great care should go into selecting the right make and model.

A cheap electric collar is not only unsatisfactory in performance but can do harm to your dog, such as releasing an electric shock when it is not wanted. If a dog is in the process of pointing a bird, an unwanted shock can be almost disastrous. My personal experience with a variety of cheap units has been very unsatisfactory. I went through half-a-dozen shock collars of different makes before I found a reliable unit. Like everything else in life you get what you pay for. So check with your local professional or someone who has experience before you invest a considerable sum of money in the acquisition of a shock collar. The shock collar that I use, the one used by most professionals, is manufactured by Tri-Tronics Industries.

What are the advantages and disadvantages of a sportsman keeping his bird dog as a house dog and companion, as opposed to kenneling him strictly as a hunter?

Versatile hunting dogs are companion dogs. They are much happier in the surroundings of your family than in the isolation of a kennel. I would go so far as to say that many of the Versatile breeds are not good kennel dogs. They are very unhappy and react by chewing, barking, general running. The environment of a family is always beneficial to the hunting dog. It just isn't true that a dog cannot be both a pet and a hunter. The relationship between the owner and the hunting dog is strengthened very much if the dog becomes an active member of the family.

I always feel sorry for a Versatile hunting dog that is kenneled in isolation with no companion, fed once or twice a day, and never given any exercise until the actual hunting season has approached. So if you have any means of making the hunting dog a member of your family, you will be the winner by having a much better dog.

If for some reason you cannot keep the dog in the house and have to provide a kennel, there's nothing wrong in that either as long as you pay sufficient attention to the dog. There can be a compromise that works out well if the dog is kenneled in the daytime and spends the nighttime in the house, or vice versa. At least he spends some time with his family and gets more close contact with his owner.

The only disadvantage I can think of is that the house dog might not be as weather-hardy. If you hunt under extreme conditions, he might feel the cold more than the dog that has been kenneled outside without heat.

Based upon your extensive experience, would you give some off-the-cuff advice, odds and ends of information, pet peeves, tips, remarks on conditioning, etc., that weren't touched upon in previous questions?

The Versatile breeds as a whole are relatively easy to train and seem to have a great capacity for learning. Yet very few dogs reach even half of their potential during their life span. One of the prime reasons for this is that Versatile dogs also need a fairly firm hand. Most amateur dog trainers are just too softhearted to command the respect of their dogs.

To be a successful trainer, one has to be boss-man at all times.

PART 3

Retrievers

Ed Carey

Growing up on a southern Wisconsin farm, Edward M. (Ed) Carey trained some hunting dogs as a boy and in 1949 began his career as a professional trainer, specializing in retrievers but training all types of hunting dogs.

He has started or finished literally dozens of field trial champion Labrador and Golden retrievers and as an indication of his versatility has also trained and handled a German shorthaired pointer and an Irish setter field champion and once won the Wisconsin state beagle championship in the 15-inch class.

Ed Carey spent fifteen years as a trainer at the Fin-N-Feather Club, Dundee, Illinois, and dropped out of field trialing about three years ago to concentrate on developing class shooting dogs. His wife, Sanna, who has trained and handled retrievers in amateur competition since she was a girl, became a professional upon marriage to a pro and continues to handle some trial retrievers. They have six children living with them at their summer training farm near Woodstock, Illinois, and winter training quarters near Green Pond, South Carolina, on an 11,000-acre plantation owned by Mr. and Mrs. Gaylord Donnelly. Donnelly is president of Ducks Unlimited.

The kennel at Woodstock, where dogs are trained from April to mid-November, accepts dogs for boarding during the winter but the southern climes make continuation of training a twenty-five to thirty dog string easier in the winter and coincide with the quail and duck hunting seasons.

The Careys can be reached at Lakeridge Kennels, 1308 Thompson Road, Woodstock, Illinois 60098 (Phone: 815—338-5536) from April to mid-November and at Ashepoo Plantation, Green Pond, South Carolina (Phone: 803—844-2817) from mid-November to April.

Trainer Ed Carey.

Loral I Delaney

Some puppies start young and so do some dog trainers. In the case of Loral I Delaney, at age thirty-eight the attractive Minnesota professional can look back on almost thirty years of training dogs for pay and proven success with hunting, field trial, and stage performing dogs.

Daughter of Fred Armstrong, a pioneer game farm and shooting preserve operator, and wife of Charles "Chuck" Delaney, also a pro trainer and gun club operator, dogs, guns, and game have been the young woman's life. She made her first on-stage appearance with her father's dogs at the age of five, started training her own dogs at age nine, at thirteen took over the kennel end of her father's operation, and was on her own at age eighteen.

Now the Delaneys operate an extensive boarding and training kennel with 280 acres of grounds, working with 250 to 300 dogs annually, and Loral I appears in three to six sport shows each year nationwide with a troupe of gun dogs that demonstrate, on stage, many things hunting dogs are required to do in the field.

Successful women professional gun dog trainers are rare in the United States and Loral I has been successful with all gun dog breeds as well as retrievers, including having trained German shorthaired pointers that have taken national laurels in trials. She also ranks as one of the nation's best trapshooters and does her own taxidermy work. She has hunted upland birds and waterfowl from Texas to Canada and has bagged a buck deer with bow and arrow. Loral I and Chuck have a fifteen-year-old daughter, Sherry.

The Delaneys can be reached at Armstrong Ranch & Kennel, 8404 161st Avenue, N.W., Anoka, Minnesota 55303 (Phone: 612—427-1777).

Loral I Delaney and yellow Labrador retriever friend.

Orin Benson

   While Orin Benson may be best known for his work with retrievers, he not only has trained virtually all breeds of dogs but is a premier animal trainer as well, proving his capabilities by producing fox, pheasant, hawk, skunk, and other wild and domestic animal performers for movies.

   For more than thirty years his gun dog demonstrations have graced stages at the nation's sport shows and other outdoor exhibitions. A native of Minnesota, he has been training retrievers since before the first trial for retrievers was held in his adopted state of Wisconsin in 1936. Benson quickly established himself as a leading trainer and handler of field trial retrievers, his top dogs including FTC Black Panther, whose record number of 172½ points gained in American Kennel Club Open competition was unchallenged for many years.

   In recent years Benson's efforts have been devoted to gun dog training at his kennel and game farm in the Kettle Moraine area of southeastern Wisconsin. He is one of the few men in the nation with an understanding of wolves, having bred, raised, and *trained* them. Kepa, his first timber wolf, was trained very much as a dog is trained and is the subject of at least one book and numerous magazine articles. Benson is widely versed in all aspects of the dog world—breeding, training, trialing, showing, grooming, boarding, and merchandising dogs—and is a valued consultant for other pro and amateur trainers, shooting preserve operators, and movie producers. Benson and his wife, Lucille, who has shared the supervision of varied dog operations with him, have a daughter, Lynn. Benson can be reached at Benson's Eaglewood Kennels, Eagle, Wisconsin 53119 (Phone: 414—594-2313).

Trainer Orin Benson with one of his timber wolves.

What were your reasons or what influenced you to decide to specialize in training retrievers primarily, rather than other breeds of gun dogs?

Carey: First I guess my decision to train dogs was a great love for the dogs. I saw what the dogs could do and what other people could do with them, and I saw an area of competition. I saw a great deal of self-satisfaction in trying to train the dog's basic qualities into something extraspecial.

Another thing was the people who were involved. When I was a kid, a young trainer came to our house frequently to have dinner. I admired him quite a bit. It was Orin Benson. He was a wizard at handling dogs, getting a dog to do things I didn't think the dog could do. He was just a great trainer. It was a matter of the nice associations with the people as well as the dogs themselves, the whole thing, that made it totally attractive to me.

Delaney: I grew up in the field of dog training. My dad was a trainer and I can remember trying to be a trainer ever since I was about three years of age, copying him, watching him, having something to do with the training end of it.

Orin Benson, shown with Finnegan, an Irish water spaniel, in dry, full coat, has a soft spot for "grandpa's duck dog, the old Irish rat-tail."

I really started training other people's dogs when I was about nine years old, and was almost in the business on my own when I was thirteen. My dad took over a game farm and I was running the kennel business at that time. I just enjoyed it, and I guess that's how I got started.

Benson: In this part of the country we're in duck country, not in quail country. When I started, duck dogs were the big thing. They weren't all retrievers either. Anything that could swim, hold a bird, and bring it back fit to eat was a duck dog. Then, naturally, hunters started wanting a better quality dog. There was a demand for the training, handling, and care of retrievers more exclusively, although I have continued to train all breeds of gun dog from time to time.

Thirty-five to forty years ago people didn't know too much about the Labradors and Goldens. They'd had Irish "rat-tails" and American water spaniels and Chesapeakes, and that old Irish water spaniel was slow in the open water but combined the qualities of a retriever and a spaniel and was the best swamp and marsh dog and cripple catcher ever. But its coat and some other drawbacks didn't let it keep up with the other retrievers. There aren't many any more, but that was grandpa's duck dog.

In 1936, the first retriever trial was held in Wisconsin at Oshkosh. They came from all over: Dave Elliot was out from Long Island, and Frank Hogan and his group from Barrington, Illinois. For the first time in the state of Wisconsin some people saw this group of trained retrievers. So by witnessing a field trial we could see the value of a retriever as a hunting dog and now we've wound up mostly with Labradors, Goldens, and Chesapeakes.

I think the retriever is more companionable, from a gun dog standpoint, than most of the other breeds, so in this particular area and for everyday living the retriever is the best bet for a combination shooting dog, companion dog, and home dog.

There are obvious minor physical differences among the various retriever breeds—coat, color, etc. But do you believe there are any basic structural differences among the retriever breeds? If there are, explain.

Carey: As to structural differences, there's a great difference between a given standard in dog shows and an actual field requirement. Two things that might be pointed out are the length of neck in a retriever and the positioning of the front legs as they join the shoulders. When the neck is too short and the legs are too straight as they are set into the shoulder, a dog must, of necessity, stop before he picks up a bird.

I can take you down to the kennel and show you two distinct dogs within the same breed, the show-bred dog and the field-bred dog. The field-bred dog cannot begin to conform to the standards as set forth in the show ring. Many of the show-bred dogs cannot do the work to the best of their ability because of their physical structure.

The Labrador has the ability to lay on a layer of protective fat that helps an awful lot in the cold water, and the Chesapeake has slightly higher hindquarters, which provides power—important in marsh work and picking up birds—and keeps the head near the ground to help trail.

I never really thought about differences under the skin, but I think that if some carcasses were carefully examined we'd be able to see differences between Chesapeakes and the other two breeds. You'd have to study it to see it, but there are differences: the hock and the set of the hind legs, the way the back is, the slope is different, generally their heads are bigger. Maybe there's more bone density in a Labrador than in a Golden; I'm sure there is.

Delaney: Talking about the different breeds, Goldens, to me, have a different shape than the black Labs, like they've got a little wolfhound or something, I don't know what it is, in them. Chesapeakes also have a shape of their own. They seem to have higher hips that give them a sort of slant to the front. Basically I suppose there's not a great deal of difference. I don't know if there's any particular value in the build of one over the other. They all do the same type of work.

Benson: To me, under the hide, the Labrador is probably the shortest coupled, the Golden is a little lankier, a little higher in leg, the Chesapeake has a longer hindquarter and is a broader-chested, heavier dog. Plus he's stocky in the front shoulders and has an almost swayback conformation. I think if you had them all lying under a blanket I could feel them and tell you which breed was which, because there is a physical difference.

Based on your experience, can you characterize the retriever breeds and the differences between them as to temperament, response to training, ease of training, etc.?

Carey: Let's start with the Chesapeake. Maybe 10 percent of the retrievers I've worked with have been Chesapeakes, and it's been my experience that the Chesapeake is a dog that either does or doesn't. Books on how to train just generally do not apply to the Chesapeake.

The Chesapeake must be very motivated within himself to do what you want him to do. In many cases his natural ability is quite high, higher than the average of the other retriever breeds, but you cannot say "Today we're going to do such and such" and expect to do it with a kennel full of Chesapeakes. It's a step-by-step process. So that would make them a little different from the Golden or the Lab.

The Golden can be trained beautifully to a high degree of mechanical performance. He can learn obedience training much better than the Labrador, he's less trouble to house train, and will acclimate himself to groups and situations much quicker. As a breed the Golden may have a better nose than the Labrador. But the one thing that differentiates the Golden is he's not a dog you can make mistakes with.

With the Labrador you can start with a book and a program and make mistakes and still have a well-trained dog. Thus a Lab makes a good *first* dog. Goldens are more sensitive types and seem to have to know the reason, whereas the Lab doesn't. The Labrador has a lot more momentum, a lot

Left
To more closely simulate actual hunting conditions, during summer training sessions the young hunting retriever needs experience with his handler doing the shooting of flying birds in contrast to field trial training where shots are fired by a gunner at a distance and birds thrown for the dog to mark.

Right
After knocking the pheasant down, Ed Carey sends the steadied dog on his way to make the retrieve.

more thrust to what he's doing. He's tougher, and has more retrieving instinct than a Golden. As a breed, the Lab is just the type you can train a lot easier.

Delaney: The black Lab is probably the easiest to train. Labs are more natural, pick things up easier—usually. But lately I've been getting some nervous, high-strung dogs, which isn't too good for the black Lab breed. Or maybe I've just been getting some bad dogs. But if you get the good breeding in the black Lab, you get a good quality dog.

We get a lot of Golden retrievers in training that haven't had any work and they seem to be a little slower to pick up and get going on birds. Once they do get into the bird situation, the Golden likes to take a bird, possess it, even if it means trying to hide behind two blades of grass. They think they're out of sight. They've got their own thing. So, naturally, they need more force-retrieve training.

Chesapeakes are probably the slowest to mature. It takes a special person to understand them because they are so slow. Compared to a Lab, forget it as far as speed in training is concerned. For instance, you could expect a nine-month-old Lab to be way ahead of a twenty-two-month-old Chesapeake. If you try to keep your Chesapeake going with your neighbor's black Lab, you're really going to go backwards because you'll get panicky

Left
Gun broken open as a safety precaution, Carey waits as the dog returns with the bird.

Center
Having circled behind the handler the dog assumes a sitting position in front of him prepared to release the bird to hand. But with a young dog in training, Carey is in no hurry to snatch the bird from his mouth, reinforcing lessons in carrying and holding.

Right
Calmly and smoothly the handler reaches down to take delivery from the Labrador who may release voluntarily when the man's hand is on it or at the command to "Drop," "Give," or "Out."

and start pushing—and that's the last thing you want to do with a Chesapeake. You have to wait until a Chesapeake is ready to train. Some are brighter than others and will come faster, but most of them aren't.

Benson: Taking the three popular breeds—Chesapeake, Golden, and Labrador—I think the Chesapeake is known to be the toughest of the three as far as temperament and disposition. From a watch-dog angle, being possessive about a bird, he's tough all the way around. Of the three the Chesapeake is the hardest to handle. He'll do tough work, but he takes a specialized handler, someone who knows the breed characteristics, to get the most out of him. Very often the female Ches doesn't carry the distasteful traits the male will. Because a female Chesapeake is easier to handle, I'd favor a female if you have the choice of the two sexes.

The Golden retriever is probably the most mild of the three breeds, a home dog, a friendly, real easy-going pet. They've lost some popularity because of this softness. They can't be rushed or pushed by someone trying to cram everything into an hour's training. Their temperament makes them a

A proper hold on a small diver duck is demonstrated by Stormy, a large Lab belonging to Dave Duffey, who sits quietly and holds a duck he fetched from Lake Poygan as part of some in-the-field-training while actually hunting.

"three-year-old dog"—you get the most out of them by the time they're about three years old. You don't tell Goldens anything; you ask them. Consequently many Goldens are favored from the house-pet side. But as I know the temperament, if a male Golden is a "fighting Golden" there's nothing more vicious. They seem to have the knack, the awareness, the sharpness, and are very intelligent. So when you get a fighting Golden you've got a bad one.

Today the Labrador is the most popular. The same mildness comes through that you get in a Golden, plus you have the short coat. The popularity gives a better field to pick from and there's a lot of selective breeding that is responsible for excellent temperament. To me the best buy on the market today is the Labrador.

Most of the minority breeds are gone today. The Flat-coated retriever is like a black Golden—wonderful temperament and most placid style. The Curley-coated retriever, which is long gone, had a temperament comparable to the American brown water spaniel—half-way between the Lab and the Chesapeake in disposition. The old Irish water spaniel, the rat-tail, the swamp dog, a hot-tempered dog, will challenge and fight anything, and has the weight and brains to know how.

All those old duck dogs took more rigid handling than the breeds of today. So today's methods and everything else goes by the temperament of the different breeds. Consequently the tough breeds are on the way out, the mild breeds on the way in.

Do you have a preference as to which of the retriever breeds you prefer to train? Explain why you do or do not.

Carey: I really don't have a preference, but if I had to select one dog for doing all the work a retriever ought to do it would probably be a Labrador. Yet, I've had Golden retrievers that worked every bit as well as any Labrador I've ever trained. The same applies for Chesapeakes. I would get much more success, be a better dog trainer, have more happy customers if all of my customers owned Labradors.

Delaney: I might be an odd trainer, but I have no preference for any breed, no matter what it is. I like a good quality dog. It can be of any breed; it doesn't make a bit of difference. I just enjoy training. Naturally, I like a dog that has some intelligence and some potential to go somewhere, but you'll get that in every breed and also a bad one in every breed.

Right now I'm into German shorthaired pointers and working a lot with them, handling in field trials. Maybe I have more Chesapeakes around than most trainers, not just because the Midwest is duck country but be-

A neat, clean delivery from a sitting position is made to Orin Benson by a Golden retriever during a training session on pigeons.

cause I had a real good one, Fritz, that made a big contribution to my act when I started working sport shows and I keep looking for another like him even though they're hard to find.

Benson: I'd say the Labrador is the preference, considering the availability and hereditary traits. Years ago we had to train everything, whatever was there. But today given all the qualities, temperaments, and choices, it boils down to the Labrador. With the present civic restrictions, having to transport dogs around in cars and boats, and with dogs spending a lot of time in the house, the short coat and nice temperament make the Lab the all-around pick of the retrievers.

Recognizing individual variations, as you did in making your observation about the general breed differences among retrievers in a previous question, at approximately what age do you prefer to have a dog brought to you for training? For what reasons?

Carey: Years ago, before the advent of all the scientific research on how dogs should be trained, we figured bring them to us when they're a year old. The good ones made it, the bad ones didn't. Now it seems they're all supposed to make it, and if they don't it is something that didn't occur right when they were a certain age.

I have started to train dogs much earlier than a year of age. I like to do some training when they're five, six, seven months old. Before the male lifts his leg I feel there are a number of things that should be done; before the bitch has a heat period there are a number of things that she's taught to do much more easily.

But you wonder sometimes if we wouldn't be better off not to attempt to train any of these dogs that don't have a great deal of ability. If that was the case, then we'd take them at a year of age.

Delaney: Past the puppy stage, naturally. I don't like a Lab much before ten months, better a little older. Same goes for the Golden and the Chesapeake. It doesn't make that much difference. You just have to see what you've got before you get going.

Benson: I like to start them young, conditioning or exposing them to the water and the field at about four months. That doesn't mean it's necessary to send them in for training at four months, but if someone will take the pup, collar break him, lead break him, expose him to the water, get him swimming, that sort of thing, getting him familiar with the field before putting him into a professional's hands, which naturally is going to cost money, it will help get the job done much faster. At six months a puppy should have exposure to birds and the gun. By about eight months the young retriever puppy should be ready to do something in the hunting field. Some of them are pretty good at eight months.

There are things the average dog owner doesn't have right at hand, like the birds, the gun, and the water. If he doesn't, some concentrated work on those three things by a good professional will make that pup a usable dog for the fall hunting, and by ten months old, after a month or two's exposure to hunting in the field, you can get an awful lot out of him.

Can you generally count on any breed being slower to develop or to start learning at an early age?

Carey: The Golden starts on a lot of the mechanical things early—the sit, the come, the heel, the stay. You can start to teach the Lab even though he may not learn as well. You have to let the Chesapeake come at his own rate. Some Chesapeakes that looked pretty bum when they were one year of age can be super dogs at three.

Delaney: The Lab is going to be first, the Golden second, and the Chesapeake last as far as age when they start to catch on.

Benson: Each of the three popular breeds has some characteristics that require you to work on certain things more than usual. Of the three, the Chesapeake has to be taught more to hunt, to search for game. He's got to be schooled early to seek game. I'm talking about upland cover or crippled ducks. Another thing is the mouth condition; if you start a Chesapeake early and get him retrieving early, before he's too tough in the mouth, you're going to have a lot less trouble with the common characteristic of hard mouth.

The Golden is slower and, being placid, it takes a little longer to develop him. Again you have to elaborate on the hunting, game-seeking qualities. Some Goldens are very soft in the mouth and will drop their birds on the retrieves, so this requires more work. You start early in conditioning a Chesapeake to handle a bird softly, you take a Golden and condition him to handle and carry a bird more rigid, have a good delivery. So you have two distinct opposites in your Ches and Golden. The Lab is in between. You don't quite have the problems of hard mouth or dropping birds. Conse-

Well-bred, well-trained retrievers, like this Labrador, should be eager, proficient water retrievers. When expected to work out of elevated blinds, they must be encouraged or taught to leap from the blind into the water below. (Larry Mueller photo)

quently the Lab is usually just about two months ahead of the Golden and Chessie in the start of retrieving game birds.

What steps can a dog's owner take to help ensure that the pup will be trainable and the formal training job made easier when he brings the dog to you?

Carey: You could fill a library with what's been written about this. Basically, a dog that is eight or nine weeks of age should be housebroken quickly. By the time he is three months of age, he should be wearing a collar. After that drag a light string or something and eventually make a leash out of it. He must learn to come when he's called, before he develops any independent ideas. Put him in a sitting position and have him sit and stay by the time he's four to five months of age.

By the time he's four months of age, a retriever should know to retrieve. He should go and get a ball and bring it to you, pick up a dummy with a bird wing on it, things like this. By the time he's six months of age, given the proper circumstances—calm day, shallow, warm water—he should be introduced to water, learn to like water. By the time pups are nine months of age, I like them to be steady to a shot bird, to sit and watch it go. In all the training that is ahead, that's required.

Delaney: When you get a puppy home get him used to being in the crate, and by being in the crate you housebreak him and teach him to go outside to do his business. You're starting the training right there. Teaching a pup to stay in one room in the house is some form of training, but you can't be too hard on him. Then you get him used to the collar and leash, taking him around the neighborhood, or wherever. From there you go into the first phases of retrieving, encouraging the natural retrieving.

In the summer get the pups used to water, grass, weeds. We have some dogs that come from the city and when they see a bush they jump 10 feet high. Let them know what the world's about. Get them used to riding in cars. Just plain social living is what a pup needs. Don't do as some people and throw sticks and balls until the dog is so crazy about them he won't pay any attention to a bird. But it won't hurt to get a pigeon and start him on a pigeon. Also, always remember when you get a pup into water make sure it isn't too early in the spring or too late in the fall so it gets the dog sour on the water because it's too cold.

Benson: People having a puppy at home can help an awful lot. The dog has to accept being restrained by the collar and lead to make him staunch when you're training. Take him for walks, take along a dummy, throw it out in the cover so the dog gets away from eyeballing it all the time. Get him to recognize his name, to come, to follow you. Let him learn to backtrack you. Lie down in the grass, hide behind a tree, let him worry a little about losing you, see if he can find you. Expose him to water, get him to swim.

Just living with the dog and teaching him three or four little things before the concentrated yard work starts will help the trainer a lot and will save the owner a few bucks.

Top
A strong-swimming Labrador approaches a pigeon shot during a training session. Pigeons are flown and shot over water in summer to train for the upcoming duck season. (Larry Mueller photo)

Bottom
Duck grasped firmly but gently, a Labrador heads back to deliver the recovered bird to the hunter. (Larry Mueller photo)

If an owner chooses to train his own dog, are there ages or stages a puppy or young dog goes through when he will learn certain things more readily than at any other time?

Carey: To give an example, let's say you want to teach the pup to sit. You take him out alone, not with a group of other puppies and show him how to sit. (I'm talking about a pup twelve weeks of age.) Have him sit and stay and put his feed pan down and do not let him go to it until you release him. You can develop this in a puppy very quickly, and if he has any sense at all he'll learn that quickly.

Coming in and out of doors is another way to teach a puppy to sit and stay. Don't let him go through a door until you call him through.

Teaching him to come when called, faultlessly, by the time he's six months old is done in short sessions and is extremely important. Don't tell him to come a thousand times and then turn him over to a trainer and say, "Please teach my dog to come," because you've already taught him *not* to

Left

Dave Duffey demonstrates a conventional hand-held dummy launcher. These devices give a trainer numerous advantages when training alone in giving longer falls than can be provided by even the strongest throwing arm, and simulating shooting as it is done while hunting. Note use of protective gloves. With long-range loads the recoil can batter bare hands. (Mickey McLinden photo)

Right

The expression on the trainer's face indicates the noise and recoil of a dummy launcher are hardly pleasant. Care should be exercised in using launchers until a dog is well accustomed to gunfire for the noise they make is more bothersome to an inexperienced or sensitive dog than blanks or live shotgun rounds. (Mickey McLinden photo)

come. That's what you want to avoid—untraining, detraining, bad training.

Delaney: Lots of times one of the retrieving breeds, only six or eight weeks old, will swim right out to a mallard the first time they ever hit the water, like they've been swimming for years, and they'll grab that big duck and tow it in toward shore. Everything's natural. Then if a person doesn't keep them coming along, just drops it there, leaves them in a kennel up to about six months, when they get into about the teen-age stage both male and female puppies get a sort of wanderlust attitude. If you don't get them started on that retrieving part, involved with birds, they get to thinking it's just more fun to bum around.

I know of a particular example of one of those six-week-old natural pups; the people took this pup to live with them, brought him back for training, hadn't done much with him, and at between eight to ten months old that dog couldn't swim, he was afraid of birds, and he was just a bum.

The use of training dummies reduces bird costs in retriever training but young-sters should be familiarized with feathers before the hunting season and trained dogs brushed up with real birds during off-season training sessions. This is Stormy with a canvas dummy; the short rope attached allows flinging it farther.

Why he became that way I couldn't tell you because he did everything nat-urally when he was little. But somewhere along the line he just lost his interest—a sort of dropout.

Benson: It's easy for an owner, before he takes the pup to a trainer, to take him out and see what he likes and dislikes in the hunting line and what the dog has naturally inherited. A pup that has to be coaxed and coaxed, you have to put on hip boots and wade out with him, just doesn't care too much for water at his initial exposure, even though he's a water-bred retriever. Sometimes that is hereditary—if it hasn't been man-made by some guy taking him by the back of the neck and throwing him out in the water. When he's a little short on water, you'll have to work on that end of it. If you expose him to a pigeon, if he runs in circles and barks at it, then you'll know he lacks the guts to go up and get hold of a live bird, so you elaborate on that. I've seen pups that as soon as they got into belly-high cover were afraid of something and would duck back.

If you're a died-in-the-wool duck hunter, pick a dog that loves the water. He might not do anything else, but he's going to make a better duck dog than one that has to be coaxed and forced into the water.

When the owner brings a pup to a trainer, it's a shortcut and a great help if the owner is truthful about the dog and tells the trainer if he won't go in the water, if he mouths his bird, grabs an object and just chews it,

103

won't come to him, all those things. If the owner has fired a blank pistol around the dog and the dog ran over and sat by the car or by the owner, then the trainer can try to overcome either the shyness or boldness or whatever is causing the trouble. So truthfulness about a pup's faults may help more with a puppy than just telling us how good he is.

Naturally there is a difference in dogs of the same age, even littermates, between one that has been ignored and one that has been lived with, taken from his kennel, and periodically played with. You can see the difference between one that has been a buddy-dog, has ridden in a car, been out for a walk with the guy. If a dog is used to being around you, he'll follow and do things with you that he enjoys. A dog first out of a pen is going to be wild. Everybody takes them out of a kennel and expects them to "Heel! Sit!" bang-bang-bang. But they have to have that walk, especially young dogs. So the owner should live with the dog, not have the idea that "I left him in the pen because I didn't want to touch him and do something wrong." Live with the dog and you'll get a better job.

Assuming that for different people there are different choices, under what circumstances will someone buying a dog be best satisfied with a puppy, a started dog, or a trained dog?

Carey: The big question is, what does the prospective owner know about this whole thing? What does he know about dogs? What kind of empathy has he developed over a period of years? If he's had dogs before has he learned from his mistakes? Can the owner take a thoroughly trained dog, pay a good price for him, and then get out of the dog what he has in him?

The trained dog is one whose basic inborn instincts have been properly curbed. If a dog will not deliver to hand, or breaks shot under every situation, if he is allowed to retrogress, and goes back to things he has been taught not to do, can this new owner step in and correct such problems? Or is it better for the new owner to start with a little puppy, to learn with the puppy?

The answer depends on the owner and on his ability to handle a dog and get with him. Some people would be better off, because of their physical condition or lack of knowledge about dogs, to buy a five- to six-year-old thoroughly settled retriever that knows his job and has been doing it for years, maybe knows more about it than they do.

On the other hand, a fellow just getting started in shooting might be better off to get a puppy, bring him along, follow directions, try to train him, consult with a professional. So it works both ways. I'd put the started dog about in the middle.

Delaney: A person interested in buying a dog would have to analyze himself. If he has the time, he can do a lot with a dog from the time the puppy's little. But if he's a busy guy and can't give a pup lots of attention, he's better off buying a started dog from eight months of age on. Then the owner knows what he's got, how the dog likes birds, how he is with the gun. If you can afford it, buy one that's already started. I think you're

A well-trained, even-tempered retriever used as a gun dog may have to be even more adaptable and steady than a field trial dog if he does work like this yellow Labrador does for his owner, Jack Wilson, Fredonia, Wis., shooting mallard in a cornfield.

money ahead. Or, better still, buy a trained dog. Then you really know what you've got. I definitely would buy a trained dog if I had no time to put in on a young dog.

Benson: To tell what age bracket of dog would be best suited to an owner is difficult without knowing the way of life this dog is going to have to live under. A fellow who likes his dog, lives with his dog, he can get along with a puppy, especially if he's capable of doing something with it.

A man whose time is limited to maybe weekends can get a partially started dog that takes only two or three evenings a week of rehearsal. An elderly man who still loves the sport of hunting, the work of a good dog, but doesn't want to go chasing after a dog in the field, should buy a trained dog. If a man hasn't got the time to rehearse his dog during the off-season, someone who just cannot or doesn't want to spend the hours that should be spent with a dog, he'll be better off with a fully broke dog, particularly if he's a preserve or duck club shooter. Actually, I think anyone, no matter what his situation, should be able to find a few minutes a day to devote to his dog.

So you'd try to match the age and capabilities of the owners and dogs, and sometimes we have a lot more trouble with the owners than we do with the dogs.

Describe a started dog in terms of what the buyer of such a dog might expect with regard to obedience and hunting ability. In other words, what has a started dog learned and what can he do?

Carey: I would consider a started dog as a dog you can look at and say, "This dog is going to be a good water dog"; you see him on birds and say, "This dog is going to have a tender mouth." A started dog knows, in a quiet situation, to sit, heel, come, and stay, knows his name and has been put through just basic obedience. A started dog is one that can be said to have no major faults and isn't gunshy.

Because my professional reputation is at stake, when I sell the dog and I call him started the dog must fulfill those requirements. Some dogs are better than others and some started dogs are just going to be started. They're not ever going to reach great heights. But then, of course, that's what the man pays for. You don't necessarily buy a dog that's going to be a field trial champion.

And started at what age? That's important—whether you're talking about a started dog eight or nine months of age or a started two-year-old. The younger dog has more time and is likely to develop further. The two-year-old may have progressed as far as he's going.

Delaney: In my opinion a started dog would be one that would pick up a pigeon, a duck, or a pheasant, on land or water, can swim and is not gun-shy—that's a sort of beginner's started dog. In addition, a started dog would be one that will heel, sit, stay, and come when he's called, one that would have had force-retrieve work to hold and carry a dummy or stick. All that would be required would be to put it together and put a little more polish on his marking.

Benson: A started dog is a dog that has a start in the field he's going to undertake. In a retriever, a started dog must go into the water willingly and retrieve an object, either a dummy or a bird. He must acknowledge the firing of a gun, looking up in the air to see if anything's falling; he must have a certain amount of gun exposure and know what the gun means. He should walk at heel, sit on command, and stay under moderate conditions. He should be acquainted with field cover and in the case of upland hunting should go out looking for his birds, but not run over the hill. Staunching or steadying has begun, and after the dog is started from then on it's a matter of perfection coming up.

What tips would you offer for the selection and purchase of a puppy to help assure the buyer that he will be getting a sound, healthy pup that should be potentially trainable?

Carey: As important as anything is the dog's health. Buy a dog that's in good health; he shouldn't have to go into a new stress situation with a belly full of worms or any kind of infection. A complete veterinary examination at the time of purchase is my recommendation, or the understanding

A Labrador retriever is "given a line" by Loral I Delaney demonstrating the hand signal given to send a dog straight out to a bird he hasn't seen fall.

that the purchaser will take the dog to the vet within a reasonable time after the dog leaves the seller's hands.

The dog should be structurally sound and out of structurally sound parents and grandparents. The Orthopedic Foundation now allows for a lot of checking on hip dysplasia, and I think it's important that all breeding stock go through this thing to ensure that they don't turn up dysplastic.

There must also be some proven ability on the part of the dam and the sire and the granddams and grandsires to be reasonable retrievers. And the dog must like water, like to retrieve in water. A dog shouldn't be picked for appearance or what a good house pet he'll make.

Buying from reputable breeders who have been in the business many years or from people who have stock from such breeders is the best way to approach this thing.

Delaney: Selecting any pup is one of the hardest things anyone can do. Your best bet is to get good breeding; you should know that the sire and dam have produced good pups before. Those are the ones to dive for. You can sometimes get pups out of field trial champions that are not producing anything like themselves, just so-so dogs. It will pay to find out what is producing a top-quality dog.

Benson: Picking a puppy can be a pig in a poke proposition. When you look at a litter of pups, though, there are certain things that catch the eye:

timidity, alertness, willingness, tail wagging, cowering, or not flinching at sharp noises like hand claps. Check pups out. At the first approach of a stranger, does the dog hesitate or come wagging up willingly? Does he go willingly after a little glove and carry it? Is he proud to carry something, anything, even a stick or rolled up cigarette package? A dog's willingness to carry even as a little untrained puppy is a reflection of what he's going to do the rest of his life.

With a litter the hardest thing to do is to pick one out of four or five pups playing together and disrupting each other. So pick out three you'd like to see and watch for little differences. Then get down to one. Taken away from the litter, how does he react? If in a few minutes he's friendly, companionable, wags his tail, acknowledges just you alone, he'll get along better in a home away from his litter. A dog frightened by being alone is a problem dog. You have to depend upon his ancestry to make him a water dog, a retriever, a hunter.

Do you have any particular guidelines or rules of thumb in your approach to training retrievers that govern your actions around dogs and make training efforts easier, quicker, better? Some do and don't suggestions?

Carey: It's a sort of philosophy of training that you're talking about. I don't feel that dog training is a science. I think it's an art, a creative thing that is done with each and every dog. So when we start to work with a dog we have a general idea of what we're going to do, but we change our minds quite often, as things come up.

The dog's basic program changes to some degree. If I start four or five dogs out of the same litter, I'll probably be doing three or four different methods of training. Even though they're all littermates, they're all different.

Throughout the whole thing, I try not to apply quite as much pressure and force in the early training as the dog can take. I try never to lose my temper. One thing any animal—dogs, horses, cows—can't stand is panic. I feel it is readily transmittable. Whether the trainer or the dog panics, the learning process at that moment stops. Or if the dog learns anything he learns bad—bad things, bad reactions. That's what you have to avoid.

When a dog is a little older, perhaps a year or a year and a half depending upon the individual dog, he has to get more training than he needs. You have to reinforce some reactions and activities so he'll perform almost automatically rather than on command, because sometimes dog owners do not give the command at the proper time. Holding, not dropping, an object, whether dummy, duck, or pheasant, must be force-trained. Nobody is going to stand up in a duck blind and order "Hold it! Hold it!" So once a dog picks up a dummy he should be force-trained to deliver to hand—without question, perfectly. Before you can call him a finished dog, he also must be overly trained when it comes to handling and taking directions. He must be steady to wing and shot and must learn to sit and watch birds fly off before he can do well in the exciting temptation of having four or five birds over your decoys and two or three people shooting at them.

Big, tough, and slower to develop, once a trainer gets through to Chesapeakes, like these two monsters from Minnesota trained by Dave Duffey, they are unbeatable for pulling off the most difficult retrieving tasks.

Delaney: Never threaten your dog, never let him really see when you plan to correct him. I always like to have my corrections basically a surprise. Say you have a dog in the house and he's chewing on the corner of the couch, you could sneak up and really crash him a good one. If you did not give him any warning you were going to do it, he'd automatically feel that the couch did it to him. That's an example you can follow through on heeling, sitting, stopping to the whistle in the field when he takes the wrong direction, and it goes into the deepest part of all training.

Benson: To get the most out of a dog, remember that a dog will absorb your mannerisms easily. A very important point is the speed with which you move around animals. Around any animal, you go slow. It's a hereditary trait for an animal to think fast movement is a predator. All predators move fast, all dogs in a fight are fast, so consequently your movement and actions should be slow around an animal.

When you reach down to pet a dog, don't rush him and grab at him. He'll flinch. When the dog comes in with a bird, don't reach out and snatch the bird out of his mouth. Pet him and take it gently. He's going to be a gentle retriever. To me the greatest thing is gentleness and slow movement, not that it takes you forever and a day. Sometimes a guy can move too slow and the dog will drop something or get away from him when he reaches down. When you open a gate, get the dog's attention and let him see you're coming. Don't just fling open the gate and rush in. Don't reach quick and grab a dog when you go into his kennel. That means harshness, which they don't like. But don't be lazy about it either. Just be mild mannered and you'll get more out of dogs.

What, if anything, must a field trial retriever possess to a greater de-gree, regarding natural ability, than a reasonably good hunting dog? Or is it primarily the type and quality of training that makes the difference?

Carey: It's much easier to train a field trial retriever that has a pretty thick skin. I mean the ability to accept correction any number of times for doing the same thing wrong under entirely different circumstances. He must be able to stand an awful lot of repetition. Not many dogs are born with the ability to remember three or four marks, and then pick out one of the four at the handler's command, retrieve that first one out of the natural sequence in which they fell. No dog is born with the ability to do 300- to 400-yard blind retrieves down channels with the banks 6 feet away from either shoulder into the wind. The dog has to learn to do this in order to beat other dogs in the trial.

He has to have a particularly tough, unreasoning attitude toward train-ing. He doesn't ask. And as I said earlier, you'd better give your Golden retriever a good reason, and with a Chesapeake, you'd better take him at his own time. Both of these attributes make it a little harder for these two breeds to win as field trial dogs.

Unfortunately, lately, the winning dogs in field trials have not been chosen because of their style but because of their ability to obey. A nice, fast, brisk walking dog under perfect control sometimes gets a higher score than a dog with a lot of dash and a lot of snap, that slips a whistle or two. It's easier to train these slow, biddable dogs than it is hard-going, tough dogs to do these terribly difficult tests. So field trials may be taking a bad way, a wrong direction there.

Delaney: I think the field trial dog is superior in mind, brain, desire. The brain means memory, cooperativeness, style. You've got to have every-thing going for you before you even start, as far as I'm concerned, to make outstanding field trial dogs.

Benson: Qualities that have to be considered when you're talking about a gun dog or getting into the field trial aspect include the fact that the common gun dog is a slower, more mild-tempered easier-going dog. It takes an exceptional gun dog to make a trial dog. On the other hand, all trial dogs don't make exceptional gun dogs.

The gun dog is more for the amateur. A field trial dog needs a man with a lot of know-how. That dog has to have a lot of durability to take the corrections over and over in order to do it right. The field trial dog must have an awful lot of birdiness, desire; he must almost be on the tough side to rehearse over and over, for six months or more, until he gets it right, to last and remember. A lot of field trial dogs peter out under the pressure of training.

So there is quite a difference between a field trial dog and a common gun dog from the working attitude. Certain dogs have it, come along good in their training, but if a guy overdoes it, the dog may become common and may wash out as a potential field trial dog.

Of the many dogs you have trained to be reasonably good hunting

dogs and field trial competitors, what percentage of all dogs that were suc-
cessfully trained had the potential to be field trial winners?

Carey: I would say, at the most, 2 percent that are winners. I don't
mean ones you just take to the trials. I mean the ones people know are at
the trials.

Delaney: We probably go through maybe 250 to 300 dogs every summer. Out of all of those dogs, some stay here only a week because they
have no ability to go on. Out of all the run-of-the-mill dogs that come in
for gun dog training, there's so few that come up to field trial standard. I'd
say only one in 900 dogs would classify as a possible field trial dog.

Benson: Despite differences between field trial dogs and gun dogs, I
advocate all of them being gun dogs. Give them the gun dog training at the
start, then put the finesse of the field trial dog on them. At about a year,
you're going to see if they show some field trial potential. As you put the
training attitude into them—perfection, staunchness, steadiness, directional
work—you'll see the dog either hang in or start to quit, sour. If a dog can't
take half an hour of rigorous training without tucking his tail or running
over to lay in the shade, you'll have to settle for a gun dog, if that. A trial
dog must have enthusiasm, the guts and go, at the end of your training
sessions that may last from fifteen minutes to an hour.

I've always advocated that all trial dogs should be hunting dogs. As a
matter of fact, one time I had to have a dog just on weekends to run in
trials because the owner hunted with him all week. But we still made a field
champion out of him. But there is a difference and probably not 25 percent
of the good blood retrievers today would make field trial dogs. The average
probably was better years ago when we had wilder, tougher hunting dogs.
But because of civic restrictions, living in homes and so on, the gun dog you
see today is more mild-mannered and comes up short of being a field trial
dog.

Field trial standards have been established, but what constitutes a
good hunting dog is largely a matter of personal opinion. What are the
minimum requirements, what should a dog be able to do, to be considered
a reasonably good hunting retriever?

Carey: I'll answer this question as though the dog was leaving my care
to be a good hunting dog. To qualify as a good hunting dog, the dog has to
have a good nose—and know how to use it. Without that he cannot trail
cripples. A retriever is supposed to find game we would not be able to find
otherwise. That's his job. We don't need a hunting dog for a bird that falls
out in the cornfield that we can walk out and pick up or that we drop dead
in the decoys and can go out and get later. We want the dog to do the
things we can't do.

A good, practical retrieving dog should be able to hunt upland birds
and flush them. He should know how to quarter, know how to hunt the
ground in front of the hunter and be under good enough control to be
called back when he gets out too far. This is particularly true on released
birds on preserves. In sloughs and marshes, birds will burrow in, perhaps

not run so much, and you can get away with a hard-driving dog that doesn't have too much control. But you've got to have him under control to hunt released birds.

One reason for the great popularity of the retrievers is that you can use them for waterfowl shooting. In the northern states they're used for pheasants, for waterfowl, and sometimes for grouse. In the South they're used for dove and duck retrieving. A waterfowl retriever has to have practical experience and training, as a young dog, in trailing birds. It's not enough for him to just hunt a fall for something he's seen hit the ground; you've got to have something you can use, a dog that will find the birds for you.

Delaney: My opinion doesn't really have an awful lot to do with it. It's usually the opinion of the owner that has everything in the world to do with how any particular hunting dog is going to be.

For most people, a reasonably good hunting dog should have the desire to search around for a bird, and in time his desire should build with the experience that makes a good dog. But a dog that I might not want to even waste a shell on may be just ideal for another individual. This has happened over and over. If the dog has the ability to get out there and find birds, stumble on them, however he does it, and satisfies that particular hunter, then you're doing all right.

Before he starts training a dog, a trainer should find out how much hunting a person does and what quality of dog is wanted. Then if the dog meets up to those standards, go ahead and train him. If he doesn't match their idea of hunting and so on, it's best to tell an owner he'd better find another dog.

Benson: A good hunting dog today has to be a good companion dog. If he's a duck hunter, going into the marsh, he's adapted to the boat and blind and will sit in either under moderate restraint. There are some dogs a guy hasn't bothered to train right that have to be restrained by a leash or rope in the blind. That's not the worst fault in a good hunting dog. But he should be companionable enough to go in the car, travel quietly, go in the boat, sit in the blind and be that guy's buddy for the day, stick with him, help him with his duck hunting.

Naturally, the good gun dog is not just a duck dog. He's got to be a pheasant dog, maybe a quail dog, anything. The dog has to be knowledgeable about going out and searching for game in the field, staying within range, keeping track of the hunter so if the hunter changes directions to go hunt a fence line the dog goes over there to hunt; he must be familiar with the game cover and the game he's pursuing. I don't require a gun dog to be staunch in the field. In the boat or blind, yes. He should sit until given the command to go after you've knocked down the ducks, so he doesn't knock you out of the boat.

In the field you'll learn to read your dog, when he's on a bird. Some move runners very quickly and you may have to move fast when he's trailing to get a good shot. I don't expect a hunting dog to be steady to wing and shot, like a spaniel or field trial dog would be. But when the bird comes up, if the bird comes down, he's there and got it. If it's missed, he'll come back. There's nothing wrong with giving pursuit for a short way but he should come right back to the area of the hunter when a bird is missed and start over again. Sometimes it takes quite a bit of work before a gun dog quits chasing everything over the hill. While that's not asking an awful lot, it does take time and repetition to get him to abandon the missed bird and come back and start hunting again.

The dog should keep in contact with the owner, always in his sight, punching out there a few hours a day, not needing the stricter manners required in water work but not having to be whistled at and yelled at all the time. A lot of whistling scares birds right out of the country. A dog that responds without having to be whistled and commanded all the time so you can enter a field or marsh quietly makes a good gun dog, whether on upland game or waterfowl.

Can one dog be both hunter and field trialer? How often does this actually occur? If it is usually impractical for an owner to expect to have a "two-in-one" retriever, what factors prevent this from occurring more frequently?

Carey: It's been my good fortune to have trained some of the highest-scoring field trial retrievers in history. The most notable was Tigathoe's Mainliner Mariah, field trial champion and amateur field trial champion, the highest-scoring Labrador bitch that's ever run in field trials anywhere. I would no more have thought of taking Mariah out in the Horicon marsh* and then expect her to win field trials than I would expect to fly to the moon. It would be almost like taking Secretariat out and saying "Let's go for a pleasure ride." When a dog is trained to perform a certain series of activities perfectly and it's necessary to keep up that type of performance week after week, he's got to be grooved.

A professional goes to field trials to win. So a professional's advice ninety-nine times out of one hundred would be "forget it." I had the occasion to shoot over a retriever within three days after he won the National Championship. He had won six consecutive open all-age firsts but he was a poor shooting dog. He was just too much to handle. A field trial dog is bred to do a job quickly, briskly, and under good control for a relatively short period of time. A gun dog, just like a pleasure horse, paces himself, moves fast when he has to, slows down when he doesn't. He knows he's going to have to run two or three hours, hunt pheasant on a hot October day. Field trials are a game we play, hunting is a recreation and a sport—and they're two entirely different things.

Delaney: I think it's a general opinion that you can't have one dog do both things, hunt or field trial, mainly because in field trials they may not

---

*"Horicon marsh" is a famous waterfowl refuge and hunting area in eastern Wisconsin that hosts thousands of ducks and over 250,000 geese, mostly Canadas, during the fall and spring migrations.

Facing page, top
This Lab is approaching a floating, live bird. Note release trap at the right for containing one or several birds to be flung into flight.

Center
The dog bumps into and properly ignores a decoy as he concentrates on the downed bird just ahead of a second decoy, teaching him to make his retrieves with no regard for the "blocks" used to lure waterfowl on actual hunts.

Bottom
A wounded bird eludes the dog and stimulates him to swim after it and catch it, which will pay big dividends in the collection of cripples that would otherwise get away and be wasted during actual hunts.

This page, top
After catching the live bird, the Labrador turns and starts his return with the bird.

Bottom
He clambers up into the blind toting the bird securely but gently to deliver to Ed Carey's hand, completing a job he will be asked to repeat hundreds or thousands of times during his lifetime of wild-game hunting.

A nice, clean delivery while standing is just as admirable a job as the showier sit-to-deliver. This is Junior Berth and Joe, a young Labrador belonging to L. W. (Bill) Johnson, Scandinavia, Wis.

have to use the wind in certain tests that would be a natural thing for a hunting dog to do. But I imagine if you had a super-good dog, you could have an all-around dog that could handle both things. In the pointing breeds, some dogs realize when they're in a field trial and when they're hunting. They become biddable and change their style. But on the other hand, I think a real trial winner has too much fire.

Benson: Years ago almost all field trial dogs were hunting dogs during the open seasons because our field trials blended more toward hunting tests than they do now. Heavier cover was used, there was more than one dog on line, more shooting by handlers—it all blended more toward a hunting dog attitude. Today's trials have a different, machine, attitude to them, and today it's almost a handler's test as well as a dog's test. A handler with an ability to mark a fall so he can pinpoint the dog on it is very important. Years ago dogs were judged on ability to hunt out a fall, they could circle and circle and if they stayed in the area of the fall they were graded a very good score for ability to remember and stick to the area of a fall until they got the bird. Today if the dog doesn't pinpoint, he's unlikely to be back for another test. I'd say very few gun dogs can be trained into field trial dogs because of the length of time required to get perfection. And when a dog has been field trial trained exclusively, sometimes there's a problem getting him to go out and range for pheasant hunting.

The field trial dog makes a perfect duck dog, but if a man also likes to hunt pheasants and the dog has been drilled to walk and sit at heel and only go after birds he's seen come up and fall down, the dog has lost a little bit of the hunting quality he needs to go out and work as a spaniel would do. After two years of trial work, a trial dropout usually finds it difficult to adjust to working for the normal hunter. So today we're short of gun dogs being field trial dogs and field trial dogs being gun dogs.

If there are variations in your approach to training a hunting retriever and a field trial retriever, other than more intensive and longer training for the competition dog, what procedures do you emphasize, add, or eliminate in training the hunting retriever?

Carey: To win a field trial a field trial dog is required to remember doubles, triples, and quadruples and make those retrieves without handling. A fine shooting dog can be perfectly satisfactory if he can remember a single and then handle to the other two birds that are down, if he can get in and out with the bird in a short time, rather than hunting around for it. Extensive memory for doubles and triples is not required in a gun dog.

A finished gun dog will sit in a southern dove field with ten or fifteen gunners shooting at various spots at the same time and not care what they shoot, only being interested in the birds his owner shoots. Field trial dogs would go just batty under those conditions. A dog trained to be quiet, go easy, he's fine. He's used to it.

Delaney: With the hunting dog I would probably emphasize more obedience, but really there probably isn't that much difference. The basics are very much the same. Some hunters like to let their dogs break consistently, so there again it's up to the hunter, what he wants.

Benson: Training a hunting dog is different from training the field trial dog. You must have exceptional field trial stock to start with before you ever think of trials. You wouldn't take the hereditary traits of most common gun dogs. So if you're going into field trials, buy field trial stock that is high going, jittery, but loves to retrieve and can take the work over and over.

It takes about two to four months of work on the average retriever to make a common gun dog, but six months to a year of work to make a retriever for retriever trials. A puppy from five months of age would be set on a leash, held back, and just mark falls in the field. He'd never be permitted to go out and range in front, game-seek.

The attitude and things put on the field trial dog is a whole different slant on training from that of a gun dog. I don't know how many dogs a guy would have to go through before he gets the field trial dog he wants—maybe one out of ten. Many are great as two-year-olds but never finish out.

With a gun dog the slant is different because when you walk off with him at heel you don't care if he's right up next to your side. The obedience and the steadiness aren't that important. The staunch strictness, perfection under judging, you don't have to worry about in a gun dog. As long as a gun dog stays in your immediate area as you walk down a path, he's perfectly manageable. A little whine of eagerness in the duck blind isn't a serious fault unless it gets to the point where it's disturbing you or the ducks. I think a gun dog can be judged on how many birds were shot and how many birds the dog retrieved during the year, not how fast he did it, or how much speed and style he had. As long as he gets the downed bird home, he's a good gun dog.

Outline your method and the procedures that work successfully for you in teaching a dog his name, Come When Called, No, Sit, Heel, Kennel, or whatever your basic commands are.

Carey: I don't believe I have ever knowingly thought I was teaching a dog his name. We just use his name in relation to the dog. Like I see Lincoln [a cross-bred terrier sitting on a bench across the room] over there and if I use a certain inclination to my voice, he looks at me and I say "Come!" and he'll come. It's a question of your inflection and how you use his name. You call him when he's to be fed. You actually use his name to have him come.

With a young puppy who hasn't been detrained or poorly trained, coming when called is pretty easy. It's just a question of a few lessons, on a rope, followed by a suitable reward when the dog does come to you. You try to teach him to come as soon as he'll learn, whether it's twelve weeks or six months. Always be in a position when you give this command, or any other command, to correct the dog if he doesn't respond. Don't yell "Come!" fifty times even though the dog doesn't come. What you are doing is teaching him a conditioned response to do exactly the opposite of what you want him to do.

The command "No!" is generally accompanied with some form of punishment, mild or severe, depending upon the dog's attitude and the trouble. An excellent time to teach "No!" is when a puppy is chewing—chewing you, your socks or shoes, the bottom of furniture, or other things. Also, when housebreaking, the word "No!" is excellent. You are enforcing with a swat from a newspaper or with some rigorous movement out the door, and so on.

"Sit!" is generally accompanied by a downward thrust with your hand of the dog's rear end, putting him into a sitting position. It's a command he will anticipate after he's been pushed enough into that position so he'll sit down before you push him down. "Sit!" can be taught early, and the earlier the better.

"Heel!" is a movement command in a certain place, generally done with a leash. Then you move yourself and change your direction having the dog move with you, always on the same side and in the same position. You sometimes have to be careful with this command as to when it's introduced, estimating the drive and desire of your training prospect. Because some dogs are loath to move out and put up birds, they may decide the heeling position is the greatest place in the world for them to be and the easiest. Some dogs are better off not taught to heel until after they're taught to hunt in front of the gun.

To teach "Stay!" use the same basic thinking as the "Sit!" command.

Use a long leash, having the dog stay for only a short distance, then move away 2, 3, or 4 feet in front of him. Then return to him, rewarding him for remaining in the same position. The command can be given with an upraised hand. I don't like to do this because we like the dog to move away from us, go back, on hand signal. So sometimes a dog is confused if we say "Stay!" with an upraised hand.

"Kennel!" is just a question of doing it, over and over again, accompanied by a lead, putting the dog's front feet up on the back of a station wagon or pushing him into his crate. At the kennel door, make a sort of ritual of pulling on his collar and pushing him in. Repeat with the command. It's a good idea to have him sit before entering the kennel, after he knows that by saying "Kennel!" you mean to go in. It's another form of reinforcement of control.

Delaney: My method is very simple. I believe in using the rope and leather choke collar. The rope is about 6 feet long and I can do all my basic training on that. Actually the dog learns sort of naturally his name, how to come, sit, with the help of the rope. I use the word "Sit!" to mean "Stay!"

When starting a dog on heeling, depending upon the dog, how he acts, if he's a real rope puller and it's difficult to even get him into a heeling position, on that particular dog I'll work on just coming. When he's about ready to hit the end of the rope, I'll flip him over and tell him to "Come here!" Once he settles down, starts feeling "Well, I should respond a little bit" then I go right into heeling. I teach to heel on the left side.

Like letting the fish take the bait, I give the dog the opportunity to make a mistake. When he wanders off, I set the hook, give him a good yank, and say "Heel!"

If the dog's never been taught to sit, you just naturally push him down and say "Sit!" several times so he gets to know the word. After he knows the word "Sit!" you only tell him *once*. When he's not looking and you know he has the idea, give him a rap with the end of the rope and surprise him. He didn't know this correction was coming, he thinks it came out of the sky. Pretty soon he's listening real well.

After he's heeling and sitting, you can go right into "Stay!" even if it's the same day. I use the word "Sit!" to mean "Stay!" and hold the leash up with no tension on it but ready to give a little pull to correct him on the sit when he makes a mistake. The thing to remember is always correct the instant they make the mistake; otherwise they forget what they did wrong.

Some dogs get buggy when you go around behind them, the first times they're sitting, so it's good to scratch the back of their heads as you walk around. It gives them a little assurance and gets them used to sitting. Once you can walk around them, you can drop the rope, move away, give them hazards, like running around, and every time they get up put them back in the same spot.

If I think they need more correction, as I swing them around into position I also swing the end of the rope around to hit them on the rump. That way, being in movement, they don't really see it coming and, as I stressed before, I prefer not to have a dog see a correction coming so he won't get blinky or afraid of you. You always want a dog happy, enjoying his work, and he'll respect and respond easier if he's having a good time even though you do correct him.

"Kennel!" would mean to get into the kennel or crate or car. I teach my dogs to lie on the front floor, which is a form of obedience. If they get muddy and dirty and you don't have a crate, they won't get your seats dirty. Every little thing you can do, like when you come up to the car have them sit and stay before you say "Kennel!," is good practice and if they don't want to get into the car or the kennel just push them in to start with. They'll quickly learn that part.

Benson: When you say his name if the dog is rewarded with food or petting, something pleasant happens to him when he hears that name or syllable. So he'll walk into his pen to you or get up off the floor and come to you when you call his name. You send him for a retrieve by calling his name. The dog learns that when his name is mentioned attention is focused on him, just like if I said, "Bill, look!" you might not pay any attention but if I said, "Dave, look!" you would.

To teach him to come when called, naturally his name is called and then you can say "Here!," which is close to "Heel!" if he's already been trained to that. Then give him a reward of some sort, maybe a pat, when he comes. There are different methods—the check cord, a reward, a goody, changing directions. Different dogs may respond to different methods. The belligerent one that doesn't care to be with you naturally will have to be restrained physically with a check cord or some other device or instrument. The dog that loves to be with you will look up and come when you call his name and he sees you walking in the opposite direction.

The word "No!" covers a big field. For a man who is a heavy disciplinarian the word means the dog should stop whatever he is doing. If you use it, forget about using "Whoa!" with a dog on point, for example, because the two words sound so much alike. If you've previously disciplined him with the word "No!" and you yell "Whoa!," you might drive him away from birds or get him to thinking birds are bad and should be avoided. You should consider using some different command, like "Stop It!," "Unh! Unh!," or anything that wouldn't be confused with "Whoa!"

But whatever the command, it means "No, just don't do it!" and you have to administer some mild physical hurt so the dog knows you mean business. I use it very little, only if the dog is doing something real bad. If a dog will sit on command, I'd rather tell him to sit. If he sits he's no longer doing wrong. "No!" is a harsh word and I think there's a a lot more words adaptable to a dog's mind other than just a big old No!

Teaching to sit is just a form of living with the dog. Before they ever have the leash on, some little puppies can be coaxed to sit if you stand there with a bit of food, say "Sit!" and then give them a bite when they do. You don't pat some other dogs on the head until you say "Sit!" and they go down. When you're training to retrieve, you say "Sit!" and the dog doesn't get to chase out and fetch until he does. There's any number of ways. Every dog is different. You may have to lift the leash, give a reward, or push the

All puppies can be play-trained to retrieve at an early age by using some small, soft object that won't stick in their teeth, like the glove Dave Duffey is teasing this pup with.

rump down on the word "Sit!" Some of them love to sit and appreciate sitting. Others have to be forced into a sitting position, with a collar and lead, a slap or push. But I like the ones that will sit in anticipation of something good happening after they do sit.

Heeling is done on a leash. I don't know of any better way than to put a dog on a lead, say "Heel!," restraining him with the leash if he stretches out or pulling him up if he lags. If a dog is properly lead broken, he accepts this quickly. On little puppies I use a flat leather collar, not the harsh slip-chain collar. They'll tug and tug and tug. Use your judgment about when to move up to the chain collar to give a little more discipline if the older dog really breaks away hard defying the "Heel!" command.

Certain commands can be cut short or eliminated. "Stay!" is one of them. It's nice if you have a dog that can accept a lot of talk or conversation. But to me the business of saying "Sit! Stay!," which a lot of people do, is just conversation. When I say "Sit!" to a dog he's sitting and he's staying, so why add another word to it? So when you say "Sit!" he sits and stays until his name is called or you move him out to walk at heel or whatever. I see no need for words like "Stay!," or "Steady!," or "Wait!," or all the other words that are thrown at a dog. It's a great show when a guy talks in sentences to his dog, but to me commands that are short and simple seem to be the best.

The word "Kennel!" is the same as "Get in There!" making a dog go into confinement. We just say "Kennel!" to little puppies brought to their kennel gates and throw a little tidbit in ahead of them. The throwing motion, a hand wave, is going to come to mean they should go in there and find something. In a short time they grasp the word and the meaning, get in there whether there's something to find or not. They've learned what it meant but sometimes there'll be something they're more interested in than a tidbit and won't go in.

When a dog gets belligerent you bring out the collar and the lead, bring him to the gate and force him in with the lead. It's like having a dog lie on a certain rug. Once he gets the word and gesture down, you can point to a crate in the back of the car and while it's not his kennel the word and gesture means get into whatever I point out. If I want a dog to lie in the corner or on a rug, I use "Down!," "Sit!," "Heel!," "Kennel!," and "Come!" These are all the commands the average dog has to know.

In teaching retrieving, do you make full use of the natural inclination of most retrievers to pick up and carry, while making sure they know they must retrieve without fail? Or do you as a matter of training routine use a methodical and/or mechanical force-training procedure to teach retrieving?

Carey: I'd like to say we do both.

Delaney: When I start a dog I get as much out of his natural ability as I can squeeze out of him, try him on birds, a dummy, whatever. But even though the dog naturally picks up the bird or dummy and comes back, one day he's going to let you down. It may be six months from now, it may be in the duck boat when he's got to go through some heavy mud, some way along the line if there's no way you can tell him to fetch or hold, whatever your command is, he's going to spit it out because that's the easy way to go.

I always like to follow through with the force-retrieve method, at least to make him carry and hold until I take it. If he's a nice natural retriever, you can maybe skip the force part to make him fetch it off the ground. But you should at least teach the dog to carry and hold until you take it.

Benson: In retrieving I like to bring forth the natural characteristics because I'm a stickler on good breeding, on natural ability. For gun dog work a dog that loves to carry and carries willingly will be a better dog if you don't tap the vitality and style of the dog. Any dog that will carry an object willingly will make a better retriever, unless he gets into that bracket where he refuses to do this and lots of time that's from overwork.

If any forced measures are necessary, I think I'd use a modified force. I insist that a dog hold an object until I take it from him. But to start right out, taking a puppy and forcing something in his mouth to carry, no. I don't believe in that. I take advantage of the natural ability and the willingness and then just perfect the natural ability.

Recognizing that you may use both methods as circumstances dictate, why do you generally prefer one method over the other?

Carey: I don't want to say I favor one over the other, but I think one complements the other. I don't see much point in force-training any retriever unless he has a good amount of natural ability and natural inclination to retrieve.

To force-train a dog so he'll retrieve properly off bare ground won't help much when it comes to Horicon marsh, or some other place like that. What I like to do is take a puppy and develop his ability to retrieve, the *desire* to at least go and find and grab dead ducks, pheasant, pigeons, dummies, and just see how much he'll do on his own or with natural methods of training before I start force-breaking.

But the force-breaking comes along at the same time as the obedience training, incorporated in the same package. We use the dog's foot to encourage him to say "Ouch!" and when he says "Ouch!" we say "Fetch!" and put the dummy in his mouth. After a while when we say "Fetch!" he reaches out and takes the dummy, picks it off the floor, goes out and gets it when we throw it out. With a dog that is a good, moderately aggressive retriever, this falls right in. After he's force-broke to do these lessons in the yard or kennel, you take him out and use the same retrieving objects to get him to come out of water and deliver without shaking off. Also there's so much obedience—the heeling, sitting, staying—right in with it.

Delaney: I definitely favor the force-retrieve method because it assures of a positive retrieve and clean delivery to hand. Every trainer has some special things he emphasizes and force-retrieving is one of my specialties.

Benson: I prefer the natural method because of the happiness the dog's expression gives me. The minute you apply force, lower the boom on him, you take quite a bit of style out of the dog. Because he's afraid of dropping a bird or object, naturally he focuses on you and loses a little bit of the pleasantness he comes in with. A dog that comes in with a pleasant expression and gayness about himself when making delivery is more impressive than a dog making a perfect delivery with his tail between his legs, or slowing down when he's coming in for fear of dropping a bird and being corrected harshly.

Also, when the dog is sent home with an owner who is not a trainer, the dog that loves to carry and come in and deliver happily will do it for anyone. So many times a dog that is force-broke, if the training is not continued, will drop what he's fetching, walk off, and then just refuse to pick up.

If the dog drops the object on the ground, I just give it a kick with my foot to show it and tell the dog to fetch it. Then he goes happily after it again. So if you do happen to have an object on the ground, you can say "Fetch It!" but it doesn't mean to the degree of "Fetch and Hold!" discipline. In force-breaking a dog you go all the way and you must continue, relate it back to the owner. The dog could quit and if the owner doesn't know how the dog was force-broke he'll have a hard time getting that dog to pick up that object.

Describe the procedures you use to instill reliable retrieving.

Carey: First of all, do not advance faster than the dog can do it. I spent fifteen years at a shooting preserve and I have seen some of the dogs I have trained retrieve 150 to 200 times out of water. I know how they were developed. I've seen others quit after fifteen or twenty retrieves. I also know how they were developed. When you start with your little pups, after they're coming along and you are getting some mature, decent retrieving from the pup at eight to ten months of age, you shouldn't have the dog become bored. Give him what he'll take, but no more. Starting to do retrieving in the field should precede the water retrieving.

We try to perfect a sloppy retrieve at first with the same retrieve under the same conditions, immediately following the poor retrieve, the second one, the third one, to get it a little better. Once the dog has it down pat we go to another spot to have him retrieve. A good retriever is one that has had *experience* retrieving. A good trainer must visualize and understand the type of work that dog is going to be required to do and put him in situations during his training that will approximate the work he's going to do when he's through.

I like to start a puppy with a ball or with a bird wing tied on a small dummy, things like that. I like it to be totally fun for that pup to retrieve, to go and get it. When you start your training, always put him in a position where he can't run away from you. Never try to develop anything but some sort of good delivery. If you know he's going to run away, put him up against a fence so he has to come back to you. Watch his mouth. Watch so you aren't going to have a dog that is going to be shaking, tearing something up. A good mouth to carry properly is an important plus.

Delaney: I just like to socialize them. Maybe I'm not as good with pups as some other people because basically my job, my whole life, has been

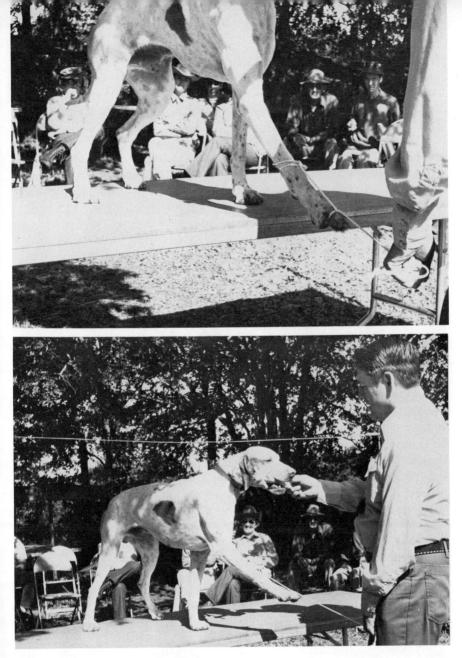

Top
A technique used in force-training to retrieve is to loop a cord around a dog's middle toes, as illustrated, pull, and when the dog opens his mouth to protest the pinch, insert an object in it. (Larry Mueller photo)

Bottom
The pull on the cord pinching the dog's toes and the insertion of a retrieving buck in the dog's mouth is demonstrated on a training table by an instructor at a training seminar. Once the buck is in the dog's mouth the tension on the cord is released and the dog quickly learns to take the object to stop the discomfort. (Larry Mueller photo)

training dogs that were ready to train from a year on. That's when I like to take over a dog and that's where I've had the most experience. I've raised a lot of pups and had good pups come out. But here again the quality of the dog is what really makes any retriever a great retriever. The person doesn't necessarily have a lot to do with it. I think they're born the way they're going to be.

I've had dogs I've done nothing with until they were a year old and they turned out to be sensational retrievers. I've also had pups that I did a lot for from six weeks on. For example, I had a lot of luck starting one Chesapeake on just a crumpled piece of stationery; seemed like the noise really stirred him up. It was naturally there. I didn't have to do much. He was fun to work with because he liked to do it. I also had a Chesapeake that didn't like to pick up anything and I figured she'd grow out of it. I gave her every opportunity in the world, even let her chase clipped-wing pheasants. She loves to hunt, loves to find them, but she's got a problem that no person has anything to do with—she just doesn't want to pick up and carry. I'm going to experiment with her via the force-retrieve method. The experiment will be interesting, but I think these dogs are going to be what they're going to be whether you touch them or not.

Normally, as a general rule, to start a pup on retrieving, take a wad of paper and roll a ball across the floor. As soon as the pup can handle that, go out in the yard where you can get him going farther and farther and the minute you have him going good in the yard you've got to get him immediately into cover. This is necessary even at a very young age so the pup doesn't always rely on his eyes. Do as much as the dog's ability lets you go ahead with. The main thing is to keep improving. Don't throw just 10 feet every time, just because he is little. You might be amazed that puppies will do more and more for you as long as you progress.

Benson: To encourage a dog that has the natural habit of retrieving, loves to retrieve, wants to retrieve, the most important thing is to know when to quit the exercise—before he quits.

Any deviation—his wandering away, dropping it before he gets to you —is an indication that he wants to quit. So that means short sessions. Maybe three or four times he'll come direct to you, be happy about it. Don't be in a hurry to take the dummy or the bird out of his mouth, don't grab it out of his mouth. Give him a little praise when he does bring it to you. Let him stand! Don't worry about sit to deliver and all that show stuff, how perfect he is. After about the fifth or sixth time, if he falters off the line, starts looking into space or someplace else, quit. That's his limit per session. Then try again, later in the day or the next day. Always try to close with the dog wanting to come to you with the retrieve. Then you can change directions, change fields, change objects, go to water, anything to keep his interest.

Facing page
A good gun dog may have to hunt in any kind of weather, including cold, snowy days in northern climates where game-bird shooting is a frosty proposition.

When you go out for a fifteen-minute session, only do a short session on one thing, then go into another, to keep his interest up.

Doing the same thing over and over is one of the worst things you can do to a dog, other than when you're working toward perfection in a field trial dog. With a gun dog, give it to him just as long as he is willing and sharing the joy in what you're doing. It takes a little more time, but in the long run is better for the average owner.

As the puppy gets older, when you're at the point of giving him staunchness training and restraining him, if the dog still wants to bring it to you and has no reason to go off because he still enjoys what you're doing, then you can start restraining him by the collar. The minute he feels you've restrained him or given him any harshness, he might quit. He might have done ten retrieves right up to you fine, until you've held him back. Then you've got to be smart enough to know that because of the restraining he doesn't like you and he'll start goofing off on the side. When this happens, you'll have to go back and do two or three retrieves before he quits so he doesn't have any resentment of being held by you. That's when a change of objects is good, from the dummy to the bird, or with a puppy the glove. Pups just love praise and love to hang onto the object when they come in. As they get older, you can take it from them immediately.

I'd say repetition is the best way to instill reliable retrieving. Have the dogs come to you willingly and continue that right on along the line according to their age, amount of training, and how they are doing. Some dogs are faster than others; gradually move into advanced stages of training as long as the dog is coming willingly.

A hunting retriever should seek and flush game for the gun as well as fetch game after it is shot. Describe the procedures you use to instill "hunt" and "birdiness" and accustom a retriever to quartering the field in a controlled pattern to find and flush game.

Carey: In some instances, with some retrievers, after finishing a thorough course in retrieving, I even have to take the dog out, have him sit down, dizzy birds and put them out in front of him, and have him *see* just exactly what I'm doing. With some of them a desire and ability to hunt in front of the gun doesn't come naturally.

I wait until the bird is walking and able to fly before I put the dog in, and in the first five, ten, or fifteen retrieves I let the dog break and chase. Shortly after I have the dog started in his desire to run in the field and look for something that's planted, hunt for it and flush it, I start teaching him to stop to the whistle no matter where he is running so he'll stop and sit. This is taught sometimes with the aid of a check cord, sometimes with the aid of an electronic collar, sometimes with a lot of leg work and a lot of running. In the yard, as part of his yard training, I have him sit to one sharp blast of the whistle, have him start for dummies, stop when he's halfway to them. So he learns to put himself in a sitting position when he hears that whistle blow.

Letting kids and pups play together is good for both and makes formal training of bird dogs easier. This is Kathleen Duffey with some pups out of a litter by Cannonade X Seairup Twist.

Then I'll have him flush a few birds that I will *not* shoot and have him sit, so that he will flush the bird, sit and watch the bird fly away.

Teaching to quarter is a combination of doing two things. First I get him hunting and seeking in the field. Then I move in a crisscross or side-to-side pattern myself, generally into the wind, getting him to turn if necessary by the whistle, when he's approaching the edge of gun range on my right or left.

This isn't done easily or quickly. With retrievers it can take a good deal of time. Although they do not have the natural quartering instinct spaniels do and there's a lot of pottering involved, if that type of movement and type of training is introduced, they acclimate to the idea of working back and forth in front of you.

This, of course, is diametrically opposed to the field trial retriever's idea of taking a straight line out on command. This is another reason why it's difficult to make a field trial retriever out of a dog that's already been taught to quarter.

Delaney: I'm assuming that the dog is retrieving birds you've thrown by hand or had someone else throw, right? But he hasn't had the chance to find birds by himself in the cover. This is something you have to do artificially quite a bit. Take a couple of pigeons, dizzy them, throw them into the grass where they'll stay long enough for you to go back and get your dog, your dog not having seen where you put the birds.

You want him to come out, work into the wind. That way you can get him quartering. Start on a 30-foot rope where you've got a little control and can guide him, get him right in on the bird. What you're trying to do is to get the dog not to just automatically look for a bird coming from somebody that's throwing it. Once the dog finds out there are birds in the field cover, he's going to start hunting, quartering. Then you can put your 30-foot rope on him to guide him, turn him when you say his name, give him the whistle, or whatever you decide to do to signal him.

The dog has learned to sit and heel. I send him on to hunt and hang onto that long rope for a while until he learns to quarter, turn in any direction I want. If he's over to the far right and I want him to swing to the left, I'll wait until he's about at the end of his rope, say his name, toot the whistle, or whatever. I prefer the name because I hate to fumble around for a whistle. I give a good yank on the rope and have him come over to the left. Then I go back and forth until he gets the idea.

When you guide them into birds, they get to rely on you a lot—"That guy knows there's something around here." There's another little trick I learned accidentally. If you miss a bird and the dog chases after it naturally, because he's young, when he's about ready to come back throw another bird up in the air and shoot. All of a sudden he'll think all of the action is around you. It helps that dog tie in what you want him to do—hunt for you.

Benson: Some retrievers are going to have more ability to seek game on land than others. How fast a dog learns to seek game depends a lot on the natural ability of the particular retriever you're working with. During your walks with your dogs you'll see your retriever pick up something in his nose, and he'll seek it. It could be a mouse, a rabbit, a gopher, or anything. But you'll be able to see what he's doing naturally. If he's got a natural way of going out looking for field mice, all you've got to do is change his mind from field mice to birds.

You've probably done your yard work with a dummy in light cover where he can see it, eyeball it. Then by putting the dummy out in cover that conceals it, holding him back so he doesn't go right with the throw, you make him have to search a little bit. Do it against the wind so if he is short of where the dummy fell his nose will bring it in.

Once he's really finding the dummy in heavier cover, throw it, hold him back, lead him away, bring him back up again and then send him, delaying his memory so he'll have to look for it harder. To develop the game-seeking habit, you just can't go out pheasant hunting, throw a bundle in the air and say go out and hunt pheasant. So by taking objects, dummies, pigeons, placing them in the field without his seeing them, then making an arm motion in that direction to send him, he'll probably think you threw something. You get more use out of your birds and encourage pups to run around searching the field and they'll get a dummy or another object and bring it in to you. Another way is to take a clipped-wing pigeon and let it walk through the grass. You'll be surprised how far a pigeon walks. Put the pup on the track so he game seeks it. A clipped-wing duck is another bird that can be used to walk off and encourage a pup to hunt.

If a dog goes into cover on an arm motion and finally gets the object he's seeking, he's going to continue that. Then you use live birds to put scent down so the dogs learn to go out and look and look without having seen an object fall.

Naturally, before you start having him seek stuff hidden in the grass, he's had the practice of bringing thrown dummies to you. The proper procedure is that after you have him retrieving an object, you put that same object in the field without his knowing about it and he just goes out and searches for it.

The dog should know the difference between just a walk and a hunt. Many people try to condition their dog to hunting and say "Oh, I walk him 5 miles a day." Well, by just going and walking you can be creating a lot of bad habits. But you want the dog to know something's up on that day you take the gun in your hands.

When I want to take a leisurely walk, I don't give any commands, let the dogs do what they want, as long as they stay reasonably close to me, follow my direction of walk. But when I go out to work, I take a gun, show them the dummies and then they'll put their mind on business. You have to give some indication of what's up so the dogs will adopt the proper attitude as to whether they're out to work or play.

Describe your method of "steadying" a retriever that will be used at heel, from a boat or blind, strictly as a nonslip retriever, as in waterfowl, driven bird, or dove shooting.

Carey: The basic command for instilling this steadiness is "Sit!" and/ or "Stay!" After a dog is retrieving properly to hand, we teach him to sit and to be released on a command, whether it's the common term "Get Back!," accompanied by the waving of an arm or the pointing of the hand in the direction of the bird, or any other way.

Trained retrievers are steady under all circumstances and requiring them to stay put while another dog works is one way of achieving steadiness. These are two Nilo Kennels Labradors being worked by Harry Pershall.

But he must learn by being called back, pulled back, or held restrained in some way that he must not go for this tempting dummy just thrown out on the lawn. That's the time you study your dog—you are always studying your dog—to find out just how much you should do. I don't like to see a dog steadied until he'll also retrieve well in and out of the water and develops a lot of desire to go out and retrieve good distances. Then, without the gun, without anything particularly enticing, we just teach him mechanically not to go before he is sent. Later on we build up to have him watch shot birds or clipped-wing pigeons flown away from him while we hold and restrain.

At some time during his training before you can say he's steady, you and he in most cases are going to have a head-on confrontation. The use of a whip, spike collar, check cord, leash, or some type of force is going to have to be used if he's the average high-powered, hard-running dog to make him realize he has to stay there under any conditions.

I use walking birds, birds on fish lines flying around the dog, running clipped-wing ducks, all types of enticements, including another dog retrieving, while the dog in training remains steady. Make him realize he cannot go, in fact must wait for your command.

A hunting retriever, to be a good one, must be a lot steadier than a field trial dog. Maybe that sounds crazy. But only rarely does a field trial dog see a bird that he doesn't retrieve. It's only two or three seconds at the most from the time a bird goes down and the dog is ordered to retrieve. In a duck blind or in dove shooting you may knock a bird down, and not send your dog for several minutes, maybe not at all. And when a retriever honors another dog's work, it is generally done only once in the trial and then generally after the honoring dog has made a retrieve of his own, but a hunting retriever may be required to honor under all kinds of different and tempting circumstances.

Delaney: If your dog has learned to sit and stay and he's staying well with someone else throwing and shooting a bird, you got him to this point because every time he breaks you get that rope on him and he's dragged back, rapped on the rump. This is achieved by simple repetition, making him sit when he's supposed to sit.

When he's got a lot of desire and is heeling off the leash but still breaking on you, have your rope over your shoulder and try to swat him as he breaks. That's one way. Another way is to have the rope or lead attached to his collar and make a hitch that will slip around the belly, with you holding the end. When he gets about 10 feet out there, he's suddenly snubbed up around the belly. That's pretty effective also.

You have to set up hunting situations and tempt the dog to misbehave before you get out in that boat.

Benson: After the dog knows the fundamentals of walking at heel and sit, for getting staunchness I've been using with amazing results some clay target shooting. After they're familiar with gun fire and are retrieving well, naturally you aren't going to want them fetching clay targets. But you can use them to steady up a dog.

Keeping sanitary, neat, and up-to-date kennels like these at Woodstock, Ill., is a costly undertaking and part of a professional trainer's expensive overhead in turning out gun dogs for sportsmen clients.

A dog has to learn he isn't to jump out of a boat or run out every time a gun goes off. I'll bet at least 50 percent of the ducks shot at are missed. So he's got to get used to a lot of shooting when there's nothing out there to bring back.

So you take your dog out, sit him down, restrain him on leash, have someone throw and shoot clay targets, and every time the dog tries to go out to chase, jerk him back and sit him down. Every once in a while, after

When young retrievers are being steadied on shot birds, they are held on a short leash attached to a slip collar so they can be jerked up and reseated if they break, as Orin Benson demonstrates here.

he's become steady, just before he loses interest because you're shooting and shooting and there's nothing in it for him, throw out one of the live pigeons you've brought along, shoot it, have him remain sitting and then send him to fetch it. That way he'll develop a habit of sitting while you're shooting and being sent only when a bird is down.

Another way is to shoot a gun in the air and throw a dummy out into the water, restraining the dog on a leash until you send him. Very few dogs

I know of can learn this without having the leash put on them, so they can be reefed back when they jump to retrieve. You graduate from the leash to a finger hooked in the collar so he knows he's being restrained.

Lots of times when you first make them sit and stay in a sitting position you walk away from them so you're facing them and throw the dummy behind your back, then go back to the dog and send him. But don't send him from where you're standing. Always go back to the dog before sending him if you want him to be steady. That way he'll learn he cannot make a retrieve unless you're right at his side.

There are all kinds of ways to teach a dog to sit and wait until he's told to go. If you don't have the clay targets set up to work with, the restraint with a leash on the collar when dummies and birds are thrown is about the most effective way of doing it.

Describe your method of keeping a hunting retriever within gun range and preventing wild chasing of flushed and missed birds by a retriever seeking game to flush for the gun.

Carey: We talked earlier about quartering and teaching your dog to stop to the whistle. Both are very important. I use a number of birds that fly away, deliberately missed, gun fired into the air and what not until the dog learns he should not chase endlessly every bird he sees.

I also like to teach my dogs to take and handle runners, and after they become proficient in this, stop them while they're trailing, have them sit, wait until we get up close to them and then send them on again. These are all advanced training procedures. Even though there is a lot of time involved, they aid in training the really finished gun dog.

When a dog decides he's going to chase a missed pheasant to the horizon, it's important that the hunt stop, the hunter unload and lay down his gun, go out and get that dog and bring him back and do what is necessary to be sure that particular dog understands he should not chase birds that are not dropped. After a dog goes through a session of being steady to wing and shot, steady to flush and shot, the shooting of birds that he's flushed up, not retrieving them until told, when you put him into shooting birds you should at least be able to call him back off of birds he starts to chase.

Delaney: Again you use that rope, a long light nylon cord is what I'm talking about. You've got to give the dog the idea with the rope and collar before you can expect him to have any idea of what you want. If he's not too hard a dog, sometimes taking a slingshot and popping him now and then with a marble without any birds involved will do the trick. Then you gradually work him in with birds so he doesn't get any ideas that it's the birds giving him the cracks.

That sliding hitch around the belly is also good. Jump on that and snare him out there.

To prevent the wild chasing on flushed birds, I think it's all obedience before you even get out there in the field. You have to do as much training as you can before you get out there. You can't beat that. When you hit the whistle, that dog's got to know he has to come back. It's the training before you get out there, with the slingshot or the rope, that makes the difference.

Benson: To keep a dog in gun range—well, I'm a silent hunter. I despise whistles for turning a dog in the field because that alerts the birds to run. I want the birds to think they've got a chance by hiding until the dog reaches them.

The easiest method to teach a dog to change direction coursing a field is for you to change direction, with maybe an arm motion to wave the dog over so he cuts a figure eight or hits all the brushpiles alongside you. If he gets out too far, turn and walk in the opposite direction and the dog will realize he's out too far.

Another way of making a dog hunt close to you is to go into a clean field where there's no chance of him ever finding a bird, and when he's out there 40 yards drop a clipped-wing pigeon in there 20 yards ahead of you. As he comes back he will find it in your immediate area. With a dog finding birds only within your immediate area, within gunshot range, he's going to pick up the habit of hunting close to you. If he gets out 100 yards and finds nothing, he's not going to go out there very often if he thinks every place you go that 15 or 20 yards in front of you there's going to be a bird on the ground. He'll be inclined to hunt right around you because he'll get the idea that you know where the birds are. Then it's up to him, with his nose, to find them. You can easily shorten his range by making sure he always finds a bird next to you.

Just letting him run across it, in your immediate area, is a lot better than a whistle and a command. Sometimes a dog will be out there busy with something else and you might have to toot a whistle or call his name to tell him that you've changed direction. He might be on a deer or a varmint or just fooling around, and you'll have to resort to a whistle or a yell to turn him and show him his direction.

Just to go out and not blow a whistle or not yell at a dog in the field is nearly unheard of, too. In training you're going to have to blow the whistle and yell from time to time. But I don't like the constant blowing and turning of direction to make a dog seek game. If he's doing something he wants to do best and you want him over, you're going to have to stop him to get his attention and show him that's bad. Then if he finds a bird in your immediate area, the next time he's going to come back a lot faster.

To stop him from chasing wild game, let him try it and not catch it. But this is particularly hard when working on game farm birds that fly 200 yards and go down and the dog chases and catches them. That's the worst thing that can happen. Any time a dog runs and chases, and wins, that means it's going to be twice as hard to stop him next time. We use what we call fly-back full-wing birds that will get up and fly back to the buildings.

Pigeons are the best birds to use. They get up quick, fly high and far and light in trees. This prevents the dog from winning his objective by catching and retrieving one. But if your basic training has been sound, once the bird gets out beyond where it is ever likely to drop if shot, you should be able to blow the whistle and stop the dog before he chases too far, bring him back and start him game seeking again. If he's properly whistle broke, he will come back. But to create a pattern without a whistle or voice command, you have to use flying birds that get away, firing a blank pistol as they fly off, so he'll know they don't always come down even when shot at. Invariably he'll start watching when a bird flies. If it comes down, he'll go after it; if not, he'll come back to you.

Do you expect a retriever used to seek and flush upland game or jump-shoot waterfowl to be steady to wing and shot? If you do, or were asked to put this finish on a dog for a customer, how would you proceed in making him reliably steady on birds he's flushed?

Carey: It may be begging the question, but this type of training is a type used in field trials, expecting a field trial standard of excellence. The only way that's maintained is by continuing to put the dog into training situations where you can develop him and have him continue, all the time. You must be in a position to enforce your command and correct your mistakes; otherwise your dog is going to start breaking. Any *good* dog is going to start breaking on flushed birds unless he's actually kept in training to keep him from doing it.

I'm not talking about an odd bird or two the dog flushes hunting. I'm talking about shooting fifteen, twenty, or twenty-five birds over a dog on a preserve. Under those conditions, if you do this day after day, it's very difficult to have a dog stay steady.

Do I expect this steadiness of a dog? Yes, in his training procedure carried to the end he should be well steadied to flushed birds and should not chase birds that he has flushed whether or not they are shot at. He should stop when he flushes, and if you shoot them he should retrieve *when told to*. But not until commanded to.

Practically speaking, keeping a dog in that stage, without constant training reinforcement, is impossible if he's a good dog. However, this early training should keep a dog so that he will come back from chasing a flying bird or runner. That's the big trouble—chasing these running birds down corn rows and putting them up out of range.

Delaney: Most hunters, it seems, barely can make a dog heel and sit. The customers I've had haven't really been interested in having a dog steady to wing and shot. If I were to train one to that requirement, I'd go with the procedure mentioned in answer to previous questions—until the dog was absolutely steady to one blast of the whistle.

Benson: When you have your dog so he is everything you want in a gun dog, but you want a bragging dog, a little more perfection, then you'll want him to stop to wing and shot, similar to spaniel training. He's already a perfect dog in the duck blind, already trained to sit when a duck is shot. So then go out and release birds in the field, sit the dog out away from you and shoot a bird down. If he'll stay where told to sit, you can down a bird at a distance. By having him coursing the field and throwing a bird, not one he flushes but one he sees thrown, and yelling "Sit!" at the same time he'll soon learn to sit when a bird flushes and will stay for shot until sent to retrieve.

But to my knowledge there are very few retrievers trained today for hunting or preserve shooting that sit when a bird gets up.

What hand and whistle signals do you use? Describe the procedures you follow in teaching response to those signals.

Carey: The signals are the same as we teach for field trials in that we ask them to stop and take directional casts, to the right, to the left, or back. We use the word "Over!" with a wave to either side and "Back!" accompanied by a hand held high over the head. We just don't expect to thread needles with these shooting dogs at 200–300 yards. Simply try, as in the case of pothole shooting, to get the dog downwind and below the bird. Get him into where he can use his nose and hunt.

A finished retriever should have the basic idea of how to handle, how to stop, and how to cast. While it is one of the easiest things to teach to the right pupil, easier than many of the other phases of training, some dogs never will learn it, because they're not smart enough. They can learn a type of training in a given spot, maybe learning a little bit about stopping to the whistle. But some of them just do not have the ability to take directional casts.

At the same time we are teaching the shooting dog to quarter and move back and forth in front of us, we are also teaching him to stop to the whistle. After we shoot a bird and he's retrieved it, we can go out with the dog and, visualizing a baseball diamond, put him at the pitcher's mound and throw the bird to first, second, or third base and cast the dog to the bird with the common "Fetch!" or "Over!" or whatever.

The handler directs the dog from home plate. Then there are sessions with two to four birds or dummies, giving the dog several alternatives, starting him off in one direction, stopping him and casting him the other way after he has become proficient at going to retrieve with the hand signal.

Sometimes this is difficult to get started. Sometimes the dog doesn't want to leave and you have to start sending him from very close to you. Gradually you move back with the dog staying in the same place. While the dog's interest is high, start to step away from him so he'll leave, looking at you in one place and the bird in another, and not try to come to your side before being sent. The thing you have to get across is that the dog must move from his position to the bird without first coming to you.

Delaney: Just an ordinary hunting dog that will go from right to left and left to right on signal, either name or whistle, is what most hunters want. To have an ideal dog that will go out on a blind retrieve, where he hasn't seen the bird knocked down, that involves advanced training and handling, which goes into taking lines, the baseball-diamond method, just about like you'd train a field trial dog.

Remember that when the dog gets the idea from your baseball diamond to go to the right, left, and straight back, when your dog has that much base, this is important training in your yard work, maybe more important than anything. (When you can't get out to the field, you can do this training very easily in your backyard.)

When he's got the basic left, right, back, when you knock a bird down and he's found out you can signal him over there, you'll be surprised how fast he will start taking directions in the field. It's not field trial caliber but it gets him there and he's happy to do it because he has found something exciting. He even thinks you're pretty super because you're able to direct him over to it.

Benson: When you start the hand and whistle signals on an average gun dog, I'd say it's most important in the water work. To be given hand directions out of a blind when he can't see a fallen bird is very important for a gun dog with one or two seasons of hunting behind him. It's nice to have a gun dog that will go on farther when you tell him and take directional signals on land, but it's not as important as in the water.

In water work probably the most important thing is for the dog to go out away from you into the marsh or open water. If you get your dog to go back far enough, his chances of winding a bird out there are that much better. Then when you've got him going back, you have your lefts and rights.

To teach a dog to go back far enough on what we call a line, probably the easiest way for the amateur trainer would be to have the dog pick up dummies or birds he's seen fall, then you throw out another one but take the dog back away from where you've been sending him. After a long delay bring him back to the blind or spot you're training from and he'll come back with about half a memory of having seen that last dummy fall. Then line him out to that, sending him on the word, "Back!" If he hesitates when he gets into the water, an overhand motion and the word "Back!" should encourage him to keep going and help refresh that half a memory.

By repetition, using "Back!" and the half-delayed mark, sooner or later he's going to think "I didn't see him throw it, but it must be out there, though."

If you don't have water you can go out on the lawn, sit the staunch dog down, throw the dummy over his head, walk back 20 or 30 yards, and with the overhand motion and "Back!" send him to pick up. He should wheel around, go back and get the dummy. Keep repeating until eventually he'll have it down pat.

To train for lefts and rights, make up a baseball diamond. Sit your dog on the pitcher's mound. Put a dummy on first base and a dummy on third base. You can stand on home plate. Motion toward first base with your right arm. The dog should go to first base and get the dummy. Take the dog out to the mound again, throw the dummy over by first base. But make a gesture toward third base with your left arm. If he starts to go for the first-base dummy, stop him with a stop whistle or a sit command, make him go over to the third-base dummy by walking and gesturing in that direction. In a short while he'll get to know the motion to right or left means that's the direction he's to take. And to work in the "Back!" direction, the dummy goes on second base. Then it's repetition until the dog invariably responds the correct way. When he starts off the wrong way, a whistle blast or the word "Sit!" should stop him. Keep at him, stopping him if he

Two Chesapeake Bay retrievers and two Labrador retrievers flank Loral I Delaney late in the Minnesota duck season. Those two breeds rank at the top for being able to stand up under tough working conditions.

goes wrong and resending him in the direction you want him to go until he does it right.

How do you introduce a hunting retriever to actual birds and familiarize the dog with game birds? How do you progress from this introduction to actual shooting of birds over the dog?

Carey: One reason I like to start early with a puppy is I like to have the pup have the idea and feeling of feathers in his mouth when he's young so it becomes a natural thing for him. If we can start with wings over a sock or dummy, anything a dog can easily pick up and like, we're way ahead of the game. But if we have a dog that's a year or a year and a half old and has never seen a bird, particularly if he's a little faint of heart about this whole thing, it's a good idea to have some foresight of what might happen or what could go wrong.

I've used the "monkey see, monkey do" routine—have them watch another dog carrying the bird around—once in a while with these dogs, just to be sure. Have several trained, nonaggressive dogs run around with the pupil in training, dogs that will fetch, drop a dead pigeon, and pick it up and carry it, so there's no chance they can become afraid, flustered, or blink this bird at the first opportunity. If they should do these things, chances are you've got trouble.

As part of my training procedure after a dog is thoroughly force-broken on dummies, I also like to have him pick up dead, cold birds so the dog comes to think it's a good thing and doesn't have any bad experience with feathers. From that, with the aid of an assistant and a .22 blank, I have a dead, cold bird thrown in a place where the dog has previously picked up dummies, *without* firing the gun at first. After the dog has made half a dozen of these bland, easy retrieves, then perhaps I'll throw the bird and have the assistant fire the gun at a distance, so the dog doesn't get gunshy.

Always do this when the young dog is in an aggressive, stimulated frame of mind. Generally we move up from dead birds to clipped-wing birds, and in some cases put masking tape around the wings so there isn't a lot of fluttering. Most dogs will go from dead pigeons to clipped-wing pigeons to shot pigeons without any trouble. But you have to worry about the one that might back off on you; then you've got trouble.

Do the same thing with ducks in the water—dummies first, then dead ducks, then live shackled ducks. Remember to put a rubber band around a duck's beak; if they get to pecking a dog, they can hit him pretty hard sometimes when he approaches. It's just a question of studying and knowing your dog and trying never to put the dog in a position where he can become afraid of what he's sent to pick up.

Delaney: With a dog that's never had a bird before, you'll have some strange things happen. Number one is, some dogs treat a bird like it was a snake in the grass—they pick at it, throw it up in the air, throw it away, nip at it, they might even eat it. Don't get all upset and worried about it. It's very rare that a dog will actually eat a bird, but it can happen. Don't get mad and correct him for it. It's just an old instinct that made him do it.

142

Maybe the next day he'll treat it just as soft and just as tender as you'd want a dog to.

The way I start a dog is by tossing a clipped-wing pigeon out. The majority of the dogs we get are afraid to take hold of it. They'll smell, maybe just leave it. You have to get them interested and keep them interested and finally they'll pick it up, maybe just by one wing, and carry it around. But every dog's a little different and I like to start with a fresh bird to see what they'll do. Dead birds just don't compare to the fresh bird you'll knock down in the field.

We had a particular dog we shot a lot of birds for in training and it just happened we killed every one of them. Then one day after he'd probably had twenty birds shot over him, his owner took him hunting and the first bird he shot he wounded but didn't kill it. That dog never did pick up the cripple, which is what you need a dog for. It was something screwy. So I like to start on a live pigeon, which has a close resemblance to other birds. Once they pick up a pigeon, go on to duck and pheasant, introduce them to all the birds you're going to go out and hunt before you go hunting.

The thing to remember is to do no force work with the bird. You've got to quit while the dog still has some interest. Try the dog on two or three birds, put him away when he still shows some interest, take him out the next day, over and over. But don't force, especially when the dog doesn't know if he likes birds or not.

Benson: I introduce a gun dog to birds early. I take a four-month-old puppy or one six months old, whenever they're in for training, to see his reaction to a bird. He might just get out and play with it. You then know he's got a willingness to go out and get a bird but doesn't have the fundamental training to bring it back. You do just enough to get the interest up in a puppy. One or two bird retrieves, when he's real young, are sufficient as compared to half a dozen with the dummies.

The best thing today for a trainer is pigeons. So once he's retrieving, every now and then check him out with a clipped-wing pigeon, toss it in the air, shoot a blank with it, naturally he'll pursue it and get it when it lands. Use the birds in short cover, in tall cover, then go back to dummy work. Live bird work with a small puppy is very limited. It's stepped up when he's learned to fetch and deliver reliably. Birds should be introduced at a young age, but not too many of them.

Do you teach a hunting retriever to track and recover crippled birds? By what means?

Carey: I absolutely do. Conservation is the whole thing here. If a dog has no previous knowledge of cripples and runners before he's taken afield, you just aren't going to recover many birds until he learns how. It's a lot easier to teach dogs to recover cripples in July and August training season than on a hot October day in a cornfield when the bird is gone.

I do a lot of things. I mentioned Orin Benson before and I think he was the first to teach me how to handle a dog on runners and what to do with them. He showed me the idea of first dunking a duck in a pail of water and then turning it loose in a field. That makes for a lot of scent and a dog with previous marking and fetching experience will quickly smell and recognize the duck scent. By walking along with the dog, sometimes on a check cord, taking him over the scent line again and again, he'll learn to follow the duck scent.

Also, when I put out pheasants, I generally hobble them for young dogs with a piece of surveyor's tape about 6 to 8 inches long. I make one loop over each leg, dizzy the bird, and set it out without its head under the wing. The bird will become entangled a bit in the first few bunches of grass it comes to, if it does run. Since I don't knot the tape, if the bird flies the tape pulls off and the bird isn't hobbled for life. The pheasant will leave a track and if scenting is extremely bad I use water on the pheasant. One part anise oil with six to eight parts vegetable oil on the bird's feet seems to accentuate and carry scent much better.

If the young dog doesn't catch the runner, but flushes it, it's terribly important that you shoot it so the dog has a retrieve. Over the past few years when there's a shortage of birds I've used bantams and Baby Reds [domestic fowl] that I keep in my bird yard. I take them considerable distance away from the barnyard and put them out in the grass. They're small birds, they fly back to the barnyard when flushed to be used another day. Anything that you can do along those lines to get a young dog to follow scent is most important.

Delaney: Ordinarily I don't go into the training to track and so on, but it certainly isn't a bad thing to do. I think if you shoot enough birds over a dog, you give him plenty of opportunity to work crippled birds. Or you can duplicate it by taking a dead bird and dragging it around; this is a good way to get them started to track.

Benson: It's very important that a hunting retriever learn to track and trail a cripple. That's a way for him to find out how birds walk around after they're crippled. It also helps him game-seek. Naturally a blood-scent bird is a lot different than a live wing-clipped pigeon or a duck. Only through repetition in the field will a dog learn by himself.

In training you must use a brailed pheasant or a wing-clipped bird, anything that can't fly, or when a shot bird isn't killed outright, use the opportunity to give experience trailing cripples.

Let the dog see a wing-clipped pigeon or duck fall, but delay in sending long enough to let the bird run 30 or 40 yards from where it came down. Then let the dog work it. He may have to track a bird that can fly only 10 or 15 yards before it gets up. But a real or imitation cripple will run and hide, move and stop, and take quite a while to catch.

Describe your procedure in introducing a retriever to gunfire, assuring that the dog will not be gunshy.

Carey: I'm firmly convinced that gunshyness in almost every instance is man made, not hereditary. I like to introduce gun fire after I have the dog retrieving and enjoying it, at the point where he'll happily retrieve clipped-wing pigeons that can be thrown by me or an assistant 10 to 20 yards

Intelligent, rigorous training makes it possible to control more than one dog at a time. Golden retrievers have to be given a reason if they are to respond properly to training, according to Ed Carey, and this Golden seems to be asking Ed for a reason why he ought to sit still like his kennelmates are doing.

away from us, downwind so the bird will flutter maybe 30 to 40 yards away into medium cover.

The dog sees the bird practically all the time. While he is running in full force, intent on the bird and has passed the assistant, we fire the gun. He maybe hears it out of the corner of his ear, so to speak, but he just doesn't care about it. After we've done that a few times and we know he's receptive to that, then we hold the dog, throw the bird and while the bird is in the air, before the dog is released, fire the gun. I'm talking about a .22 blank pistol. Eventually fire first, then throw the bird. If he gets enough of that kind of work, you can generally go to a shotgun, providing you don't stand right over him when you shoot.

Delaney: I don't introduce the gun until the dog is competent with his birds, is really gung ho. If the dog is scared of the bird and connects that noise with it, you'll have a dog that is both birdshy and gunshy.

I introduce the gun before I steady them but let them break when I shoot. I start with a .22 blank. If that seems to bother them I take them to the field, getting them to quarter and find birds in the field right off the bat so they'll associate it with the hunting right away. With just a flick of the ear some dogs will tell you they're touchy about the gun. You really have to look for it, most people don't see it. If the dog is that touchy you'll have to ride the birds out, have the dog in full chase and really intent on the birds before you shoot. If conditions aren't right, don't shoot. Just let him chase the bird over the hill, say "Goodbye," and go to the next bird.

I've seen dogs go gunshy on a bird shot too close. Shoot too close and you get a big puff of feathers. Some dogs that had other birds shot over them okay see that puff of feathers and something snaps in their minds. So don't shoot your bird too close.

When you go out to shoot with a sensitive dog, don't go on a dark, cloudy day. Maybe the gun makes twice or three times the sound, or something's gloomy and doesn't fit in with the dog's attitude. It's to your advantage to go out on a sunny, crisp day, even with a slight breeze, so you can shoot with the sound being carried off away from the dog.

Naturally, having introduced them with a .22 blank, don't go to a heavy load shell or heavy-gauge gun out in the field. Use a 28 gauge or .410 bore to start with, or a light load shell if you have to use a larger gauge.

Benson: We introduce the gun at a very early age, even at three to four months with a group of puppies. I like to do it before six months, before they've learned a sense of fear. When they're all out there galloping around, that's a good time to shoot. In the company of other dogs they've got their minds on something else. Fire a blank gun. You'll see if a puppy's dauber goes down, if he notices the shot. Maybe after four or five .22 blank shots he'll keep on going just like he never heard it. That's good. It's better not to go out with a dummy or bird, throw it, and shoot for the first time. If he's got a thing about the noise, he might associate it with the object.

Later on, when the puppy is older, shoot and throw. If he doesn't pay any attention to the shot, pretty soon he'll look up and see that dummy and associate the shot with something that's going to come down. I believe in an early introduction before you do a whole lot of other things and only then find out your dog is allergic to gunfire.

Do you break gunshy dogs? If you do, describe the procedure. If you don't, why not?

Carey: As I said before, the gunshy situation is man made. Very often a dog is brought to me and the owners will say the dog is gunshy. When I ask what happened, they'll say "Well, we were out hunting, the dog was running around, the birds got up, we all shot at them and that's how the dog got gunshy. He's afraid of it now."

Most probably the dog had no proper introduction to birds, no proper introduction to retrieving, was just taken out. In some instances, where there has been no pretraining of the dog before hunting, by simply giving him that training and forgetting all about the fact that he's supposed to be gunshy, you can have a good dog. But if the dog is definitely afraid, I don't think it's worthwhile going on.

Delaney: If a dog is really gunshy you can pretty well tell and you may decide it isn't worth the money and time it will take to break him. But there are some ways I'd suggest the owner try. Let him gamble on it. The dog should be taken to a fenced-in area, he should chase down some wing-clipped pheasants and get so built up and so crazy about birds that the dog just overlooks the noise.

Some sort of freakish things can work out, too. A wounded squirrel will bite a dog when he grabs it and some dogs with gumption seem to get so aroused and angry over being bitten they connect that with the shot and in effect sort of fight back to overcome fear of gunfire by fighting and killing the squirrel. There are all kinds of methods, but it is a hit or miss thing with gunshy dogs.

Benson: Years ago we used to spend a lot of time on it, when we didn't have a field to pick from. Gunshyness breaking is a long procedure. With the cost of training today, cost of shells, what not, the dog has to have an awful lot of something to be worth spending time on, especially if the gunshyness wasn't man made. For what you have to spend to correct gunshyness, you can buy another dog.

Describe the procedures you use to induce a retriever to willingly enter water to make a retrieve.

Carey: A young retriever should learn to think of water the same as land—as just something to cross. His first water should be very shallow to make it easy to walk around in. The bottom of the water area should gradually recede so for his first swim it's just a few strokes, with no question of panic, no question of going over his head and becoming afraid of water. It's a great help if you can be in the water with the dog, just wading around.

The dog should soon find something else to do besides look at the water and one of the best things he can do is to retrieve. In water retrieving you have a lot of control over the dog because he's going to go out into the water and he's going to come back. Sometimes a dog with just a fair amount of interest in retrieving on land will have an awful lot in water. But the introduction should be done quietly in a little, still body of water; a half-dried out little pothole is the kind of place to start.

Delaney: I have a very simple procedure—get them so nuts about the bird on land they're just going to go into the water after it. If the dog's got a lot of natural desire, he'll overcome a fear of bad swimming. Naturally, I start him where he doesn't have to swim. He can reach the bird by wading out to it. Gradually it's tossed into swimming water. If the dog has trouble swimming, you can give him some practice behind the boat.

Benson: Whether taken alone or in a group, I like to introduce puppies in a way so they associate the water with fun. If you've got an older dog, use him to lead the puppies into the water or have your kids run out into the water with the pups.

Don't try to say "Swim" and expect they'll do it. Don't force them into the water. Walk out in the shallows. They'll follow, wade, get to like it. Just expose them to water and you'll see the ones that like it.

When you throw out a small object for a pup to retrieve, toss it just a few feet at first. As you lengthen the tosses always throw into the wind so the object will be brought closer to him rather than drifting away. His nose will also help him scent it and give him a little more guts to go. The best way is to play with him in the water, give him fun and confidence, before you try him fetching.

If a dog dislikes or has developed a fear of water, do you force-break so he'll enter water on command and retrieve? If you do, describe the methods used.

Carey: I don't feel that a shooting dog should be forced into the water. I know it is 100 percent necessary for field trial retrievers to go into any water, any time, under any conditions, when ordered to. That's just what it is in many cases—an order. This can be accomplished with ropes, whips, continuous repetition, going in yourself with the dog, all kinds of rather forceful methods. But I don't think it's worthwhile in the case of a gun dog.

Delaney: I don't really care to force a dog into water. I feel you have to work him into wanting to do it. Sometimes just going in and swimming yourself develops some fun for him. But if a dog doesn't have enough desire for the bird to go into the water for it, he isn't much of a dog.

Benson: A dog that doesn't like water will sooner or later quit you. We don't always know if it's man made. A puppy that has been sufficiently exposed to the water but continues to hesitate, it takes a lot of demanding before he'll go, sooner or later when that water gets cold he's going to quit. Years ago we used to force them into water, like we used to force them to retrieve. I've seen them tuck their tails and go in out of sheer fear of a boot in the behind. But they freeze out on you, never go willingly. For the average gun dog owner, who's not a trainer, that dog will quit. So I like the natural water dog. I don't force-break a dog for water unless the person who's going to live with him can make him do it.

If a dog refuses to pick up and carry, do you try any playing or encouraging method in an effort to get the dog to do it naturally of his own volition, before resorting to force-training him to fetch?

Carey: I attempt to get all of our dogs to do it naturally, before I force-break them, because I know I'm headed for trouble if they won't do it naturally. We make a game out of the retrieving, rubber balls, all sorts of things like that, if the standard dummies don't work, before we start the force-training.

Force-training is a misnomer in a way. There is force and we are training. But there ought to be another name for it, really.

Delaney: I try to get the dog to pick up the bird in a natural way, but if that doesn't work I go to the force-training methods. The natural way would be to play, toss the bird around like a ball, something like that, to get the dog excited, interested, and grabbing.

Benson: Any pup, at six months to a year, that refuses to carry an object—a glove, a hat, a dummy—or go near a bird, to me isn't worth the money. You're going to have too much expense in it. There are ways, like using a flopping bird to encourage the dog to catch and hang on and carry, but dogs today, the way the market is, should have the natural ability to carry an object. In any puppy of good breeding, it should be hereditary that he carries objects.

If a dog picks up and carries, but runs away with a dummy or bird instead of coming to you with it, how do you get him to bring it to you?

Carey: As part of his obedience training the dog should be taught to come when he is called. In cases where a dog will come well when called but when he gets a dummy will run away, use a check cord to start with to show the dog the proper way to deliver.

Walking at heel carrying the dummy is a very important means of assuring delivery to hand. Getting it through the dog's head that he should pick up a cola bottle, a bed spring, a bird, a dummy, any object you drop on the ground in front of him and say "Fetch!," is a good way to ensure proper delivery.

Delaney: If the dog runs away, take the long rope, start reeling him in, get him in the habit of coming. A lot of times just backing away or running in the opposite direction will get him to come in to you. But those are the easy ways to do it. If they don't work you'll just have to go into your obedience and force-training.

Benson: Picking up an object and running and playing with it is not the worst fault in a dog. All you have to do is go away from him and he's going to start chasing you. Then if he has the check cord on his collar, you can step on the cord when he runs past you and snap him back. Don't take the object away from him quickly, let him hold it for a while, praise him. He enjoys it. There are other methods. But the check cord is probably the best and easiest way to make a stubborn pup come to you with what he's fetching.

If a dog picks up the dummy and carries it back toward you but drops it before he reaches you, how do you assure delivery to hand?

Carey: You take the dog to the spot where he dropped the dummy, and if you've done your force-training properly tell him to "Fetch It!" He should reach down, pick it up, hold it. Then you walk back to the spot you sent him from and take it from him.

If you haven't force-trained him that way, you're going to have to pick it up, put it in his mouth, and somehow make him hold it all the time he's walking back to that same spot. I am very much in favor of force-training, because if he drops something within 10 to 25 yards from you you can tell him "Fetch it up!" and he'll reach down and grab it. That's retrieving the way it should be.

Delaney: Plain force-retrieving.

Benson: A pup that drops a dummy when he's coming in, is it after one or two retrieves, is the object too big for him to handle it? The solution might be simple. But if he's fresh into training and big enough to handle the object, make him walk at heel with the object in his mouth. If he drops it, give it a kick and tell him to fetch it. Then reach down and pet him and

149

praise him when he has it in his mouth. Having him carry it alongside of you is probably the easiest way to get him to deliver all the way.

If a dog mauls, roughs up, tosses, and plays with a dummy or bird, how do you teach him to carry firmly, but gently?

Carey: I pick the object up, show it to the dog, and I scold him. I say "Look what you did to this thing! What's the matter with you?" And then I put it in his mouth and let him hold it. In the case of a force-broken dog, if he holds it for twenty minutes or half an hour, he's happy to give it to you. You've got a chance when the dog is force-broken.

Another thing I use is a sock around a big, square automobile sponge with nails through the sponge; then I cover this with bird wings. This can be used by those who don't believe in force-breaking, who try to get the dog to pick up, hold, and deliver naturally. The dog starts chewing and these big nails hurt his mouth.

But watch for and hasten to correct it when a dog starts rolling birds in his mouth. Insist on the dog's holding firmly but gently.

Delaney: By force-retrieve training. The force-retrieve is the most important thing in the whole business. The steps I use in force-retrieving are pretty much the standard ones—pinch an ear and when the dog opens his mouth to protest put the dummy or stick in his mouth while you tell him to "Fetch!" or whatever command you use; make him keep it in his mouth, gradually lengthening the time he holds it and so on; or open his mouth with your hand and stick the dummy in it, telling him to hold it, working at it until he'll pick up whatever you tell him to and bring it to you. There are a lot of little variations to this system; some take longer than others. I think I can usually get the job done with three or four days of work.

A really dumb or stubborn or resentful dog that is inclined to bite may have to be stood up on his hind legs by throwing a rope attached to his slip collar over something like a hitching rack, putting the stick in his mouth while he struggles and letting him down when he takes it and holds. If a dog is going to act buggy about this and bite, this makes him fight with himself instead of you and saves your hands.

Retrieving is the dog's job. Force-retrieving will often eliminate mauling, hard mouth, the playing, anything the dog does wrong. What it is is obedience in carrying an object, and that's why almost all dogs need it.

Benson: If the dog goes out and deliberately mauls and chews the object and doesn't want to follow you, you've got to use a check cord on him. As soon as he lies down with the object, make him follow and get out of that spot. A lot of puppies just lack the natural quality of carrying an object right. But the check cord comes in handy with the young dog. The old dog is a different story.

Sometimes you can use water with a young dog that wants to lie down and chew. Throw the dummy in the water and you stand in knee-deep water in hip boots. I haven't seen a puppy yet go out and stand in one place or lie down and maul in the water. By standing in the water yourself, you can create in the dog a habit of delivering right to you.

You've outlined a way to introduce a dog to feathered game so there is little chance of a retriever becoming hard mouthed. But if a dog does start to crunch his birds, what method is best for curing that fault?

Carey: I've had dogs go through the field trial until the last bird and actually go out and eat it when they could have won the field trial if this hadn't occurred. I think that bird eating in field trials by otherwise good retrievers results from a pressure situation. The whole thing gets to be too much for them. For shooting dogs, direct training methods are the best.

First of all, I will feed the dog a good meal before he goes out to sit in that blind and then I watch him. He'll pick up a few birds, but I never let him play with the birds in the blind. In the training situations, back at the kennel, I will force-break the dog to realize it's his responsibility, his duty, to carry that bird, and the only relief he will get from carrying that bird is when I take it, without snatching it, from his mouth. If he's stuck with this thing, knows he's going to have it in his mouth for a long period of time unless I take it from him, the dog will certainly want to give it to me and he won't crush it.

All kinds of things, like wires, nails, having him carry wire brushes, may be helpful. With a dog that's a good retriever, has plenty of desire, when he starts bearing down too hard, sometimes the electric collar can stop it.

Delaney: Guess I'm kind of stuck on this one answer: it is force-retrieve training.

Benson: Hard mouth is probably the most difficult thing to prescribe a remedy for without seeing the dog. Why is he doing it? Is he enjoying it? Is he attacking it? I don't have the answers without knowing the dog.

The old check cord, carrying at heel, standing on a tail, holding a bird in his mouth, swimming or wading along making him carry a duck, chastising him every time he chomps down, they all work on some dogs and not on others. You have to get out with, see, and know the particular dog you're working on. Every one's different. I have no cure-all method for hard mouth.

If a dog seems deficient in natural marking ability, is there any drill that can be given to improve his ability to make long single retrieves and to mark and remember multiple falls?

Carey: Most of this marking ability, particularly for doubles, is a matter of repetition. One thing to remember about the drill is to make the areas of the fall short enough so you have success, get it perfect. You should throw the dummies on something like a football field or a big lawn so the dog can see the object to be retrieved from the time he leaves your side. A strip of white adhesive tape around the canvas dummy will highlight it.

Generally speaking, with regard to multiple retrieves, a theory I heard from Chuck Morgan [the late Charles M. Morgan, a pioneer midwestern retriever trainer] applies. And that is, the visual impressions the dog gets in regard to marked retrieves are something like a camera in his eyes or brain.

Left

Loral I Delaney demonstrates use of choke collar on this stubborn Chesapeake. Rope is readied to hoist dog that refuses to take and hold dummy.

Right

The dog quickly learned that if he opened his mouth, took the stick in it and held for a short period he was let down from this uncomfortable position. In less than ten minutes the dog was not only accepting and holding the stick, but reaching toward it.

Say you are at home plate with the dog and your assistant on the pitcher's mound throws dummies to first and third base in that order. When you send your dog he will immediately run for the last thing he saw, the third-base dummy. After he's brought that back to you, you can almost watch the dog wait until the film develops in his head and he remembers what he saw before and then he'll go to the first-base dummy.

Sometimes you have to throw a lot of dummies to first base before you throw one to third base, so the dog gets the habit of going out there by remembering from repetition. Any kind of dog training is really just repetition and drill. But the first thing is to get the dog to develop this image of what he's seen before and when he is ready, and not before, send him.

You can do a lot on water with dummies out at 45 degrees, easily seen, if the dog is a willing water dog. When he becomes proficient at remembering, then you can start putting your hand down and sending him on command. That will help in the steadying of the dog and later in teaching him

Satisfaction in completing a tough and unpleasant training task successfully is mirrored in the trainer's face, and the dog's attitude has been converted from surly refusal to cooperation and an acceptance of discipline.

to take a line and observe hand signals. Eventually he won't go until you put your hand down and say "Go Back!" as you thrust your hand toward the area where the dummy lies. Out of habit, he'll take off in the direction you indicate with your hand even if his memory of the fall isn't clear.

Do not send for the second bird until you are sure he is ready to be sent in order to avoid the fault of recasting a confused dog.

Delaney: Some dogs don't have the ability to remember anything past a single. It's sort of rare, but it does happen. The thing you can do is just give them retrieves in different areas. Some dogs get bored with the same area and need a different terrain to make them concentrate. Try to make all your retrieves interesting so the dog has something to look forward to.

Benson: If a dog only goes out 20 yards on a 40-yard fall, work him directly into the wind so his nose will bring him on out. Work him on flatter terrain or even up a hill. Uphill will give him better vision than downhill or flat. He's more likely to see it there, if his eyes are normal.

If he's short on dummies, give him live birds. They'll give him a little more guts and he'll see them farther down. Throwing the bird high, rather than low, will help him mark. You might have to let him go before the bird drops. Then later restrain him, keeping him steady until sent.

153

Describe the best method to teach a dog to "take a line" to a downed bird he has not seen drop, doesn't remember, or has mismarked.

Carey: The best way to teach a dog a line is to have him run to a place he knows about and will go to willingly. Starting with just you and the dog and a dummy or two, walk the dog out to second base, throw the dummy there, walk him back to home plate and say "Fetch!" or "Back!" Have him sitting and send him with your hand signal at the same time as the verbal command toward second base—something he absolutely knows about and will remember.

After he's learned that lesson well, returning several times to that same area, take half-a-dozen dummies, go out to center field and drop dummies at staggered distances, in line, as you walk back to the dog at home plate. Send the dog so he'll pick them up one by one, passing the areas where he's

In giving a retriever "a line," the direction the handler wants the dog to take is indicated with the hand before the signal is given sending the dog on its way to retrieve. (Larry Mueller photo)

Depending upon the trainer's preference and the individual dog, a retriever may be sent to retrieve from either the left or right side as Ed Carey demonstrates here. (Larry Mueller photo)

previously picked up dummies, running in a straight line. You do this down the left-field line, the right-field line, and straight out over second base to center field, until at your choice he will take any one of the three lines. This might take you *weeks*, but it should be done.

Delaney: Best bet is to start them on a road, with the dummy or bird out there as short as you need to get the dog to go on the word "Back!" and increase the length of your line until it's up to maybe 100 to 150 yards. The idea is to have a clear path, so the dog will get in the habit of going straight in the direction he's sent. The main thing is to have something at the end of that line to fetch, so he knows there's going to be something out there if he keeps going.

Once he's going good for the dummies he's seen you place out there, put them out where he doesn't see them and send him just like you did before. Through the repetition he knows there's something at the end of that line and with constant practice he will keep going on a line until he finds it.

Benson: On land, you can utilize an old grass road, trail, or path, giving him a designated area to run on—any easy running path. Naturally you hide your birds or dummies on the upwind side of the path so when he's running down that path he'll whiff them from the side. Then he'll get the habit of continuing on that straight line until he runs across scent.

Aside from the necessity of using good judgment, is there generally a time to punish and a time to praise? What forms should punishment and praise take and when are they used to discipline and reward a dog?

Carey: There are darned few dogs that are going to be trained well unless they're happy to be with the person they're with. Praise and reasonable affection should be given the dog just for being with you. By that I mean just sit down and pet the dog while he's with you, tell him he's a good dog. Reaching in your pocket and getting a piece of biscuit or fried liver or something can really wake 'em up. I remember Chuck Morgan often talking about just taking long walks with the dogs, both old and new ones, and it pays off in the long run.

You're never going to train a dog if he doesn't trust you and know you. By all means, don't go out first thing and find something he'll do wrong and punish him. Very few, if any, professional trainers get a kick out of thrashing dogs. We much prefer to do it without that sort of thing. The problem a professional trainer faces is *somehow* instilling in the dog some conditioned reflex that is diametrically opposed to one he's learned for long periods of time before he came to the trainer.

There has to be times for rather forceful, attention-getting disciplining or punishment. But it has to be timed properly; otherwise the dog with a brief attention span just doesn't connect the trouble he's gotten himself into with the punishment. Severe punishment should be meted out only by someone who knows what he's doing.

It leads to an idea of animal and human communication. There has been quite a number of books written recently about such communication. We do a lot of things we don't know we're doing when training. We assume a lot of postures that have meaning to the dog and sometimes our emotions convey attitudes to him that we don't want him to have. It's also possible on occasion to get a dog to perform the exact action you want him to by simply changing your body posture; for example, instead of being aggressive and giving oral commands, simply turn away, almost ignoring the dog. But it's a pretty good idea, both in punishment and praise, to be low keyed.

Delaney: It's always important to use good judgment because every dog is different. There's always a time to reward the dog, even with pleasant *thoughts*—what's in your mind will reflect in your attitude toward your dog. When it comes to punishment, you only punish the dog when he's in the act of doing something wrong and you know that he knows what you want. Sometimes just a slight correction is enough. Another dog might need heavy correction. I try to keep my corrections as simple as possible.

When the dog does right, I just naturally do a little sweet talk with that dog. I really don't know what I say. I just say what I feel like at the time. If the dog needs some encouraging, is the type of dog that feels that petting is the big deal in his life, maybe a couple pats or a scratch behind the ear stimulates him a little bit. Some dogs get right down to business and don't need talk, petting, or anything. They're willing to do their work and happy to do it. I don't think tidbits are necessary in field work; maybe if you're teaching tricks or something like that they will be helpful.

Benson: A dog's got to have praise and he's got to have discipline. I think a dog needs 90 percent praise and 10 percent discipline at the beginning of training. Praise the dog when he is doing good and hold your discipline for when he pulls a real baddy and needs physical correction. A sharp, instantaneous hurt in correction is worth a dozen slaps to discipline a dog. You have to use good judgment in deciding if the dog can take the discipline. If he shuns it, then you've got to do it mildly.

Probably the most innovative and well-publicized training device to appear in recent years is the electronic shock collar. Based on your experience, can the electronic shock collar be of much aid to an amateur training his own dog? If it has drawbacks, how should the person using it exercise caution to achieve the most from this device?

Carey: The electric collar is one of the best means to help dog training that we have. It gets across certain ideas without the handler being in the position of being the bad guy. However, it should be introduced and used properly before taking the dog into the field for the first time and pressing the 5,000-volt button. The dog should wear the dummy collar for a long period of time and put through his obedience paces and corrected electrically for things he does improperly, like not coming when he's called. When he does come he should be praised and not put back to the same position where he got the shock. Sometimes one shock a day once a week is plenty.

The electric collar should never be used to demonstrate dog obedience or "I'll show you how this works" attitude on the part of an amateur. He should almost never use it, but have it ready. That's the only attitude for an amateur to have and not ruin the dog. For example, the dog can see a man carrying a gun at the same time he gets the shock and perhaps become afraid of men with guns the rest of his life. It's that type of thing that you must be wary of.

The brand of collar is also important. The one I've had outstanding success with is the Tri-Tronics collar. Some I've had for five or six years and they've given me very good service.

Delaney: The electronic collar can be a pretty good idea for the amateur. If the dog knows how to heel or whoa, he will soon learn that if he doesn't do it instantly that shock is coming. Some get a little upset about it. But they cool off once they learn what it's about—that if they don't obey the command they'll get a shock.

The thing you must remember is not to overdo it. Use it as an aid only when it's absolutely necessary, as a last resort when everything else fails. Use the rope first, then the slingshot. Go to the electronic collar only if those things don't work. It's better than shooting with a 12 gauge because there's less chance of seriously hurting the dog.

The brands I use are Ability and Tri-Tronics, and I've had good and bad luck with both of them.

Benson: The electronic collar of today is a great help, one of the finest measures of discipline at a distance there is, when correctly used. It's not a cure-all, it doesn't make the dog a better hunter, but it does make him a better mannered dog. It's helpful for stopping a gun dog from running deer, skunk, varmint, or rabbit. Otherwise you'd have to catch up and discipline him with a choke collar, leash, or whop him.

It's great for making a dog stay in "shooting preserve range" where you have neighboring gunners and your dog tends to run over to other people. It's probably the most humane method of harsh discipline you can put on a dog. It's not even that harsh when it's used right. I think an amateur should have its use explained and the dog conditioned by one who knows how to use it. You don't have to use it often for it to be effective.

My most satisfactory experience with a specific brand of electronic collars has been with the Tri-Tronics collar.

What are the advantages and disadvantages of a sportsman keeping his retriever as a house dog and companion, as opposed to kenneling him strictly as a hunter?

Carey: The advantage is that the dog is with the person who then has the enjoyment of the company of the dog. But that must not overshadow any lack of discipline that might result when dogs are not required to do a certain thing at a certain time. If the dog is going to be untrained or detrained by a bunch of other people—family, friends, whoever—while the trainer isn't at home, the best place for the dog is in the kennel, at least through the early formative years. I mean a home kennel, not a boarding kennel.

In some cases, for various reasons, some people keep dogs with me until the hunting season, then pick them up and have them with them for a

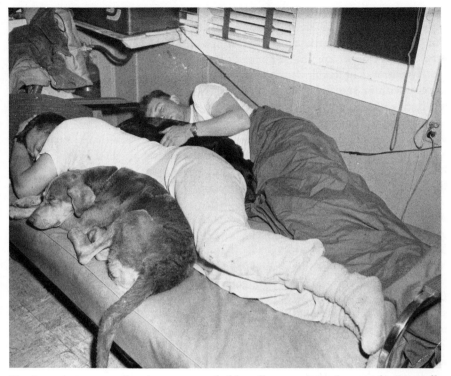

Getting next to your dog is recommended by all pro trainers but maybe Joe Kelly and Dave Duffey are carrying it to an extreme with Sport, a Chesapeake, and Clinker, a Labrador, on a Mississippi River duck-hunting trip.

few months. They feel this is much better than no dog at all. But, really, the house is the best place if it's a good environment for obedience for a young dog, not a place where the dog will learn a million bad habits and can get away with disobeying.

Of course, dogs kept outside develop better protective coats than dogs that live in artificially heated houses and they become better adjusted to outside temperatures they'll be encountering when hunting.

Delaney: It would depend a lot on the people who have the dog. Some people can follow through with training in the house and the dog can learn a lot. But many people get sloppy, let the dog have his way and do what he wants. Or they'll baby the dog too much. Then I don't agree with him being in the house.

I guess I'm always a trainer, no matter where I have a dog. But some people aren't. You have to judge yourself. If you aren't going to train while he's in the house, I'd suggest keeping him in the kennel.

I also believe dogs like their privacy. It's all right to have them in the house for a while but they enjoy their own home, they enjoy the outdoors, it's better for their coats. So everyone has to make up his own mind.

Benson: I think that all gun dogs, where it's feasible, should be companion dogs, house dogs. I don't say that staying in a good warm house is best. Actually, the best way is to have the dog sleep in a kennel outside, but let him come in and enjoy the afternoon and evening hours with you and the family. From another standpoint, a dog in the kennel is a better watch dog than a dog in the house. He warns his people of intruders when they enter the premises. The dog also gets used to going in and out. Generally the dog should be adapted to a little household living, but he should stay outdoors the better part of the day.

Based upon your extensive experience, would you give some off-the-cuff advice, odds and ends of information, pet peeves, tips, remarks on conditioning, etc., that weren't touched upon in previous questions?

Carey: One thing we do wrong with dogs is we keep forgetting they are dogs. We give them human attributes, human ways of reasoning, and we read into their personalities an awful lot of feelings they don't have. That makes life a lot tougher for the dogs.

The type of testing in retriever field trials is becoming unreal, emphasizing only trained, acquired characteristics rather than natural attributes the dogs are born with. And bird dog trials, like the retriever trials, are pretty far afield from what we can do practically. It's too bad that one is so different from the other that we're getting all kinds of different dogs. Trying to select a bunch of fine pleasure horses from a bunch of Kentucky Derby hopefuls is no way to do it. But that's what we're doing.

The advent of good food and good veterinary care compared to what we had years ago results in many more dogs that should not be bred being bred—producing pups for money reasons, for the children, and so on. We're getting a lot of bad dogs. I hope there won't be the overall decrease in ability in the dogs over the next twenty years I feel there's been in the last twenty. We're just not breeding shooting dogs as much and the best of the shooting dogs is not a field trial dog, which is something else. This is especially so in regard to retrievers. The way game and places to hunt are decreasing, it's too bad we have a lot of dogs that can't be trained as well as they ought to because they weren't bred properly.

Regarding retrieving conditions, one thing to consider and think about is heat problems in handling dogs. Always be sure you carry enough water along for your dog to drink and to get him cooled down to prevent heat stroke, particularly when dove shooting in hot weather. Even in the northern states, running a dog for long distances in warm September or October weather can easily break a dog's wind and it may adversely affect him the rest of his life.

It's also a good idea to give the dog a period alone before training. Getting a newcomer, I usually put him off in a kennel by himself, in semi-isolation for a day or so before I take him out or go to his kennel to pick him up. That gives him confidence in me as the first friend he sees. I also use a dog wagon or truck to haul my dogs to the field so the dogs in the compartments are pretty much by themselves on their way to training. Invariably dogs that are driven to the field work better than those that walk

When hunting dry upland cover, spaniels and retrievers should be watered frequently or at least be given refreshment when brought back to the car in which water can be easily carried. Dave Duffey waters Poncho and Flirt. (Tom McNally photo)

from the kennel to the field. They pay attention, they get along better, and seem more ready to work when they come out of the box.

So for any amateur it's a good idea to have a car crate, have it enclosed, not open on the sides. If you want an open crate for your dog, also buy a canvas cover to put over it.

The training methods we've discussed here are my own methods that I've acquired and stolen and borrowed and learned from people in this business, both amateurs and professionals. They work in my particular circumstances and geographic area and in some instances may not be *the* way to do it; and they may not be the way in some cases that I'll be doing it next year. Things do change and you always keep learning.

Delaney: One place where amateurs who train dogs can run into problems is watching trainers who may be too tough on dogs. People who watch other trainers tend to copy a lot. You may copy the wrong thing. It's better to train by yourself and not get involved in other people's thinking, other than if they're really good at it. Then you'll learn something. But don't rely on everything the man down the street says just because he has one or two dogs and thinks he's a great expert, when he really isn't. You can maybe destroy your dog by doing things he does that you shouldn't do.

I don't like to see people correct dogs by hanging them by their ears. I think it's a very unnecessary correction, and might be harmful to the dog.

In picking dogs for my shows, I like field trial type or potential dogs. They've got special class, are above average, and have a consistency about them that I can depend on. I guess they could be called field trial potential, something with a little class.

I think working dogs can be a satisfying hobby. You get them out two or three times a week and the conditioning is just naturally going to take place—swimming, running in the field, and so forth—for a certain amount of time. Have them heel while you ride a bicycle but be careful not to have them run too hard on tar roads. I learned through experience you can run a dog's feet raw that way.

All training and conditioning is mostly using common sense, logic, being persistent, and enjoying everything you're trying to do with the dog.

Benson: They say every dog has his day and I think every dog probably has to have a kick in the tail once in a while. But my pet peeve is the person who whips a dog and enjoys it, or whips a dog and gets mad.

Another dislike is pulling ears for discipline, grabbing a dog by the ear and wrenching it or dragging him and twisting his ear or shaking him by the ears. He's got to hear you and there's too much injury done by pulling ears.

If he's got to be restrained or shook, take him by the back of the neck and the loose skin on the rump and shake him up, pick him up like that. But stay away from his eyes and his ears, sex organs, and things like that.

PART 4

Spaniels

Dave Lorenz with two-time National Champion Gwibernant Ganol, owned by John T. Pirie, Jr.

Dave Lorenz

Dave Lorenz, with a solid background in training various breeds of hunting dogs, is a sure bet to finish one of the string of English springer spaniels he handles "in the money" at any field trial in which he competes.

There are probably less than a dozen professional trainers in the United States who regularly compete in field trials and train gun dogs for hunters as well, and Lorenz is one of the veterans.

His record of success speaks for itself. Between 1964 and 1975 he has handled three Springers to four National Open Championships, back-to-back wins with Gwibernant Ganol (owned by John T. Pirie, Jr.) in 1964 and 1965, Brackenbriar Snapshot (owned by Brackenbriar Kennels) in 1967, and Dot of Charel (owned by Dr. Charles T. Curdy) in 1972. During an over thirty-five-year career he has handled many other fine competitors to field trial championships and placements in trials throughout the country. With the retirement from active training of such luminaries as Steve Studnicki, Cliff Wallace, and Elmore Chick, Lorenz rates, along with Larry Mac-Queen, as the dean of spaniel trainers in the United States.

Assisted by his wife, Mary, daughter of the late Martin Hogan who is generally credited with popularizing the Labrador retriever and Springer spaniel in the Midwest upon reaching Illinois from Ireland, and son, David Lorenz, Jr., one of the better trial guns now shooting over Springers, Lorenz operates a public training and boarding kennel.

He can be reached at The Hogan Kennels, Sullivan Lake Road, Ingleside, Illinois 60041 (Phone: 815—385-6311).

John Isaacs

John Isaacs got a late start as a professional trainer of English springer spaniels, but has come up fast in qualifying dogs for National Championship competition by placing them in trials throughout the country.

John Isaacs with two winning English imports, Pinewarren Warloan, left, and FTC Bricksclose Sprigg, right.

Pro dog training is a second career for Isaacs, who retired after serving twenty years as a maintenance specialist in the U.S. Air Force, and with the aid of his wife, Nadine, and their four children, his public kennel specializes in Springer spaniels, but accepts pointing breeds for training as well.

While on a tour of duty in England, Isaacs purchased and trained his second Springer, Pepe of Shrewsbury; and when brought to this country the young dog impressed John Buoy, a United Airlines pilot and one of the top amateur spaniel handlers in the United States. When Isaacs shipped out for a second tour of duty in Spain, he sold Pepe to Buoy. The talented amateur guided Pepe to his field trial championship and in 1969 placed him third in the National Open, following up with a second in the same stake in 1970.

When Isaacs opened his kennel in 1971, in an effort to get the Kentucky-born trainer interested in trialing, Buoy returned FTC Pepe of Shrewsbury to his original owner. With that start, Isaacs was off to the races, establishing himself as a competitor and competent trainer of gun dogs.

He can be reached at Guadaira Kennels, Route 1, Box 66, Amanda, Ohio 53102 (Phone: 614—969-2686).

Alan Hurst

Alan Hurst learned gamekeeping from an uncle in England prior to World War II and served in the Royal Navy during that conflict. He came to the United States in 1975 to manage a private estate and train dogs for its owner, J. A. Puelicher, Milwaukee, Wisconsin.

Alan Hurst and Tom (Ardnamurchan Mac), an English Cocker field trial champion.

Following his discharge as a navy officer, he served in a fire brigade and worked as a gamekeeper in England and Wales. With his wife, Jo, and their daughter, he established his own breeding and training kennel, specializing in spaniels, both Springer and working Cocker, taking a black Cocker, Ardnamurchan Mac, to his English field trial championship.

Hurst also put English titles on Stanley Regis Premier and Sari of Gorsty and won in British competition with Cutnook Coxwain and Layerbrook Sultan. Stanley Regis Premier also won his United States field trial champion title under the whistle of New Jersey pro, Larry MacQueen for owner Mike Kurkjain.

Hurst is a close friend of Keith Erlandson, generally recognized as the top spaniel trainer in the United Kingdom, who recently authored a book on his experiences and training techniques. With his background, experience, and contacts, Hurst is well qualified to detail British training techniques and philosophy.

He can be reached at Willow Creek Club, Route 2, Wild Rose, Wisconsin (Phone: 414—787-3515).

What were your reasons or what influenced you to decide to specialize in training spaniels primarily, rather than other breeds of gun dogs?

Lorenz: Actually I ran Labradors in trials before I did Springers but after my father-in-law died I just sort of took over the clients that we had and continued on field trialing Springers. I like Springers best of all the breeds because while they are harder to train they're also more interesting to train. Their dispositions are such that it's just more rewarding to work with Springers than any of the other breeds.

Isaacs: I had Springer spaniels for personal hunting dogs. I enjoyed working with them, enjoyed training them. I thought that I trained them to a high standard for a hunting dog. Working alone, using my own methods and using your book [*Hunting Dog Know-How* by David Michael Duffey, Winchester Press], among others, I found myself at a stage where I could win with a dog in the amateur trials, so people came to me wanting me to train a pup for them. One thing led to another and we gradually built up to where we had people wanting us to handle a dog in the open all-age stakes. I then ceased handling in the amateur stakes.

It was Charles "Chuck" Goodall's book, *The Complete English Springer Spaniel*, that first got me interested in the breed, and after reading and gaining some knowledge about the various breeds I decided I'd try an English springer spaniel.

I was in England and bought an eight-week-old female puppy and left her with a gamekeeper to be trained, to get her started. Then, when she was six months old, I picked her up and started working with her daily. I was fascinated by the way she'd respond. She was always right there, doing what I wanted done, and from then on I was in love with Springers. At nine or ten months old she was putting up pheasants and bringing the shot birds to hand. With only dummy work in the summertime, the first bird that was shot for her, the first feathers she ever had in her mouth, she brought the bird to me just like she did the dummy. I was impressed with the value of a breed that could do those things in such a short time.

Hurst: As a gamekeeper in England, where our cover is often very thick and heavy, it was obvious that none of the retriever breeds was good enough to use on shooting [hunting] days. Obviously something else was needed, a fast, clever, close-hunting dog. The Springer, basically, and the Cocker spaniel to a degree, fulfill this need.

Do you look for any physical traits that might give an individual dog an edge in his training and work? Are there traits of temperament or disposition that indicate to you that the dog you are dealing with may be relatively easy to train or be difficult? In effect, describe your kind of dog.

Lorenz: I've had very good luck with puppies of our own breeding. You know the sire and the dam and then you can pick out a puppy whose markings resemble the sire or the dam. If you have a good sire, for example, and you pick out a puppy with similar markings, very often the puppy will carry the same traits that made the sire good. It's worked out real well.

I like a larger-type dog, especially in a male. With females it doesn't make that much difference. The dog shouldn't be too soft, but should have lots of what you call "trainability," one that wants to please you more than one you have to be correcting all the time.

Isaacs: The number-one thing in a dog is the temperament. After that I look for natural ability, a desire to hunt, to stay with me. I don't want a dog that's aloof or one that wants to run on his own. Physically, I want a good-looking dog. But mostly I want a dog that shows an eager willingness to work with me, a dog that will accept training, and if he requires discipline will accept that and respond.

When I handle a puppy and put him down, I like him to go about his business, not cower. I have no use for that. I'm a very gentle handler with dogs but every dog has to be disciplined at one time or another. I want a dog that will respond to discipline and accept it, not the shy one, or the dog that has to be disciplined every move he makes in the field and is still pig-headed enough to go ahead and commit the same offense again.

Hurst: I require a hard-hunting, fast, stylish spaniel. This type of dog has the drive and the stamina to do the work in heavy cover. Over ten years a particular type of Springer has emerged in Britain. These puppies basically come from Hale's Smut and it is now recognized that there are two distinct types of Springer. I prefer that which is known as a Smut-type dog in Britain, which is a thick-set, not too tall, hard-going, stylish dog, with great amounts of speed in contrast to the slower type of dog that does not stay the ground and slows up much more quickly.

At approximately what age, recognizing variations in individual dogs, do you prefer to have a dog brought to you for training? For what reasons?

Lorenz: The best puppies are always the ones you have from the beginning, that you can start working with at six or seven weeks. But that's not always practical. If I'm going to take a dog in for training, and assuming that the people who own the puppy have socialized him and worked with him, I usually take the puppy at about nine months of age.

Isaacs: I first ask the owners what they have done or what they can do for the puppy. If they say, "Well, I don't have time" and so on, then I want that puppy between the ages of eight weeks and twelve weeks, just as early as I can get him. But if they can get this pup out daily, can take a knotted handkerchief or a stuffed stocking and get the puppy to retrieving in the hallway or on the lawn, if they will take him out in the field to fetch a dummy, if they can teach him to sit and stay and come and heel, then I'd like to have the puppy at a year old or after. But he has to be trained from a puppy, either by the owner or by the trainer.

Hurst: I prefer to start training a puppy between the ages of seven and nine months, by which time he has gotten over his initial puppyhood and will learn and retain what he is taught. If training is started earlier than at this age, puppies tend to be repressed.

What steps can a dog's owner take to help ensure that the pup will be trainable and the formal training job easier when he brings the dog to you?

Lorenz: The most important thing an owner can do before bringing a pup in for training is to have him retrieving to hand, which can be started when the puppy is seven or eight weeks old. Aside from that, the owner should do what we call "socializing" the puppy, exposing him to a lot of different conditions, noises, and so forth.

Isaacs: The most important thing is the human contact with that dog. A dog shouldn't be ignored and then when he's nine to eighteen months old he's brought out with the owner figuring to go hunting or looking for some trainer to take and train the dog. The dog should be in constant human contact and should be worked with from the time he's a puppy, so when you go in the field he will love to stay with you and work for you.

An owner can accomplish this if he'll spend five minutes a day or fifteen minutes twice a week (although daily is best) taking his dog out and giving him some attention. Let the dog get out and develop his natural ability to hunt and retrieve, but bring the dog back in with a whistle and keep him under control. Pet him from time to time when you're out with him. You don't want a dog under your feet all the time, and a dog with no desire to get out you don't want around. When the dog starts reaching out boldly, start bringing him back in, establishing some control.

Hurst: Create biddability by making a fuss over the little pup, not allowing him to do any self-hunting at all, only the controlled exercises. Never let the pup go more than 40 yards from his owner during the exercises. This is achieved by bribery and the use of a whistle. Call the dog up at the 40-yard range and give him a biscuit. Let him run on again, call him up again at 40 yards and give him another biscuit. This allows the dog to develop a particular pattern without any repressive training at all.

If an owner chooses to train his own dog, are there ages or stages a puppy or young dog goes through when he will learn certain things more readily than at any other time?

Lorenz: The most important time is from six weeks to four months. This is the best time to establish a pattern that will hold through the puppy's life. If the pup's neglected during that time, it's much harder for anyone to take over to start or continue the training.

Isaacs: Each dog is an individual. There's no certain age that you can say every dog should be this or that. I've run into dogs I thought would never do some things, like retrieve or handle, but all of a sudden they do it. Effort should be made to watch the dog to see that he's ready to do what he should do. But you also need to detect whether in the long run this dog will have the ability to deliver what you want. You have to train toward that goal and you've got to understand each dog individually.

Hurst: Each puppy is an individual. Some take readily to hunting training earlier in life than retriever training, some vice versa. By early experimentation and playing, it is essential to find out what the pup really wants to do that you want him to do, and what he *doesn't* want to do that you want him to do. You then commence the training by teaching him the things that he wants to do. A certain amount of control comes with confidence in the handler and makes it possible to teach him the things he really doesn't want to do. For example, if the puppy is slow in entering cover naturally, he is taken to a piece of ground with cover and pieces of dried meat are thrown in so the puppy can see them. Throw in a reasonable-size piece of dried meat, let the puppy see the meat, let him scent it, let him find it. This goes on for a period of time until a puppy will readily enter cover looking for dried meat, ground scent, or whatever he may find in there.

Assuming that for different people there are different choices, under what circumstances will someone buying a dog be best satisfied with a puppy, a started dog, or a trained dog?

Lorenz: If a person is used to dogs and doesn't have any small children in the family, he could probably start off with a puppy and train it. But if there's small children who'll throw balls and sticks and give the dog a lot of useless commands, then it's better to buy a trained dog, one that's beyond being spoiled by the children.

Isaacs: My advice to anyone who can afford it is to buy a trained dog. But for the person who doesn't have much money to spend, but has the time, energy, and will to do it, I suggest he train a puppy himself with the aid of books and training devices that are available and with the advice of knowledgeable people he can discuss the training aspects with. If a person has less time, but thinks he has the ability to train a dog, he should buy a started dog in order to accomplish what he wants.

A busy person with a tight schedule who says "All I want to do is go

Top
On being introduced to live birds, most retrievers can be expected to take a rather gingerly hold, as Finnegan, an Irish water spaniel, does here with a shackled duck.

Bottom
With more experience, Finnegan demonstrates a "better grasp" of his subject matter, but a "butt-hold" isn't a preferred way to carry, although sometimes resorted to when catching a fleeing bird.

hunting; I don't have time to train a dog" should buy a trained dog and plan on leaving that dog with a trainer one or two months out of the year before the hunting season to have it ready.

Hurst: Undertaking the training of a puppy is advisable only when the owner is fully prepared to go to a great deal of trouble to train the puppy in the proper manner and is willing to seek advice on training and read good books on training. He must be enthusiastic enough to do this for a period of up to six months. If he isn't prepared to do this, one way out is to buy a started dog, which would require only two or three months of finishing work. But even with a started dog the owner must be prepared to devote time, patience, and energy to train the dog in a proper manner, seeking advice from the pros or information from a good book.

Somebody who doesn't have the time or the will to do it for himself should buy a trained dog. It's essential for anybody who buys a trained dog to carefully follow the trainer's instructions and see that the dog is worked in all circumstances. If the dog has been properly demonstrated in the first place and goes wrong, there is only the new owner to blame.

Describe a started dog in terms of what the buyer of such a dog might expect with regard to obedience and hunting ability. In other words, what has a started dog learned and what can he do?

Lorenz: I think a started dog is one eight to ten months old that has learned to hunt, flush, and chase birds—pigeons—and also be shot over and retrieve the shot birds back to the handler.

Isaacs: A started dog should be able to quarter and stay in range, come in to you when called, sit down and stay there until you are ready to carry on. A started dog would be one that would quarter in front of the gun with very little handling, and would have the nose to find a bird. The dog will go in and flush the pigeons or pheasants, and when you shoot a bird the dog will get it and bring it back to you. That's about 99 percent of what people need for a hunting dog, period. As long as a dog knows game scent, will get in there and put the bird out, get it and bring it to you when it's shot, you should be satisfied with that dog as a hunting spaniel.

Hurst: A started dog is one that will obey all whistle signals either to drop to the whistle, turn to the whistle, come in to the whistle, drop to shot, remain steady to shot, and retrieve dummies on command and be able to be directed to a blind retrieve. The dog must have a reasonable hunting pattern on ground but not be expected to be steady to flushed game.

Facing page, top
This seven-week-old Springer pup brings a knotted handkerchief to trainer John Isaacs as the first step in the channeling of natural retrieving instincts into reliable recovery and delivery of shot birds.

Facing page, bottom
Delivery to hand is achieved as Isaacs reaches for the first object this bold puppy has been sent to retrieve.

What tips would you offer for the selection and purchase of a puppy to help assure the buyer that he will be getting a sound, healthy pup that should be potentially trainable?

Lorenz: Before picking a pup out of the litter, take them out onto the lawn. Watch which one goes off investigating by himself instead of sticking with the pack. If you clap your hands, look for one that doesn't shrink away from the noise. I would also throw a paint roller or glove to see which one displayed the best retrieving instinct.

Isaacs: Examination by a veterinarian would assure a strong healthy puppy. In order to make the right selection, go to the kennel and see the sire of the puppies perform. That dog should be a bird dog!

Too many people buy a puppy from somebody who's been breeding for years and years and when that breeder is asked, "Do you hunt the dam?" the answer is, "No, but she's a good dog." But you've never seen that dog, so you don't know.

When you are buying a puppy by mail or phone, if you buy a dog that is sired by a field trial winner, that pup is out of field trial dogs all the way back, the percentages are great that that dog is going to make a hunting dog. But if you are told "I never saw the dog hunt in the field" and you don't know if the dog ever did anything and the pedigree doesn't show anything, you are buying a pig in a poke for sure. All you're getting is a registered dog. People get an American Kennel Club paper on a pup like this, they go to the encyclopedia and it says the Springer spaniel is basically a hunting dog. But the registration certificate does not make that dog a hunting dog.

You should see the puppy's sire hunt or know he'll hunt and the dam should be a hunter, too, or at least she should be out of hunting stock showing that she has descended from field trial bloodlines. If from personal knowledge you know the breeder has hunted his dogs and he's bringing in the game, you've got a chance to get a good hunter. But check and find out all you can about that puppy's sire and dam.

Hurst: It's absolutely essential to buy the right raw material in the first place. Investigate the pedigree, background, and working ability of all the forebears on the pedigree. Bloodlines should be carefully looked for. If you don't understand these bloodlines, seek the advice of a professional trainer.

Go look at the litter of puppies, approach them quietly, speak, clap your hands, but avoid any puppy that runs under his dog box or into the back of his kennel. Look for the puppy with the fast-going tail, with the very bright eyes that will look directly at you. Make sure there are no physical defects, such as undershot jaws and overshot eyes. The leg bones should be reasonably straight, not cowhocked at the back when the puppy is running. When the puppy runs away from you, he should have a double leg hop like a rabbit.

Do you have any particular guidelines or rules of thumb in your ap-

Cocker spaniels are small and appealing and when well trained make excellent ruffed grouse and woodcock dogs. Small, but willing, they can carry surprisingly large loads and are expected to neatly retrieve large hares in England.

proach to training spaniels that govern your actions around dogs and make training efforts easier, quicker, better? Some do and don't suggestions?

Lorenz: You have to gain the dog's complete confidence around the yard and kennel and have him retrieving dead pigeons well in the yard before ever taking him out in the field. If you do run into a problem out in the field, it is better to correct it in the yard. If they sour on something out in the field they don't ever seem to forget it, but if they get some correction in the yard it doesn't interfere with their training out in the field.

Isaacs: I've always heard that if you are going to be a dog trainer you must have great patience. I know myself enough to realize I'm impatient. However, the important thing is to be able to control your patience or impatience. If you're in a bad mood, don't go out and work the dog that you know is going to do something wrong. You won't be able to cope with it. Leave that dog alone.

What success I've had with dogs may be due to the fact that I don't demand perfection, showing people I can take out six dogs at a time and all of them walk along perfectly at heel, that sort of routine. Some people have told me they spend 75 percent of their time on yard work. I think that would get tiresome to both me and the dog. I spend most of my time training the dog out in the field, after I've done the basic yard work.

If the dog makes the slightest imperfection in his pattern, I don't run out and grab him, start kicking and thumping him, cutting him with the leash. I correct the dog, real easy correction, then I leave the dog alone. If

you're constantly on the dog in training, after a while when it's essential to get on him, the discipline has little or no effect. This business of sitting them up in a chair or on the lawn and making them hold dummies by the hour, after a while this gets old for anybody, and sure must for the dog. So I do only what's really necessary to get the job done.

Hurst: Give your puppy a playground where he is allowed to do anything he likes—this must be a confined space—and play with him as often as possible. Scold the puppy if he's really recalcitrant, shake him but never beat him. Never give a command to a puppy that you can't enforce. If he's hurrying away on a line, do *not* blow your stop whistle to stop him because he knows you can't enforce it. Never let a puppy out on his own. Never let him more than 40 yards away from you in training except on a specific retrieve command. Never at any time exercise puppies with untrained dogs.

What, if anything, must a field trial spaniel possess to a greater degree, regarding natural ability, than a reasonably good hunting dog? Or is it primarily the type and quality of training that makes the difference?

Lorenz: The only difference between a well-trained hunting dog, shooting dog, and a field trial dog is the speed and desire. A lot of dogs are well trained and will do all the work but just don't have the necessary speed and desire to place or win in field trials.

Isaacs: The most important trait the field trial spaniel should exhibit is an abundance of enthusiasm in hunting. The dog also has to be biddable. If you have a puppy that is lackadaisical, doesn't show a lot of desire to get out there, then you have to eliminate him as a field trial prospect.

You could have a puppy that is the most perfect retriever, but if he goes out slow and returns slow that dog won't make a field trialer. He may have a lot of qualities desirable in a hunting dog, but you should look for the puppy that really moves in a hustle when he's out there quartering.

When a client brings in a dog and answers my questions about the dog, its pedigree and so on, if the dog looks good I'll ask the owner, "What if this dog should show field trial potential?" If he's interested in having the dog developed for field trials, I'm going to encourage that. If the owner says he has no interest in field trials I'll offer him a fully trained dog to replace this puppy. Unless he has the ability to get the best out of the dog in the field, he might be better off with a hunting-type dog than a top field trial dog.

But any dog lover who appreciates class in dog work will want a field trial-type dog for a hunting dog. Even if he only gets half of his limit a day, if that one performance thrilled him, a classy-type dog is the one he'd want. It might not be the easiest dog to handle in the field, or the best

Facing page
In a training session to simulate ruffed grouse hunting, for which Springers are admirably suited, a sportsman encourages his Springer in the retrieving of a chukar partridge. (John Friend photo)

managed dog, but if a guy isn't worried about how much meat he's going to put on the table, wants to see exciting dog work, a dog really turning it on looking for game, then he won't settle for anything less.

If a dog produces regardless of how he does the job and doesn't require a lot of attention or handling, if he brings back a bird, then he may be acceptable to many hunters. This may be particularly true of the senior citizen who doesn't want to be chasing after a dog in the field or hurrying to keep up. A dog that stays in front and keeps moving around close would be ideal for anyone who just wants a little exercise in the field.

Hurst: The qualities a field trial dog must have over an ordinary hunting dog are style, speed, and intelligence. The small proportion of puppies from a litter that are slower than the others will make absolutely first-class hunting or shooting dogs but will never come up to the top in trials. For a trial dog you must look for a very fast, very stylish, very biddable, intelligent dog that can think for himself when he's out of sight and hearing of his handler on a retrieve. He must know that he's got to get on with the job on his own and still remain steady and workable.

Of the many dogs you have trained to be reasonably good hunting dogs and field trial competitors, what percentage of all dogs that were successfully trained had the potential to be field trial winners?

Lorenz: It happens quite often that someone wanting just a hunting dog buys a pup out of good field trial breeding and he may wind up having the most likely field trial prospect, while those most interested in trials would get some of the worst ones in the litter. But all in all, I'd say the chances of that happening would be about 25 percent. That is, if the breeding was there, in about twenty-five out of one hundred dogs the people could have had a field trial dog if they'd been willing to spend the money to campaign them. I'm talking about really good field trial breeding. Most of these fellows that come around and have a hunting dog trained, it isn't out of what you'd call top trial breeding. Most people who go to all the trouble of breeding a litter of top field trial pups just aren't going to sell these dogs to people who are not going to campaign them.

Isaacs: I figure I can make field trial winners out of maybe 20 percent of the six-month-old puppies that have field trial caliber. After they're steadied, of those pups you like well enough to consider for the puppy stakes, maybe about one in ten will make an open winner. The percentage really starts to drop. There are exciting puppies that win big, but they just can't keep it all together for the open.

Hurst: Within the past eight years in Britain there has been a great improvement in the breeding of Springer spaniels. It is now expected that out of a litter of ten puppies approximately two will be rejects for some reason or another, three will make useful top-class shooting dogs that are not fast enough for trials, the other five are expected to make trials dogs. It is to be remembered that in Britain all trials dogs are used on shooting days as well. All a trials dog is in Britain is a top-class, trained, properly handled shooting dog.

Handling a dog off horseback is a whole new ball game but both dog and handler must learn it if they are to field trial or hunt with the aid of a mount. Here Frank Smith, attending a training seminar sponsored by *Hunting Dog* magazine, gives a hand signal as David Harden prepares to cast Smith's young setter. (George Quigley photo)

I have trained some absolutely top-class potential trials dogs for owners who unfortunately were not the least interested in field trials and only wanted to use these top-class dogs for shooting. I would say that in the past eight years I have trained twenty spaniels that would have made it to the top in trials had they been given the opportunity by their owners.

Field trial standards have been established, but what constitutes a good hunting dog is largely a matter of personal opinion. What are the minimum requirements, what should a spaniel be able to do, to be considered a reasonably good hunting dog?

Lorenz: Many people bring a dog into the kennel and ask that it be trained. About the first thing they say is "I'm just interested in having a shooting dog. I'm not interested in having it trained for trials and don't want to spend the money to have it trained that way." You explain to them that the training is exactly the same, that some dogs just make it and some dogs don't. But they can't seem to really believe that.

A reasonably good hunting dog should quarter within range, either by himself or with the handler blowing the whistle, and the handler should be able to either call him off or stop him on running birds so the flushing will be done within gun range. I don't think it is necessary to have him steady to shot although we do train them to be steady to shot. But even if the owners let them break when they take over, usually they won't chase missed birds out of the country. Of course, when they find the shot bird they should retrieve back to the handlers without any detours or dropping.

Isaacs: A Springer spaniel, to satisfy me as a reasonably good hunting dog, could be taken to any part of the United States, hunted on native game there, he would hunt aggressively, produce game for me, and bring it to hand when it's shot. He would not have to be steady to shot and flush. I'd expect the dog to sit with me on the bank or in a duck blind, and I could keep the dog there with me until I commanded him to go out and retrieve from water. This to me would be a suitable hunting dog.

Hurst: To be a useful shooting dog a spaniel must hunt within pattern, within shooting distance of his owner or handler, so that any game put up would be within reach of that handler's gun. The dog must remain absolutely steady on flush, only to retrieve on command. The dog must be able to be directed to an unmarked or blind retrieve and not require constant whistling at to remain in a pattern. His pattern must be a built-in part of his movements.

Can one dog be both hunter and field trialer? How often does this actually occur? If it is usually impractical for an owner to expect to have a "two-in-one" dog, what factors prevent this from occurring much more frequently?

Lorenz: I don't believe field trial dogs should be hunted because they'll learn to pace themselves in order to hunt for hours and therefore will run much slower in the trials. But I have taken some of my best field trial dogs and hunted them for about an hour in the wintertime when the weather was near freezing and they'd run at top speed. But if you do that in warm weather, they'll soon learn to pace themselves and lose the enthusiasm necessary for field trials.

Isaacs: A dog can be both a hunting dog and field trial dog. But that's a special dog, and they are very few. They have to be the sort of dog that hasn't developed the habit of pacing themselves, or of hunting too far out. It depends entirely on the dog. There are dogs that can be hunted and then put down in amateur stakes, do a good job and win. I've had them myself. But I do not think the top dog it takes to win the open all-age trial today should be taken hunting.

The amateur who has a dog trained and handled for him by a professional should not expect to have that pro let him take the dog home to go hunting with and then bring him back for the pro to continue trialing, because there's going to be damage done. I doubt whether the owner of that dog could keep him under control at all times under actual hunting conditions. Possibly the professional himself could. But even if the owner is a fine trainer himself, in actual hunting it's doubtful if he should take that dog out. Complete, field trial control under real hunting conditions is very difficult.

Hurst: Any good, class trials dog can be used as a hunting dog. It is absolutely essential though that his handler handle him properly on hunting days, and not allow him to be undisciplined in any way. Again, all a trials dog is is a top-class hunting dog. All or most of the top-class trials dogs in Britain are used at least once if not twice a week during the field trial season for ordinary hunting. When properly handled, this improves them as trials dogs because it gives added experience.

If there are variations in your approach to training a hunting spaniel and a field trial spaniel, other than more intensive and longer training for the competition dog, what procedures do you emphasize, add, or eliminate in training the hunting dog?

Lorenz: You can train a Springer for hunting much quicker by taking shortcuts because you don't have to worry if Springers become slow on the flush, which is okay for hunting but disastrous for a field trial dog. So if I'm training a dog for hunting, I'll take shortcuts to do the training in a shorter time; whereas with a field trial dog I'll take a lot longer time, do everything I can, with the thought being that I just don't want him slowing down on flush.

Isaacs: In training a hunting dog you can greatly accelerate the training because you are not as concerned about the bold flush, the perfection in delivery, the quartering, the pattern. The effort expended in developing the field trial dog is far greater than with a hunting dog where a lot of shortcuts can be made. The time is cut in maybe one fourth in bringing around a finished hunting dog as against a finished trial dog.

Hurst: When taking a dog to train it is essential to assess the personality of the owner. Decide if he's capable of handling or willing to handle a fast dog. If the owner or handler is basically interested in using the dog in hunting, it is necessary to train the dog to be slower in his movement and thinking than a field trial dog. Otherwise his speed of brain and speed of body will outwit his handler. This is achieved quite simply in his initial training by increasing the amount of discipline and whistle training and not allowing the dog to get into a fast drive speed over game. Don't shoot any game at all over him until he's fourteen months of age, by which time he's become completely reliable and biddable.

Outline your method and the procedures that work successfully for you in teaching a dog his name, Come When Called, No, Sit, Heel, Stay, Kennel, or whatever your basic commands are.

Lorenz: Most puppies learn their names around the kennel. Our dogs are kenneled in inside stalls and we turn them into runs on the outside. They have to go through a door. We usually turn them out three times a day, so the puppies soon learn their names by being spoken to as they go out the door.

To teach a pup to come when called, I use a 50-foot nylon cord, and during the pup's yard work I call his name and whistle at the same time and bring him in to me with the cord.

In the course of training if a dog is sniffing, interested in, or picking something up, I use a sharp command "Leave It!" This command is useful in field trials also. If they are taking a bird on another course, you can get them off it with a sharp command.

Starting with young puppies three and four months old, use a light collar and a leash. After getting them accustomed to having it around their necks, I walk them slowly around the yard, give the command "Hup!" and gently push the rear end down to the ground and bring the leash up so they connect the sitting down with the command.

Heeling I don't really emphasize too much until after they're hunting well out in the field; otherwise it's hard to get them to leave your side when you do want them to go out and hunt. After they're keen about hunting, I just walk them slowly up and down my driveway with the leash in one hand, a switch in the other, and say "Heel!" and gently pull them back with the leash and wave the switch in front of their noses.

To teach a dog to "Hup!" and "Stay!" I use a light cord with a pulley attached to a tree so I can make the dog hup and stay when I walk away. If they want to follow me I pull on the cord, which brings them back toward the tree where they were supposed to sit in the first place.

As far as kenneling, if you point to the place you want them to go and use the word "Kennel!" it's just a matter of time until they realize what you want.

Isaacs: I like to have a name for the puppy when I get him at ten to twelve weeks old and I'll call the puppy by name every time I want his attention. I go for walks with young puppies, one puppy at a time, and continually call the puppy to me, using his name, always putting his name first. Then I use the whistle at the same time to get him to come to me when whistled or spoken to.

There's nothing formal about it, like in strict obedience training. It's natural when you work with puppies, spend time with them. Every time they're a little away from you, tell them to come to you and they soon learn to come.

Whenever you see a dog doing something he shouldn't, give him the command "No!" in a tone of voice that means he must quit whatever he's doing right then. That starts early also. If he doesn't quit when you say "No!," get right to him.

For sitting, after you've gotten the puppy used to the collar and lead, either by walking him or tying him to a stake for a few minutes at a time so he learns he can't get away by fighting, you walk along leading the pup and tell him to sit every time you stop. I give a little yank on the leash when I say "Sit!" and most puppies automatically sit down. If they don't I reach down and press the hindquarters right on down. As they get a little older and don't sit when told, I may give a little tap on the rump to enforce that command.

Bricksclose Sprigg, a John Isaacs-trained Springer spaniel owned by Ohioan Vincent Bolling, Jr., puts a bird into flight and is coming down in a "Sit!" ("Hup!") position. (Andy Shoaff photo)

"Heel!" can be taught by just yanking the dog back with the leash anytime he moves out from walking alongside you. By repetition, giving that yank, you will soon have him heeling right. In a little while, when the dog's out away from you, and you want him back, you can command "Heel!" and the dog automatically comes to you and walks alongside. But it starts on the leash and with being jerked back. I don't put a lot of emphasis on how close the dog hugs my leg, spins around to sit down, etc. If he stays around me and doesn't go off hunting, that's "Heel!" to me.

Staying can be taught very rapidly to any intelligent dog. You just put the dog in place, command "Stay!," hold up the hand as a traffic policeman would do, as a signal to him, and you just keep backing away from him. Any time he moves put him right back in place.

I use "Kennel!" at the kennel gate starting right off with puppies. You take the leash off them, tell them to "Kennel!," get them by the nap of the neck and put them on in there. Since they don't like being forced in that way, soon they'll go in on their own when told to. Use the same procedure to get them to load up in the truck or get into anything. Give the command and lift or boost them in until they're kenneling on their own.

Hurst: To teach a puppy his name, pick him up, make a fuss over him, and say his name. Put him down on the ground, let him run away, call him by name. When he comes to you, give him a biscuit. Let him run away again, call him by name again; this will very quickly get into the pup's mind.

To teach a dog to understand the command "No!," create a situation where he wants to pick something up that you don't want him to pick up. When he goes toward the object it is essential to catch him, gently take him away and repeat the word "No!" Anytime he does anything you don't want him to do, the word "No!" must be introduced. But you also have to physically illustrate just what it is you don't want him to do.

To teach a puppy to sit, or as we say in Britain, "Hup!," put your left hand under his chin, put the right hand over his back, and gently push him down into the sitting position and say the word "Hup!" This has to be done over and over until the puppy will do it without being pushed down. After the puppy has become reliable enough so that no matter where he is the command "Hup!" will sit him on his backside, the sitting to whistle is then introduced by giving the verbal command "Hup!" and blowing the whistle at the same time. It won't be long before the puppy learns that those two commands mean the same thing. After this has been achieved, the whistle is blown at the same time a shot is fired from a blank pistol. In the same manner the pup learns that the shot also means he must sit on his backside. After a very short time, he becomes quite reliable on all these signals. But it's essential that you vary the sequence in which these commands are given.

A spaniel must have six months of hand training starting at eight months of age. At the end of this period, you will have a well-trained but rather green or inexperienced dog. At this stage a bird or two is shot over the dog. After this, he's gently taught to walk to heel over a period of up to four weeks. Most spaniels when taught to walk properly at heel, nose to knee, will lose a lot of their drive and initiative. If the dog will walk within 5 yards of his handler, that is quite sufficient.

To teach a puppy to stay—sit on his backside while his handler walks away—first of all he's got to be taught to "Hup!" to verbal command, whistle, and shot. After the puppy is taught this, the handler then backs away from the puppy, no more than 5 yards initially, one step at a time holding his hand up facing the puppy. If at any time the puppy moves, he must immediately be replaced on the spot that he's moved from. You must continue until the dog learns to stay put. When he is reliable on a 20-yard walkaway, the handler then walks around the dog in a circle. Any time the puppy moves in this training, he must immediately be pushed back to where he moved from.

To teach a puppy to go into his kennel, take hold of him gently by the scruff of the neck, open the kennel door, push him in and say the word, "Kennel!" After a period of time it is then possible to open the kennel door and on given command the puppy will walk in.

In teaching retrieving, do you make full use of the natural inclination of most spaniels to pick up and carry, while making sure they know they

Alan Hurst giving "Hup!" command while training a Cocker spaniel.

must retrieve without fail? Or do you as a matter of training routine use a methodical and/or mechanical force-training procedure to teach retrieving?

Lorenz: I believe in developing the natural instinct in a dog to retrieve. I've been quite successful in using a check cord or a reward such as a treat to get them to retrieve right up to me. I do not use any method of force-breaking until the puppies are seven or eight months old at least. If at that time they're not good natural retrievers, I put something in their mouths and tell them to "Hold It!" I'm really not a believer in force-breaking unless you absolutely have to do it.

A dog that loves to retrieve will retrieve almost anything you throw for him. He'll never let you down on it. If a dog has to be force-trained to retrieve, he'll usually develop some other habit, such as being a little hard on the bird. Some of the speed and desire may also be taken out of him. I think if a dog is a good natural retriever, he'll always do it as fast as he can.

Isaacs: I look for puppies that have the natural ability to retrieve, to

Pride in achievement shows in this Springer spaniel's eyes as Flirt happily holds a ruffed grouse she flushed and retrieved.

carry something properly, pick it up readily without mouthing it, get onto a larger object without laying it down or rolling it. The sooner I can get them to move up to larger objects and move on to a bird the better. But if a puppy has no inclination to retrieve at all, I don't want to be fooling with him. I don't want to force-train any puppy.

A dog should be bred for an inherited desire to retrieve. You start out by simply playing with that dog and he'd better show the willingness to do what you want him to do. You toss that thing out and if the puppy won't pick it up, just go out and pick it up, walk back, and continue throwing it to get the puppy started. If you have to force-train a spaniel to retrieve, maybe every dog descended from that one will have to be force-trained to retrieve.

Hurst: There is considerable controversy about this question. Some few trainers, as a matter of course, force-train all puppies to retrieve. I feel this is a retrogressive step, for it is then possible to breed nonretrieving spaniels.

Make full use of any puppy's inclination to retrieve. I've found by experience that little puppies of eight to ten weeks of age love to retrieve empty cartridge cases. Once a puppy will pick up, carry, and run about with an object, he's then taught to come to his handler with the object in his mouth. It is absolutely essential that retrieving is not overdone. Once a puppy will pick up an object and bring it to his handler, it is advised that this not be done more than twice a week. Otherwise a puppy will tend to run away and either drop and leave or bury the object.

Most dogs object to being looked in the eye when they have an object in their mouths. To get a dog to bring what he's retrieving to you, first of all it is essential to get him to come to you any time you call his name. Throw a dummy or other object and when he picks it up immediately call his name, turn about, and walk away from him. He will usually follow and give up the object. If you face a puppy and look at him, he will generally tend to go away with the object or drop it within 5 yards of you.

Retrieving training for any kind of spaniel should be initially viewed by the puppy as a game, something he wants to do. Find out by play and experimentation which objects a puppy likes to retrieve and run about with in his mouth, and encourage this. Then take him out into the field with a dummy. Hold the dummy, show it to the dog and let him sniff it, lift it up and let him jump up at it and get the idea of the thing in his mind. Then throw it a short distance, perhaps 10 yards. He should immediately run out and pick the thing up.

Initially, don't expect him to bring it right back. Most puppies will pick up and run about in circles with it. Call his name, walk away, and hope he comes back with the dummy. If he's still inclined to play, have another dummy in your hand. Throw this one in the air and catch it a number of times. The puppy will then focus his interest on the moving dummy and will usually bring the first dummy back, whereupon you can take it from him. This goes on for a period of time until the puppy is used to carrying the dummies and used to bringing them back to his handler. At all times accept a dummy from a puppy with your back to him.

Once he's really reliable on retrieving, the discipline side of the job is then introduced. You have already taught the puppy to sit at command by the side of his handler. The dummy is then thrown over the handler's shoulder away from the dog so the handler stands between the puppy and the dummy. The puppy will immediately disobey all of his instructions and dodge in to get hold of the dummy.

The handler intercepts him on the way, catches him, takes him back to the spot he moved from, gently sits him down and gives him the word "No!" The handler then backs away from the puppy, keeping him sat. The

Dave Lorenz "presses the button" to start a perfectly trained spaniel on his field trial beat under the scrutiny of a judge.

puppy knows every time he moves he's sat down again. The handler then goes and picks up the dummy. This often takes a considerable number of times. There are occasions when a puppy will not respond to this. If he doesn't, put a lead around his neck and tie him to a stake in the ground, give him the command "Sit!" and make him sit. Throw the dummy to within 5 yards of him and command "No!" After a period of time the puppy will sit still on the end of the lead.

Each time the dummy is thrown, it is picked up by the handler. Once this has been achieved the lead is tied around the dog's neck like a collar. This procedure is continued until the puppy is really steady to the dummy. A light elastic band is substituted for the lead around his neck, the procedure continued longer. The elastic band is then taken away. Eventually the puppy remains steady.

This extensive treatment is usually needed only for a very hardheaded puppy. Normally two or three sessions will suffice to steady him. This time of training usually occurs at about the age of ten months when the puppy has had about two months of initial training. Occasionally I've found it necessary to force a dog's retrieving. I dislike doing it because it tends to repress the puppy in his later training for it takes him a little time to get over the fact that he is being forced. There is also the possibility that dogs constantly forced may become natural *non*retrievers. In later life, a forced dog can occasionally refuse a bird out of sight of his handler. This could well become a habit, whereupon shot game could be lost.

Recognizing that you may use both methods as circumstances dictate, why do you generally prefer one method over the other?

Lorenz: My reasons for favoring natural retrieving over force-training are pretty well summed up in the answer to the previous question.

Isaacs: I guess we got a little ahead of ourselves. I pretty much told you why I like the natural way better in my answer to the question about training spaniels to retrieve.

Hurst: I believe my answer is fully explained, at length, in our discussion of natural retrieving versus force-retrieving.

Describe the procedures you use to instill reliable retrieving.

Lorenz: The best way is to take the puppy into some room, a place he can't escape from like a garage, where there are no other distractions. Get down on your hands and knees and tease him with a glove or similar object. Throw the object a short distance at first. He'll go and get it and come back to you with it. Make sure he brings it all the way back to you. Just don't overdo it; with any young dog, two or three tosses at one time is much better than throwing it ten to fifteen times. I'd rather do it three or four times a day, just a little, than do a lot of it at one time.

Isaacs: I like to start with a pup at the youngest possible age. If a pup is seven weeks old and will pick up a handkerchief and chase after me with it, I start there and move up to a dummy or another object, one that a puppy can easily get his teeth in. Keep right on building up to where he'll carry a dead pigeon.

Some puppies as young as twelve weeks old will carry a live pigeon that's flopping around, will chase after it, pounce on it. But with some other puppies you have to be more cautious. When you get that live-bird business behind them, they're ready for pheasant and you should have a five- or six-month-old pup carrying around a stiff, dead pheasant.

If a puppy doesn't show good ability to pick up and carry without laying it down and mouthing it around, it's unlikely he will be field trial potential, but might develop to be good enough for hunting.

It takes a lot of repetition to properly develop retrieving. One of the best ways to get a puppy to come directly to you is to back away from him when he's coming toward you carrying the dummy or bird. Take him out in a field where you've got a mowed path, with tall grass on both sides. The only place he can go is either to you or away from you, and not many pups are dumb enough to run away from you, so you back up this path and keep telling the puppy to come.

If he is a little reluctant to come, just turn around and walk off, completely leaving him. If you look over your shoulder, you'll see him running to catch up with you. When he comes to you, reach down and take what he's carrying.

Hurst: I believe I adequately outlined how to teach reliable retrieving in my answer to a previous question.

Describe the procedures you use to instill "hunt" and "birdiness" and accustom a spaniel to quartering the field in a controlled pattern to find and flush game.

Lorenz: After a puppy knows about a dead pigeon and will retrieve it good in the yard, I go out in the field and take six or eight dead pigeons and lay them down in a staggered pattern, some on the right, others on the left. Then I work the puppy into the wind. The pup will walk along at my heels until he winds the bird and then he'll go in, pick it up, and retrieve it.

Keep on working him in this way, bird after bird. Usually, after he gets the idea there's something ahead of him to find, he'll start quartering, using his nose to find the dead birds. After he's accustomed to dead birds, I put out clipped-wing pigeons and then live birds that can fly, allowing him to find and chase quite a few before shooting one. When shooting live birds, never shoot the bird if it's flying directly over the puppy's head, even if it's high enough, because the noise is too great. Shoot only those going to the side and fire only one shot, taking only reasonably good shots so the bird will be killed. The first three or four birds killed over a puppy are the most important in his whole life.

Isaacs: Start off by walking a young puppy in the field. Try to find out what his natural pace is going to be. Some reach on out, some won't. Others you can pitch in a bird here, pitch in another there, and you get them running around in excitement looking for the birds. This develops a desire to go looking. Some puppies will just naturally start swinging, without any bird. But the thing that really builds the puppy up is when he gets a little away from you and finds a bird. Then when you zigzag one way and he comes with you, out in front of you he finds a bird. Pretty soon that dog starts zigzagging, quartering, on his own.

I use a lot of what you might call clipped-wing birds, although I've never clipped a wing yet. I always tape the flight feathers with masking tape and then, when I want to shoot a flying bird for the dog, I cut the tape with a knife, throw the bird, and it will fly.

I put these taped birds out at intervals in the field so I can zigzag through the field and know just where the birds are. As the dog gets older you do less zigzagging yourself and you start pushing the dog out on the sides. If you've got gunners out there, they can toss birds out for you while they're walking. This builds a good pattern at an early age, between seven and ten months old.

Facing page
Age is no barrier to young-at-heart spaniel men. Wally Retzlaff, Milwaukee, Wis., and Joysam's Solo Sam won both the 1975 Canadian National Championship and the 1975 U.S. National Amateur Championship when Sam was 3½ years old and Wally a sprightly 72. (Shallop photo)

The main thing is you've got to get the retrieving right. With some puppies, that takes longer. You don't want a puppy out there quartering, finding a bird, and then running down the field with it. Because you've first got to teach pups to come when they've got the bird in their mouths, the age when you can start tossing birds out for them will vary.

Hurst: To teach a puppy to hunt the game, we make full use of the rabbit pen. Dogs will tend to hunt rabbits before they will hunt any other type of game. Rabbits leave very strong lines, and any puppy will learn to run down these lines to find the rabbit in the pen, whereupon the rabbit will run away into cover. Any puppy worth his salt will follow this rabbit into cover and very quickly learn that if he hunts cover he will find a rabbit. This is one means of getting the dog hunting, and it develops his style, his drive, and his muscle.

No two puppies are alike. Start this procedure by taking a whole litter or all the puppies you have into the rabbit pen at 3½ months of age. Leave them to their own devices for a period of up to two hours, then bring the puppies away from the pen and put them in their kennel for two days. After this, the puppies are individually taken into the pen. One puppy will immediately find the rabbit, chase it into a bush, dive into the bush to look for it. Another puppy will chase the rabbit to the bush, circle the bush looking for a way in, wondering why the rabbit is gone. This puppy is then taken into the pen each day until he learns to go into the bush to look for the rabbit. The first puppy, who is natural on this business, is not usually taken to the pen again.

Describe your procedures in training a dog to be steady at flush and shot.

Lorenz: You teach a dog to be steady in the yard on thrown birds. You set the dog down, walk off ahead of him, throw a dummy or a dead bird, and shoot a blank pistol. After that is accomplished, use a 50-foot cord and work him in the field. After the bird is flushed, instead of jerking him back head over heels, I believe it's best to just slow him down gradually, using either a whistle or saying "Hup!" to him. After a few birds, the dog will learn that he's supposed to stay there, but usually you have to do quite a bit of work on the line before you can trust him off the line.

Isaacs: When I decide a dog is worth steadying, I bring him back in the yard for rigorous obedience training—sit, stay, etc.—until everything's perfect. I step back 8 to 10 feet from the sitting dog, and throw the dummy so I'm stationed between where it falls and the dog. If the dog jumps to go after it, I pick him up and set him back in place. I keep this up until I can get him to sit right there and watch, then I call his name to go get it.

Repeat this over and over, and then start throwing to the point of a triangle with you and the dog as the base corners. The dog should hold, but if he doesn't you can still get out there and intercept him before he gets to the dummy—at least he'll see you coming while you yell at him. The important thing is to stop him. I very seldom use a line on a dog, but

Being a spaniel in more than name, Irish water spaniels adapt well to jump shooting or working before the gun in the field as Finnegan is doing here for teen-age Mike Duffey.

that's another way of getting it done—jerk him back when he goes before he's ordered to. When he holds like he ought to, go up, snap off the lead, and tell him to go.

Before teaching him to steady on birds, you have to work on this until you can throw the dummy, shoot a gun off, and the dog won't go until he is sent. Next throw out a *dead* bird, fire the gun, and he shouldn't go until he's sent. Get all that down pat and then throw out a live bird that's fluttering, flying away from him, and have an assistant shoot it. You should always position yourself so you're between the dog and where your assistant is going to kill that bird. When the bird is shot, send the dog. If you're positioned right, you can cut the dog off while he's on his way, if he breaks. Once he gets to the bird it's too late to discipline him.

Of course, you're always going to be throwing out some birds that you don't shoot; you let them fly away. After you've steadied him, the dog must be taught at an early age to sit and watch a bird fly away instead of chasing after it. Once he's steadied you can't tolerate any chasing at all.

To steady that dog to a bird flying off, you've got to be set up so you can get out there and stop the dog. You've got to have gunners who know what you want done. This is why it is very hard for an amateur to train unless he's a member of a club or has knowledgeable people to help him.

Hurst: The puppy has been taught to sit to shot. When he's reliable on this, take three or four live pigeons out onto a field of long grass and plant them. The dog hunts the ground and flushes a pigeon. When the shot is fired, the dog will drop to the shot and watch the pigeon fly away. If the dog chases the pigeon, bring him back and repeat the procedure until he learns that flush means the same thing as the verbal command "Hup!" or the whistle command to drop to shot.

Occasionally we come across a pup whose enthusiasm on game is so strong that on flush of either rabbit or feather he'll forget all his training and chase. We then have to resort to—and the correct term is "resort to" —the use of a thin piece of light, strong nylon cord approximately 20 feet long. The dog is hunted with this tied around his neck and trailing over open ground for a period of time until he gets used to trailing it behind him. When he will hunt readily trailing the piece of cord, he's then taken to the rabbit pen and is hunted over rabbits in the pen.

The handler stays as close to the dog as possible. The dog hunts, finds a rabbit, and immediately chases. The handler then stomps his foot on or grabs hold of the cord, pulling the dog up with a smart jerk. We

Springer spaniels, like this young bitch, Satan's Pumpkin, are pleasant, eager-to-please dogs that will hunt their hearts out even to produce game that is really too big for them to handle cleverly, like this brace of sage chickens.

find it doesn't work to run a spaniel on a long line with the handler holding the end of the line. The dog will normally cease to hunt. This is why the line is allowed to trail along the ground. By this means it is almost 100 percent successful. Occasionally a dog will emerge that can never be steadied, but this is extremely rare.

How and at what age do you prefer to introduce a spaniel to actual game or live birds in training?

Lorenz: The age will vary from puppy to puppy. Some pups are much more advanced at six months than others. The outstanding puppy can be introduced to live birds at five or six months, maybe another one out of the same litter won't be ready until he's eight or nine months old.

I introduce them to live birds by planting the birds in the field where the pups can flush and chase them. Never shoot until they've chased five or six birds as far as they can see them. When you know they're really going to chase the bird, then shoot the first one.

Isaacs: Step by step, get the dog retrieving a dummy, then a dead pigeon, thrown. Next, toss out a live bird and let him watch it fly away. Then put down a clipped-wing bird and let the dog go in on it and catch it. He should be retrieving in such a way that when he catches that bird he'll bring it to you. That's important. The age can vary greatly, but that's how to introduce a dog to birds in training.

Hurst: Puppies are not normally run on any ground where they are likely to find wild game. Each dog is trained in the rabbit pen or on live pigeons, which do not constitute scent as exciting to the dog as game scent. When the dog will pass all tests without fail on hunting style and pattern, steady to dummies, fully conversant and obedient to all whistle and verbal commands, and will remain steady to rabbits in the pen and pigeons out in the field, by this time the puppy is usually about fourteen months of age. He's then taken out onto ground that contains game.

He's hunted on this ground without any shooting at all, and is allowed to find and flush a dozen birds within five or six sessions. After he's become steady to flushing game, he's taken out with a gun. Again he finds and flushes game for three sessions, no session lasting for more than an hour. On each flush of game a shot is fired into the air.

When the dog has become used to this he's then allowed to find game, and the game is shot for him in such a condition that he can mark and retrieve it. No game is shot for him less than 30 yards away. He's given a retrieve, he's given another find and another retrieve. This goes on for four or five more sessions. The ideal thing now, of course, is to run the dog in two or three novice trials to get him accustomed to working in company and to consolidate all the rest of his training in a short period of time. It normally takes four trials to change a dog from a well-trained but green dog to a well-trained and experienced dog.

Describe your procedure in introducing a dog to gunfire, assuring that the dog will not be gunshy.

Lorenz: A spaniel should never be introduced to gunfire unless he can connect it with a retrieve. By that I mean start the young puppy with a bundle or dummy, and fire a blank pistol when you throw the dummy for him to catch. When he gets older have someone stand about 30 or 40 yards away with a shotgun, and when the puppy is running shoot and throw the dead bird back toward the dog.

Isaacs: You can start firing a blank pistol over some puppies eight to twelve weeks old, others you have to be careful with. With the active, very bold pup that gets around and couldn't care less about things, have someone off a distance fire the pistol. The pup will probably move right up there with him. With a shy puppy, you'd better be careful, take all the precautions—have the gun at a distance, start with a cap pistol and build up. Maybe the amateur can't always determine shyness and boldness, but it's usually pretty obvious.

The dog will begin to make an association between retrieving and gunfire; at least when the dog hears a gun go off he knows something is going to be falling. When the pup is about two-thirds of the way to a retrieve, have someone fire the pistol in the air. Gradually work up until you can fire when the pup's right by you just before he's sent for the dummy.

Hurst: It's essential to introduce puppies to gunfire as early as possible in life. There are puppies that are not in the least gunshy, there are puppies that are gun-nervy, and there are puppies that are gunshy. There is no cure whatever for a gunshy pup. A gun-nervy pup is almost always successfully trained.

To find out which puppies in a litter are gunshy or to prevent gun-nerviness in a puppy from becoming stronger, you normally introduce gunfire to the puppies at the age of eight weeks when they're feeding. The puppies are fed, they're eating the food, which is something they want to do, the handler stands 20 yards away with a .22 blank pistol and fires an occasional shot. It will very quickly become apparent if any of the dogs are at all gunshy. Any pup that dives under his bed or cowers in the corner of his kennel should be immediately discarded as being a completely gunshy puppy.

There will be one or two that don't particularly like it. They'll put their ears down but will continue to eat. Over a short period of time this is usually overcome.

How and at what age do you prefer to introduce a spaniel to water?

Lorenz: Introducing a Springer pup to water depends a lot on the weather. I think seven to eight weeks is the ideal time to introduce a puppy to water, if the water is warm enough so you'd want to swim in it yourself. Even if the puppy is born at the wrong time, like fall or winter, and you're not able to put him in the water until he's somewhat older, I still wouldn't

Facing page
Orin Benson gets an English setter keyed up and intense as he works the dog on a planted bird.

introduce him until the water was warm. The age doesn't make that much difference—just so the water is comfortable.

After the pup has learned to retrieve a small bundle on land, take him to a gradual sloping, sandy part of a lake, and toss out the bundle far enough so he'll have to retrieve it by wading. Throw it a little farther each time. If the puppy hesitates to go into the water, you should be ready to walk in with him and encourage him to follow you. If the pup doesn't want to go in and you wade out yourself, nine times out of ten he'll follow you right out into the lake.

Isaacs: It depends upon the time of year, but the puppies should be into water within the year in which they are born. In July, I wade the branches with twelve-week-old puppies and get them to tag along. Pups born in the fall or winter may be over six months old before the temperature of the water is warm enough to start them.

Try running the dogs in the field, get them hot, then take them to the water and they will naturally want to go in to cool off. They'll eventually get out in there swimming around. If you do have one that's reluctant to go in, swim and wade with him. Coax him to come in there with you.

Hurst: At the very earliest, we like to introduce our puppies to water at eight weeks of age. It's essential, though, that this be done in the summer, when the water is warm. Select a clean pond with a hard gravel, not muddy, bottom.

Puppies are taken in a pack with an experienced dog to this stretch of water. One small dummy is thrown way out into the pond, two or three additional dummies are thrown no more than 6 feet from the edge of the pond. After the trained dog is sent in, the pups will tend to follow. Some will swim immediately with the trained dog, the ones that don't like to get their feet wet will go to the edge of the pond, others will wade out into the pond. We then decide which puppies need more work in the water than others.

The trained dog is then taken away, small dummies are thrown into the water no more than 3 feet from the edge. After a period of time, nine out of ten puppies will swim in the water just for the sheer joy of it.

For an owner with a young single pup, it is essential first of all to get him to retrieve (pick up and run about with) small objects. Once he will retrieve small objects, and at this stage it isn't necessary that the puppy bring the object back to his handler, we then select an object a puppy will like to carry about on dry land. The puppy is taken to a hard-bottom pond, the object is thrown onto land near the water, the puppy will pick it up and run about with it.

It's then taken away from him and thrown 1 yard into the water. The puppy will want to go and pick up this object. He will get his feet wet and sniff at it; after a period of time we expect him to at least wade out to the thing, grab it—"grab it" is exactly what they do—and get himself out of the water as fast as he can. This continues until the puppy will immediately dash in and fetch it out again. Once this is achieved the object is thrown farther, no more than an increase of 1 yard at a time, until the dog will take his feet off the bottom of the pond and make one or two swimming strokes to retrieve the object. The distance is then increased until the puppy becomes bold and swims out.

At all times the idea is to encourage the puppy to get out into the water. Once he gets to the object he will always bring it back, because his reason for going into the water has been to get the object in his mouth and retrieve it. It's very rare for a puppy to refuse the retrieve of an object when he's out there in the water.

The ideal object for this training is an empty cartridge case, with a wood or rubber plug at one end, and a piece of rag or old sock with a glove thumb put onto it. It's essential that this object be small enough for little pups to easily get hold of.

What hand and whistle signals do you use? Describe the procedures you follow in teaching response to those signals.

Lorenz: The stop or sit whistle is taught in connection with the hupping or sitting, one of the first things they learn. When the puppy has become birdy enough, the turn whistle is learned in the field. I use a check cord in a field free of all obstructions that might tangle the cord when the dog reaches the stage where he wants to punch out beyond gun range. I quarter the dog to the right and to the left and if he doesn't turn I tug on the cord and make him turn the way I want him to turn, at the same time blowing the whistle.

I use the regular Roy Gonia whistle and blow one short blast for the "Hup!" or "Sit!" For the turn whistle, I blow two "peep, peeps" that turn the dog in the opposite direction. When the bird is flushed, one short blast is used to make the dog "Hup!" If the dog overruns the fall or if I want to bring him back to me, I use a series of the two "peep, peeps."

On a trained dog the owner should use the same kind of whistle the trainer uses and use it in the same manner. Use it as sparingly as possible. A dog exposed to continuous unnecessary whistling will soon become immune to it. It just won't mean anything to him. The whistle command, like the voice command, is useless if not obeyed.

However, once the dog has learned to sit at the whistle command, in training when the dog is quartering, even if a bird is not flushed, if you give the whistle command to "Hup!" the dog will be thinking about it and it will be much fresher in his mind. When you do get to the bird, he'll sit better at the command blown on the whistle.

Isaacs: I try to limit that as much as possible. I start with two toots on the whistle to turn a dog. If I want to swing him a little when he's just standing around, I blow a "Come In!" whistle, a continuous series of toots to sort of tow him right on in, like he was on a fishing line. Quarter the field with the dog, give one blast on the whistle to mean "Sit!" and if the dog doesn't, get him and put him in place. When you're starting, blow the whistle and yell "Hup!" and soon all you have to do is give him that one whistle blast. The whistle is to come in, to sit, and to change direction.

I do very few hand signals. With a dog quartering, I'll flip out my hand to the left or right. When signaling a dog to retrieve, with the right arm I wave to the right for the dog to go that way, come across my body for him to go left, and wave straight out for him to go back. Everybody does it differently, but I try to keep it as simple as possible.

When the dog has flushed a bird, hold the hand up, like a traffic cop, to remind the dog to keep sitting there so he doesn't take off on you.

To get him to go in the direction you want, wave your arm properly and tell him to "Go Over!" in the direction you wave. If he goes wrong, circles around, whatever, sit him, then wave him where you want him to go. Keep doing this until he goes where you want him to go.

Hurst: The number-one disciplining command is the "Stop!" whistle, which is a short, sharp blast. It must always be delivered as a command. The puppy has been taught verbally to sit, he is then taught to sit to the short, sharp blast on the whistle. This is the only one of all the training commands that cannot be overdone. When that whistle is blown, no matter what the dog is doing or where in relation to his handler he is, he must at all times obey it.

The dog's got to be taught to hunt within gunshot of his owner and to work a pattern of ground. To achieve this hunting, dummies are placed to either side of the dog in a straight line and he's hunted to the dummies and back again until he has learned that when he's cast off by the verbal command "Hie-dad!" he's to begin to hunt. When the pup is initially 15 yards to either side of his handler, a whistle is blown two short, sharp blasts and the puppy is called by name. He will then turn and come back to his handler, who catches him, makes a fuss over him, pets him, and casts him off immediately in the opposite direction. Upon achieving a distance of 15 yards to the other side of his handler, the procedure is repeated. This is continued over and over until the puppy is hunting and turning just to the two blasts of the whistle. After a period of time the puppy will have developed his own width pattern and the need for the turning whistle becomes less and less until it's not needed at all, except to turn a puppy or a dog if he begins to follow a line.

In teaching these patterns the handler should walk on a small zigzag course, the dog should work on a larger one. This helps to stop any problems of puppies dwelling on lines or scents.

What are the most common problems a trainer is likely to encounter in getting his spaniel to hunt and retrieve properly and to remain under control?

Lorenz: The most common problem is getting the dog to retrieve directly to hand without dropping the bird. If the dog can be properly trained to retrieve to hand in the yard, this can be carried out in the field without difficulty. But if it's neglected in the yard, then you'll have problems out in the field.

Usually when a puppy starts out he'll hunt within range without too much difficulty. As he gets older and gains experience, the dog may dis-

A sportsman demonstrates the signal given a spaniel to indicate a direction change and school the dog in working a quartering pattern before the gun. (Larry Mueller photo)

obey the turn whistle and want to punch out. When this happens the best thing to do is stop the dog out in front of you, walk out to him, slip a collar with leash attached over his head, and give several good jerks on the leash at the same time blowing the turn whistle so he gets the connection with what he's doing wrong.

If the puppy's retrieving well in the yard and then starts to lay the bird down out in the field, the best way to correct this is to have an assistant with a handful of pea gravel follow the dog in as the dog comes to you with the bird. If the dog lays the bird down and is fiddling with it, the assistant should toss the handful of pea gravel at the dog. He won't connect that with you, so usually he'll grab the bird and come flying to you with it.

Isaacs: The most common problem is the dog that doesn't show any natural ability and doesn't want to get out from under your feet. Within a reasonable period if you can't instill a little desire in him to get out there by putting the pigeons out for him or getting him into some ground where there's some natural birds, then I'd say you'd best not spend any more time on that dog.

Another problem is getting the puppy to come directly to you. You start at an early age with the retrieving and naturally they think they're playing, they want to show off a little, they run off and hide with whatever they're carrying. But you've got to let the pup know you're serious. A lot of people have trouble getting the puppy to come in, especially if they have children throwing things and chasing after the dog.

The real birdy dog, the one with the burning desire to get out there and find birds, can be a problem, too. This is the kind you've really got to lay on to with the whistle, give more obedience training to, got to be firmer with him in everything he does. But this is the kind of dog I like. When the dog starts reaching out, you want to get him back quick. The problem is keeping the hard-going, birdy dog within range, but repetition with the whistle will teach him what his range is. Be sure and always enforce in the field what you've trained the dog to do in the yard. You give him the turn whistle, that's what he's to do. If he doesn't, get down there to him.

If you have to go out to a dog, give him a little shaking, a little whipping, like you got when you were a kid. I use a flushing whip for this. It doesn't hurt the dog, it makes a lot of popping and causes more noise than pain. But 90 percent of my discipline is picking the dog up and giving him a shaking while blowing the whistle into his ear and calling him in roughly to where he should have come to.

Hurst: The most common problem is with the puppy that picks up the dummy, runs away with it and doesn't come back to his handler at all or else comes back and drops it 5 yards in front of his handler. If this common fault occurs, the pup is given no retrieving training of any kind for a week except that he's taken out into the field and is sat in front of his handler. The handler then calls the dog's name, pats his own chest, and hopes that the puppy will jump on his back legs with his front feet on the handler. If he doesn't, the handler bends down, gently picks up the puppy by the front feet, and lifts him into a standing position. Then he is petted, talked to, and generally made a fuss of while in that position. He's put down and this is repeated until the puppy will immediately stand up on his handler to be petted. This normally takes about a week; no training session of this kind must be done for more than twenty minutes at a time.

After this period of time, the dummy is thrown, the dog immediately goes after it and picks it up. As soon as he's got the dummy in his mouth, the handler calls the dog's name, pats his chest, and the puppy comes back and stands on his hind legs to be petted. The dummy is taken out of the dog's mouth immediately while he is standing up. He's not allowed to drop it. He's petted and the performance repeated until the puppy will do this without fail. It may be argued that one does not want a dog jumping up on him on a shooting day with dirty feet on a retrieve. But later on it's simple to intercept this.

If a dog is just learning to retrieve he should be teased a bit and excited by the bird, and the trainer should toss the bird for another practice retrieve or two before stowing it away. Snatching it from him and not letting him see it again may cause him to figure he'd rather keep it for himself for a while and could lead to reluctance or refusal to deliver. (Photo by Mickey McLinden)

Take the bird off the puppy when he is a yard or two away by moving toward the dog. After all this has been achieved, the dog is taught to sit when he gets back to his handler. After a period of time he will sit, lift his nose into the air, and expect the handler to take the bird or dummy when he's in a sitting position.

To teach a spaniel to hunt, two lines of dummies are put out in the field and the dog is encouraged to pick them up. This introduces a pup to hunting and retrieving at the same time. If a dog is not terribly tempted to go for a number of dummies, which may occur because dogs can get bored with this, you will have to resort to the use of cold, dead pigeons that have been killed for a period of twenty-four hours. Almost every time the dog will seize the pigeon and pick it up.

The main problem with a spaniel is that he's got to learn to ignore lines—the line of a pheasant, a rabbit, or any game that has run across the ground he is hunting. A turn whistle is used initially to turn a dog off a line. This whistle request is not as strong as the stop whistle, which is a command.

Sometimes it is difficult to turn a dog off a line during the late stages of his training. If he completely disobeys the turn whistle, the stop whistle is tried. If he's still recalcitrant on the stop whistle, he's not allowed to go out on any ground where there is any scent of any description. He's taken to the garden, lawn, or any space that is completely scentless and is given a very severe course of stopping to the whistle.

This is done for a period of a week. He's then taken out to ground where there are lines, he's allowed to hunt, and when he begins to follow a line the stop whistle is blown. The dog will sit. He's got his nose off the ground, he's got his attention off the line and back to his handler. He's then called up with the return whistle and the procedure is repeated until he is reliable in all ways.

How do you cope with or correct problems you've mentioned?

Lorenz: Didn't I cover that in answering the previous question?

Isaacs: Guess I jumped the gun again, telling you what to do before I was asked. I think I already answered this question just a minute ago.

Hurst: Refer to the methods I just described in answering the previous question.

When a dog displays serious faults—gunshyness, birdshyness, disinterest in game, hard mouth—is there much point in an amateur trainer working to try to correct these faults?

Lorenz: After working with the dog for a week or ten days in the yard, if he still has no interest in retrieving or touching a live or dead pigeon, I think it's best to give up on that dog. After ten days if you can't develop an interest in retrieving a bird, it's useless.

Hard mouth can be brought under control, but never really stopped.

If a dog bolts from a gun, runs back to the car or the house, or otherwise displays gunshyness, I think it's useless to try to do anything about it, because usually someone has made a mistake, fired the gun at the wrong time. It takes so long to try to cure it, it isn't worth it.

Isaacs: Regarding all the mentioned subjects I certainly would spend very little time with such a dog. He'd have to have something very special about him before I'd spend much time trying to get him over any of those faults. It would mostly be a waste of time. To start with, a selective breeding program should be carried on to eliminate dogs with those faults. After proper introduction to various training methods, if you can't see any success with these problems, I'd look for another dog.

Hurst: There are two main faults that can occasionally occur with dogs. One is gunshyness and the other is hard mouth.

A gunshy dog is completely incurable of this fault. To recognize gunshyness it is only necessary to fire a shot—not too close to the dog, 20 to 30 yards away will do. A gunshy dog will immediately tuck his tail between his legs, run until he is exhausted and hide. If in his kennel he'll try to bury himself under his dog bed; fear will show in his eyes. Again, there is no way this can be cured.

A gun-nervy puppy is one that will tuck his tail between his legs and drop his ears at the sound of shot, but will not bolt. This can be cured by taking a puppy either in a rabbit pen or to an area where there is a lot of

Dr. Alvin Nitchman, a New Jersey dentist and most successful amateur handler, makes a flushing effort in front of one of his shooting dogs under the eye of a respected judge, Dr. H. I. Nesheim, a Missouri surgeon.

game scent. Allow him to hunt wild and then fire shots from a .410 shotgun. It is essential that a .22 rifle not be used for this. The whine of the bullet will definitely tend to make the pup worse. A starter's pistol can also increase this fault.

Hard mouth is the second major fault. As with gunshyness, there is no cure for this. It tends to increase as a dog becomes more used to game. A hardmouthed dog will take a bird across the back of the ribs and completely crush either one or both sides of the rib cage. Some people test for hard mouth by looking at the breast of the bird, but this gives no indication at all of the problem. The hardmouthed dog should be discarded from any competition work.

With regard to disinterest in game, the only way this can be overcome is to allow the dog to hunt wild and give no discipline training at all. This shouldn't be tried for more than three weeks. If after three weeks of being given the opportunity to find and chase game, the dog doesn't take this opportunity he should be discarded.

Sometimes, by overtraining, a dog will learn to "blink" game, which means he will find it but as soon as he gets close to it he will blink away from it and ignore it. The cure for this is to get a pigeon, tie one wing so it can't fly, put it down on open ground in front of the dog, which is on a lead, and allow the pigeon to walk away. The dog is then sent when the pigeon is out of sight and will almost in all cases retrieve the pigeon. Once he's learned to retrieve this live game, he will then go in to find other game, but must later be stopped on chasing.

Should you decide it is worthwhile to overcome any or all of the above faults, what do you do to effect a cure?

Lorenz: If the dog is out and out gunshy and will bolt for home upon hearing the shotgun, I really don't think there is any cure for him. You can get him over being gunshy to the point where he won't bolt for home, but to get him to the point where he'd go out and pick up a bird, it would take so long and cost so much you'd be much better off to forget it and start over. Even if you did work on the dog for six months, there's no guarantee you'd ever accomplish anything.

If the dog isn't too bad on the gun, if he just turns away from the bird, as the bird is being shot, you might have some luck running this kind of dog with an older dog. The younger dog will get jealous of the older dog and when the pup sees the older one flush and chase the bird, he'll go out and try to get it away from him. If you shoot a dozen or so birds in this manner and then go back to running the pup by yourself, a lot of times he'll go out and chase the bird because he found out that by doing it with the older dog nothing bad happened to him.

If the dog is introduced to the gun properly, there usually is no problem. Sometimes after a dog has flushed and chased twelve or fifteen birds and is doing well, he might all of a sudden start to back off. I think this is due to the combination of a bird jumping out of the nest, hitting the pup in the nose, flying away, having several shots fired at it, not being hit and not coming down. If this is the case, it's best to go back to the clipped-wing birds and somebody standing in the distance firing the shotgun.

When you're shooting birds it's most important for a young dog just to have one person shoot. Don't ever shoot at the bird unless you have a 90 percent chance of killing it. If you miss too frequently, you're bound to have problems.

Isaacs: With these faults, the amateur who has the time, who thinks he has the ability and will study a good book on the subject and take advice from a knowledgeable dog person, possibly can devote the time required to correct these problems. He may be successful part of the time. But as a professional I'd hate to accept a man's money for something I'm not reasonably sure I can accomplish.

Hurst: My opinions and methods were detailed in answering the previous question.

Aside from the necessity of using good judgment, is there generally a time to punish and a time to praise? What forms should punishment and praise take and when are they used to discipline and reward a dog?

Lorenz: As far as punishing the dog for breaking shot or not answering the turn whistle, I think the best way is to slip the chain collar on and use the leash to jerk him a few times. If he breaks shot, haul him back to the place he broke from, give him several good jerks on the leash and at the same time give the "Hup!" command and whistle. If you want him to quarter and after you've removed the line he ignores your turn whistle, stop him with the stop whistle. Don't call him to you. Walk out to the stationary dog, put the collar and leash on him and give him several good jerks while blowing the turn whistle that he ignored in the first place.

As far as praise, I don't believe you can overdo the praise from puppy on. If you continuously praise the puppy and he likes you, he'll do a lot of things for you because he wants to please you. If you run into a real problem where a dog doesn't want to come up to you at all, then you'd better carry some dog biscuits in your pocket and coax him to you. Reward him with a biscuit or piece of meat. This problem happens only if the dog has been overly corrected or is the shy type in the first place. But you can't overdo petting and praise. A lot of times it's not done enough.

Isaacs: Good judgment and a little sense have to be used when disciplining a dog for disobeying (for example, how bad did he disobey?). Punishment should be used sparingly, and when it's used it should be as effective as possible.

First, I'd pick the dog up, hold him by the skin of the neck, give him a good shaking, look him straight in the eye. Sometimes you don't have to shake. An eyeball to eyeball with him often has a lot of effect. You may want to give him a switch or two with the whip after you've put him down. But the degree of punishment will depend on the dog and his response to discipline.

As far as praise, I don't think these dogs know what the word is, any more than they know what "hunting" is or "good boy" is. We all have certain times when we say things like that. Just patting the dog on the head and speaking his name makes him happy. I don't think a whole lot of unnecessary talk does anything for him.

Hurst: It is required that the finished dog be a happy dog, working for his handler because he wants to, not because he thinks he's got to. Punishment and praise have to be very carefully thought out. Punishment is to be avoided as far as possible. It's essential, therefore, not to give a dog a command that won't come up in force in early training.

A dog in early training tends to be nervous and a little bit bewildered because he wonders what it's all about and hasn't yet achieved self- or handler-discipline. As his training progresses, he will naturally become more disciplined and accept his training and become bolder. Punishment is usually not resorted to in the very early stages of training, but only as training progresses and the dog becomes bolder.

The form of punishment should not be physical violence by hitting or striking the dog. The dog should be punished for whatever he's done wrong by catching him under the chin, administering a shaking with the command, "No!" A common fault of some amateur handlers is to call a dog up when he's run away, but the dog disobeys this and continues to run, and then finally comes back to his handler some considerable time later. He's then punished, and the dog believes he's being punished for coming back to his handler, not for refusing to come back when he was whistled and called. A dog must be punished while in the act of doing what he is doing wrong. The handler must go to the dog and not call up the dog for punishment. If the dog is called up and punished, he will become wary of his handler and the whole training schedule goes wrong.

Probably the most innovative and well-publicized training device to appear in recent years is the electronic shock collar. Based on your experience, can the electronic shock collar be of much aid to the amateur training his own dog? If it has drawbacks, how should the person using it exercise caution to achieve the most from this device?

Lorenz: With "soft-type" dogs like Springers or Golden retrievers, they probably should never be used. If the dog is eighteen months old or older —and then only after he's been completely trained and knows exactly what's expected of him and then ignores your commands—the electric collar has its use. But it doesn't really pay to buy an electric collar to use on a Springer because you'd only get to use it one time and after that the Springer is usually too smart. He'll never run or leave your side as long as that collar is on. It is something to be used only as punishment, not for training.

Occasionally you'll get a good pup, but spoiled rotten. I had such a young one, somebody just did something wrong with him. As long as the line was on him, he'd fetch pigeons fine. Disconnect the line and he'd run all over the place, tail going, happy as could be. This went on for quite a while. I tried correcting with the slingshot. Nothing seemed to work. He was still young, six or seven months. I put that electric collar on him, he took off, and I just touched the button. He let out a scream and brought that bird back and that was the end of it. It worked the way I wanted it that time. But it should be used only as a last resort.

Isaacs: The electronic collar is definitely an effective method of training your dog. But it is absolutely essential to use it with discretion, and above all follow the instructions that come with it. The training device can be used to control or break the dog at a long distance, where you couldn't possibly run to get to the dog. It can be used to get a dog in if you've got a dog that doesn't want to come in. Even though this isn't really harsh, there are some dogs that just won't put up with it, so you've got to be careful and watch for that. As far as drawbacks, it's bad to have a dog completely run off with the thing on him, or won't do anything but walk right at your heels. This happens if the person doesn't use discretion but overuses the shocker.

Hurst: The electronic collar is a device that hasn't been used in Britain and I have no personal experience in its use. It seems a rather violent method of training that could be used successfully with a particularly

This Brittany spaniel is restrained at the flush of a bird by the trainer's one hand holding the collar, the other over the flank. With a more exuberant dog the entire arm may have to go over the flank and pull the dog in tight against the trainer's side when teaching steady to wing. (Larry Mueller photo)

hardheaded dog. I would think its use advisable by only a very experienced trainer.

What are the advantages and disadvantages of a sportsman keeping his spaniel as a house dog and companion, as opposed to kenneling him strictly as a hunter?

Lorenz: I certainly can't see anything wrong with a hunter using the dog for both hunting and as a house dog with the exception of duck hunting in cold weather. If the dog is expected to make retrieves in near freezing temperatures, he would have to be kept outside at that time in order to acclimate himself to the cold weather.

If the dog is kept in the house he'll be better socialized, more in touch with you. If kept in the house, he should be made to behave and never be given any commands unless you make sure they are obeyed.

Isaacs: I would certainly love to keep my Springers in the house with me, then take them in the field and work them. If I owned only one dog, I would do that. I recommend that people in the city have a run attached to the garage, a place they can put a dog, even though he's a house pet. Whenever you have guests come in, a dog should have a place of his own. Dogs like to be by themselves sometimes, too. Being a house pet will have no effect at all on his ability or hunting desire and won't interfere with your training program. Some people think it does. But you don't do your training in the house, you do it out in the field.

Hurst: There are advantages and disadvantages in keeping a hunting dog as a pet in the house. One disadvantage is that a dog is brought home at the end of a shooting day, absolutely wet, cold, muddy, or whatever. He's then taken into the house, gets on the furniture, and it's difficult to get him properly dried off. The other main disadvantage is that during extremely cold weather the dog becomes softened by living in heated-house conditions. When taken out hunting in severe conditions of cold, he may refuse to enter water because it's cold or he may even get into such a very cold state during a shooting day that his work will be severely affected.

The only reason I can see for keeping a shooting dog in the house is when an owner has no facilities whatever for keeping the dog in a kennel at home.

Based upon your extensive experience, would you give some off-the-cuff advice, odds and ends of information, pet peeves, tips, remarks on conditioning, etc., that weren't touched upon in previous questions?

Lorenz: The worst thing that can happen to a young dog is to be in a household with children who throw things for the dog to retrieve and tire the dog so much he's not interested in retrieving, or perhaps the dog picks up some toy of the children's and someone screams "No!" at him so he gets the idea he's not supposed to pick up.

Another worst thing that can happen is to have a dog of a hunting breed and take him out and shoot the shotgun over him, "just to find out if he's gunshy." Even if he wasn't gunshy to start with, firing the shotgun before proper introduction was made will certainly make him gunshy.

When I first went into the business of training dogs, an old-timer told me that someone with a little experience could maybe train a dog as well as someone with a lot of experience, but that a person with a lot of experience, the more years he's trained, is going to ruin fewer dogs than the man with no experience. When I was a kid, I wasn't sure I knew what he was talking about, but the longer I'm in it the more true it's become. The more years you're in the business, the more you get to know all types of dogs and learn how to cope with different types.

If you've trained two hundred dogs you've probably learned about twenty different types, but if you've trained, say, five dogs you probably know about only one or two types. A great trainer once said, "The only

Facing page
Kennel crates provide safe, convenient transportation for gun dogs and they come out rested and ready to go to work, like this young Lab, Duffey's Irish Jig.

difference is, the more experience you have, the fewer dogs you're going to ruin."

I really think you have to have a feel for training and handling a dog. I've sold people dogs that were perfect hunting dogs, and they couldn't use their voice or their whistle to the right degree and the dogs wouldn't behave for them. They'd get disgusted. I've even had them give the dog back to me saying he was useless to them. Then I'd either give or sell the dog to someone else and in a couple of months those new owners wouldn't sell that dog for thousands of dollars. Some people just don't have a knack with dogs and no matter what they do, they can't get much good out of the dog.

Isaacs: People who buy puppies usually do two things: they try to train their puppy in one weekend or, at the other extreme, they buy a puppy and don't do anything with him.

People have to decide that they're going to train that puppy and give him some attention or they shouldn't want one. They've got to decide they aren't going to make a workhorse of the dog once a week. They're going to have to spend a little time with him daily. It's wrong to have a dog lay up in a kennel until the fall of the year waiting for some guy to go out and shoot a bird over him when hunting season opens, which nobody's going to be able to do anyway because they didn't spend any time with the dog.

Another thing, if a guy has too much time on his hands and he's too wrapped up in really wanting to train a dog, maybe he ought to buy two or three and spread his time out among them; then he won't overwork or ruin any of them. Maybe that's how I lucked out. When I started I bought three spaniels. I spent a lot of time with them but never overdid one that way.

Hurst: Over the past few years there has been an increase in the value and use of working Cockers, specifically *working-bred* Cockers. They're small dogs, useful companions, extremely good game finders, and consummate experts on rabbits and hares. Even though they are small dogs they can handle a large hare or full-grown cock pheasant with ease. It's essential to study bloodlines and pedigrees before acquiring a Cocker.

The basic difference in training methods between a Springer and a Cocker is that the Springer will have to be trained in a completely disciplined manner. Cockers tend to resent such training. With Cockers, training has to be more of a play time than with Springers. Under no circumstances, at any time, must a Cocker in training ever be hit or struck. Punishment has to be light.

One main problem with Cockers, and sometimes with Springers, has to do with retrieving. Once a Cocker will retrieve an object, dummy, or bird to hand, it's essential that the dog not be required to make more than two retrieves on each training session. If given a large number of retrieves in a training session, the Cocker has the tendency to pop away from his handler and bury the object.

Once a Cocker has learned any particular thing in his training, he will tend to retain that for the rest of his life and it's unnecessary to go over that thing again. Whatever he has learned, a Cocker normally retains that learning much more efficiently than a Springer.

On the other hand, because of his slightly nervous disposition, punishment must never be severe in training and very carefully thought out. At the end of his training the Cocker is at least equal to or better than most trained Springers.

If a person starts with two puppies at eight months of age, one Cocker, the other Springer, the discipline training of the Springer is more severe than that of the Cocker, but when both dogs reach the age of fourteen months both of them will have reached the same level.

In the words of Jimmy Wylie, the most experienced Cocker trainer in the British Isles: "One doesn't train a Cocker. One guides him."

This is the most apt description that can be stated.

The one advantage of the Cocker over the Springer for training by an amateur is that the Cocker is much easier to train to work to a close hunting pattern. In America, in the short period of time that I've been here, I've realized that the Cocker, properly trained, is the best dog that I have ever seen for shooting ruffed grouse in thick cover. The little dog will naturally work very close within gunshot range of his handler in the thick cover and will always keep within his pattern if properly trained and properly handled.

Commentary
BY DAVID MICHAEL DUFFEY

PART 1

For most hunters, one dog at a time is enough to train or handle and should be all they need. Trying to start two puppies together is usually disastrous and even when breaking in a pup with an older dog complications can develop.

But if you should be a particularly hard hunter, getting to hunt three or more times per week locally or taking extended trips for a week or more of steady hunting, whether your bird count numbers in the dozens or hundreds, you certainly will have need for more than one dog.

A tired dog is less efficient than a fresh dog. So it pays to rotate, either giving each dog at least a day's and preferably two days' rest following a grinding dawn till dark hunt, or hunt each dog only an hour or two daily.

If weather and terrain conditions are extreme, hot and dry or wet and cold, poor footing, lots of brush and hills, you may have to be even more conservative in saving your dog.

You can also rest a dog during the day by hunting him a few hours in the morning, laying him up or putting down another dog during the middle of the day and putting your morning dog down again in the late afternoon. If you follow this schedule, hunt the big, open country in the A.M. and the tight, thick covers in the P.M. After a dog has been worked hard for a period and then is "laid up" for several hours, he will stiffen. His desire to get out there to the far places will be reduced and he'll handle kindlier and work closer in the thick stuff.

You never have to worry about a sorry dog. He'll never hurt himself. And some smart old-timers get to pacing themselves, but your best dog and your young dog won't know to throttle back and quit. Sometimes circumstances force you to overwork a dog. I've brought them back from trips (where we crammed all the hunting we could get into half a week or a week) bone thin, with swollen legs and raw tails. This was working with a string of six to eight dogs. Avoid it if you can. Your circumstances will dictate whether you need one, two, or a dozen dogs to complete your season successfully.

Remember, too, that on trips, while confined during travel and subject to strange places, people, and conditions, dogs aren't really resting. They don't eat, drink, relax, or feel secure and the travel stress may be just as hard or harder on them than the actual field work.

As the experts explained, bird dog field trials are exhibitions, displays. Both dog and handler must possess at least some degree of showmanship.

Thus, there can be good hunting dogs that lack the sparkle to catch a judge's eye in a trial and excellent trainers who lack the gift of showing a dog at his best. This is not to say that the successful dogs and handlers are actors. It is to say that both have a bit more wit, style, and pizzazz than the good Lord rationed out to us average folks.

A field trial may be made up of one or more stakes (separate events) carried out in the course of a day or stretch out for a couple of weeks, as in the case of the National Championship at Grand Junction, Tennessee, where each brace of qualified dogs runs in three-hour heats. A heat, for puppies, may be as short as fifteen to twenty minutes.

There are minor field trials for mature dogs, which have a back course and a planted bird field. In some of these trials birds are shot over the dogs and retrieving may be a requirement.

But major circuit trials are mostly run on contiguous courses in one- to two-hour heats (frequently there is a qualifying heat followed by a finals heat of longer duration) and wild birds are utilized both in and out of season. Game birds are not shot in major bird dog trials. But a shot is fired into the air when pointed birds are flushed in front of a dog, testing his manners on game and proving he is not gunshy.

Formal trials have the sanction of either The American Field, working through the Amateur Field Trial Clubs of America, or the American Kennel Club. There are minor rule and requirement differences between the two governing bodies and major differences in emphasis. Most of the important major bird dog trials are under the aegis of "The Field," while the majority of single course (back course plus birdfield) trials, and those for pointing breeds other than Pointers and Setters, are within the province of the "AKC."

Derby stakes are for dogs up to two years of age. All-age stakes are, as the name implies, participated in by a dog of any age. Precocious "derbies" occasionally compete in all-age events but the youngsters are seldom a match for more mature, experienced dogs. A third stake that has turned into about the most popular event over the past twenty years is the Shooting Dog Stake.

No one has yet satisfactorily explained the difference between "shooting dog" all-age and derby performers and "open" all-age and derby dogs. Some dogs compete, place, and win in both categories. There are said to be differences in range, handling response, and perhaps the importance given to the number of game contacts; the shooting dog not being as extreme in range, more biddable, and perhaps "into birds" more often.

But all those things are relative and are complicated by individual standards and opinions held by participants, judges, and spectators and, as far as bird work is concerned, the field trial view has always been quality over quantity.

An "open" derby, shooting dog, or all-age event permits dog handling by either professional or amateur. An "amateur" derby, shooting dog, or all-age is, naturally, restricted to dogs handled by amateurs. However, most of the top "amateur dogs" either have been trained or are in the strings of professionals, sometimes competing in the open stakes under the whistle of their trainer and also in the amateur stakes for their owners or other hobby-handlers. Puppy stakes, for the very young (usually seven to fourteen months of age), are also held.

A Futurity is a breeder's stake. The owner of a bitch bets that his carefully planned mating to an outstanding stud is going to produce some top puppies. He nominates the dam and enrolls the expected litter, paying a fee or forfeit. The purchaser of an individual pup from that litter also pays forfeits to keep his hopeful eligible to enter the annual Futurity should he show the ability to win during his early development. An entry fee is also paid. Owners and breeders of the first four placing derby-age dogs in the Futurity event share in a cash purse.

Information about bird dog trials or a subscription to *The American Field,* a weekly publication with detailed accounts of all the major events, may be obtained from William F. Brown, Editor, The American Field Publishing Company, 222 West Adams Street, Chicago, Illinois 60606 (Phone: 312—372-1383).

A *45-pocket* has nothing to do with a pistol packed in a pair of pants. It refers to an imaginary 45-degree, cone-shaped pattern to the front of the handler within which a gun dog showing well does most of his hunting, the handler being at the tip of the funnel and the dog making casts and sweeps out at its widest part. Dogs will often get off to the side and may even get behind sometimes while covering a field trial course or hunting area. But even after being gone for some time, the good ones will "show to the front," ideally on course, in "the 45-pocket."

A dog that *rats* or is *ratting* may actually be trying to catch small field rodents, which are abundant in some areas. But the term also describes a dog that is pottering or messing around, working with a low head and dwelling on foot scent and often rooting out birds, if they are still present, rather than working with a high head and using body scent to locate game accurately and establish point.

A *trailer* is an overly dependent dog that depends on the dog he is braced (paired) with in the field to guide him around. He follows the other dog constantly and never strikes out independently. Some dogs are very clever about this and give the appearance of being the leader rather than the follower. But this act can be detected if the dogs are observed closely when running together.

A *blinking* dog is one that deliberately avoids or leaves something he shouldn't, usually birds but sometimes another dog on point. Too heavy discipline or shyness is the usual cause for a dog blinking birds. He's come to associate unpleasantness with birds while being taught his manners or is frightened by them. He may just pretend they aren't there and avoid them entirely or establish point and then move out without flushing them. When confronted with another dog on point, a dog may know better than to steal the other dog's point or bust the covey, but will veer off and refuse to honor the find. Overdisciplining when teaching to back or just plain jealousy may cause this form of blinking.

Trainers *road* their dogs in harness for a number of reasons, but chiefly to give them controlled exercise. A *check cord* (20- to 25-foot rope) is attached to a special roading harness, not unlike the type used on sled dogs,

With the aid of David Harden, Mrs. Felix Montgomery gets her young Brittany spaniel accustomed to a roading harness. (George Quigley photo)

and the horse-mounted trainer either hangs onto the other end or attaches it to his saddle.

Pointing dogs, particularly field trial dogs, are not generally taught to heel like retrievers or spaniels. That would tend to inhibit them when they are in the roading harness. When harnessed it is desirable that the dog pull hard against the harness, building muscle and wind. Several dogs may be roaded at one time. Trainers and their assistants are constantly bringing dogs up in roading harnesses during training sessions. While getting exercise they are also getting accustomed to horses and other dogs and experience in seeing birds pointed, birds flushed and flying, backing training, etc. Handlers often road their dogs behind the gallery (group of mounted spectators) at field trials for the same reasons or to wear down a particularly powerful or big-going dog that may be most difficult to control or will run off if not worn down a bit before he is cast off.

PART 2

The dock-tailed gun dogs of Europe, commonly referred to as the Continental pointing breeds or Versatile hunting dogs, are required to be versatile. They are expected to work at close to medium range, point birds that they find (pointing dog work), retrieve anything shot over land or water (retrieving dog work), and track and trail running game (hound dog work). In Germany such dogs are also trained to track wounded big game and to do terrier work such as dispatching feral cats and other small predators.

While closely controlled breeding programs produce dogs with great natural ability, no dog of any form, shape, or manner can become even a specialist, much less a truly versatile hunting dog, without training. There isn't one sportsman in 10,000 in the United States who will live with his dog and devote the time necessary to develop a dog that will find, point, and retrieve upland game (both fur and feather), work as a jump-shooting and nonslip retriever on waterfowl, trail large and small game, and tackle and kill predators. But U.S. hunters do like dogs that will do more than one thing and some find the answer to their likes in the spaniels and retrievers. But others like their game pointed rather than flushed. For them the Versatile breeds, such as the German shorthair, German wirehair, Pudelpointer, may be the answer.

Only through trials or tests and the accurate keeping of pedigrees and records of tests can it be determined which dogs in any breed or group are best suited for breeding, to ensure that the purchaser of a gun dog will obtain worthwhile stock to train and hunt with.

The North American Versatile Hunting Dog Association (NAVHDA secretary is Mrs. Rosie Scott, Route 4, Box 256, Brownsburg, Indiana 46112) has undertaken a program to provide such tests and service for sportsmen who own and hunt with the Versatile breeds. The breeds most commonly tested by NAVHDA are German wirehaired pointers (Drahthaars), Griffons, German shorthaired pointers, Pudelpointers, Brittany spaniels, and Weimaraners.

NAVHDA conducts two tests, a Natural Ability test for young dogs under sixteen months of age and a Utility Field test for older, intensively trained dogs. As far as the so-called average hunter is concerned, the most important of these is the Natural Ability test, designed to indicate whether or not a young dog has inherited the stuff that makes an eager, easy-to-train gun dog before its shortcomings can be covered up by skillful training.

In an effort to learn first hand what such a program is all about I entered and qualified a Pudelpointer, Wingmaster's Dillon, in a Natural Ability test. Under another trainer and owner he has gone on to qualify in the advanced Utility Field work. My son, Mike, who does some training out in Spokane, Washington, has entered and qualified a Drahthaar, Feldsturm's Obere Jägerin, in a Natural Ability test.

Through actual participation in and serving as a judge for NAVHDA testing, I've become convinced of the practicality and usefulness of the program. With a minimum of training and field experience, a young dog that will do the things asked of him in the Natural Ability tests should quickly become a dog any sportsman will enjoy taking afield. Sportsmen who want to reach a near-ultimate in top-notch gun dog field work will have it in a dog that can qualify in the Utility test. But that will require a great deal of training and devotion to the task of turning out a gun dog that can do pointer, retriever, and hound work. For those interested in doing this kind of job, a good book is available on order from NAVHDA. It is *The Training and Care of the Versatile Hunting Dog* by Sigbot Winterhelt and Edward Bailey.

Even though the NAVHDA tests for young dogs are designed to give a line on their natural ability, in fairness to the dog, some preparation is necessary. You cannot simply haul a dog out of his kennel, enter him in a Natural Ability test, and expect him to perform well. Yet, the proper instincts are so well instilled by good breeding in some of these dogs that in a recent test I judged in Indiana my fellow judge and I qualified two Drahthaar littermates just five months old! If sportsmen will do some play training and familiarization with their Continental breed puppies, they may be hunting them successfully between five months and a year of age.

John Kegel, one of this book's experts, did an excellent outline for the newsletter of the Pudelpointer Club of North America of how he prepares a pup for a NAVHDA Natural Ability test. Because it is so applicable for hunters who want to get their pups ready for their first hunting season, detailing some useful procedures for any gun dog regardless of breed, with John's permission, I'm including an edited version of these techniques.

Under my approach, training can start right from weaning and continue until the dog retires from hunting or dies. The intensity and frequency of training will vary with the age of the dog. From weaning to four or five months we might restrict our training to play training. Then after a pup's hunting instinct has been fully developed, we can progress with an intensive training program. But even the fully trained dog will require some maintenance training from time to time, especially if he hasn't been hunted for a long time.

For illustration purposes, assume your pup is a spring puppy and you take him home between seven and twelve weeks of age. The development and preparation of this pup have three major phases.

Phase I: Play training or preliminary training and introducing the pup to water. Age period from seven weeks to approximately five months.

Phase II: Building and developing his hunting desire, which will include searching and pointing.

Phase III: Tracking.

Phase I

Get the puppy used to his name and make him wear a leather collar. Make him understand the meaning of the commands "No!," "Quiet!," and "Kennel!" Teach "Sit,!" "Stay!," and "Come!" ("Here!") in that order. I don't teach "Whoa!," "Down!," or force-retrieving at this stage.

All my lessons are preceded by a five-minute play period to give the pup a chance to get rid of some of his excess steam. The playing consists of throwing a small dummy out on the lawn a few times and letting him retrieve it, or taking a fly rod with a pheasant wing dangling from it and letting the pup chase it and sight point it a few times.

I am *not* convinced that sight pointing a pheasant wing does much for a pup's future pointing. But if it isn't overdone, it is fun to watch the pup and it is also good exercise in a confined area.

The five-minute play period is followed by about ten minutes of actual training and then I take the pup for a fifteen-minute romp in the field. On nice warm days I forget the romp and take the pup down to our pond, which has a very gradual bottom slope. My first attempt to coax the puppy into the water is usually done with the rod and wing. He will readily race through shallow water and chase the wing but may be hesitant to go into deeper water.

If not making any headway with rod and wing, I switch tactics. I might throw a small dummy, a dead bird, or even a live bird into the shallow water and let him retrieve it. Here again, he may go readily to a certain depth, but as soon as he feels the bottom disappearing under his legs he just backs off. Sometimes it helps to let an older dog make some retrieves.

After four or five half-hour lessons on water, should the pup still refuse to go in, I put on my chest waders and walk into the water and try to coax him in. Failing this, my next step is to carry the dog into the pond and place him gently in the water, using both hands. *Never* throw him into the water.

As soon as you take your hands off him, he is forced to swim and usually will head for shore via the shortest route. Pick him up on shore and repeat this two more times, each time increasing the swimming distance. The forced swim will help him lose his fear of the water and by switching back to the procedures mentioned earlier you should be able to get your dog to enter water quite easily.

This is by no means the only way to introduce a pup to water. But it has worked best for me. I have used this way to introduce over forty pups to water without one failure. It is difficult to predict the length of time it will take you to get your dog accustomed to water. The majority of my Pudelpointer pups went in in less than six lessons but some stubborn ones took as many as twenty-five lessons. Oddly enough, several of the more difficult ones went on to become outstanding water dogs.

Phase II

Building and developing hunting desire is the most important lesson for a puppy. At the same time it may be the slowest and least interesting period for the novice dog trainer. Searching and pointing should be natural instincts, but we must provide our dogs with the opportunity to develop these instincts. With early maturing breeds, like the Pudelpointer, pups should be ready for this field lesson by the age of five months.

It is very important to get the pup to hunt instead of running only. In order to do that you must provide the youngster with live bird contacts from the beginning on. Since you may not live in an area where wild birds are abundant, you must do the next best thing: go to a game breeder and buy twenty well-flying bobwhite quail and one pheasant. You can house the quail in a recall pen if you have a suitable field available to keep the pen in. The alternative is to keep the birds in a small cage or pen at your home and release the birds whenever required.

If this seems costly, realize that a well-trained dog does not come cheap. A professional dog trainer will charge you anywhere from $400 to $600 for training a Versatile hunting dog. The trainer will spend a portion of this amount on birds, feed, and equipment, and if you want results you will have the same expenses.

Find a field with suitable cover 5 to 10 inches tall. Take your pheasant and, as a precautionary measure, pull four or five primary feathers from one wing and then tie a short string with an empty cola or beer bottle attached to one of the pheasant's legs. The only other thing needed at this point is a 20-foot-long check cord (¾-inch flat webbing is excellent) with a snap at the end.

Toss the anchored pheasant into a spot of very short cover so it remains visible at all times. The purpose of the upcoming exercise is to arouse the pup's pointing instinct by a combination of sight and smell.

Now attach the check cord to the pup's collar and lead him, facing the wind, in the direction of the pheasant. As soon as he sees the pheasant he will either freeze and sight point it, or try to catch it.

If he points, fine. Move up to him and restrain him with one hand holding the collar and use the other hand to pet him gently and praise him in a soft, reassuring voice. This is called sweet talk. Keep this up for about two minutes. Then get your helper (I forgot to mention the need for an assistant) to throw the pheasant out of sight.

If your dog does not start by pointing the pheasant and starts pulling hard on the check cord, calm him, slow him down, and make him stop about 10 feet from the bird. Under no circumstances should the dog be allowed to catch the pheasant.

Put your arms around the dog and restrain him in a pointing position and again sweet talk him. Don't use any restrictive commands. Just praise him. After two minutes have your helper throw the pheasant out of sight. You can repeat the lesson once more, but take great care that your dog does not catch the pheasant.

In three or four days your dog should be quite solid on sight points. Repeat these lessons two more times, each time putting the pheasant in higher cover so the bird becomes less visible and the dog has a chance to rely more on scent. After completion of this lesson, keep your pheasant alive as you will need it later for tracking.

Now your prospect is ready for actual field lessons. Take two quail and place them in birdy looking cover. Get the pup and release him with a command such as "Hie-on!" and walk at a brisk pace always facing the wind at the start. Until he learns what game holding cover looks like, it may take a little bit of maneuvering at first until you get your dog to the birds.

Don't expect a point right away. The pup will most likely show signs of making game by lowering his head and wagging his tail, flushing the bird and chasing it. This is normal and nothing to worry about. But a strongly ingrained pointing instinct will show up soon. After several flushes he will become more cautious and start to stalk and then point his game.

When your pup is approaching unfettered game he should be allowed full freedom. He should be permitted to make his point without directions or cautioning from you. This advice is not easy to follow. The handler's first impulse when he sees his dog slow down and go in with his nose extended is to "Whoa!" and caution him at every step. This just slows up the dog and keeps him pottering around when he should be advancing boldly forward with head up to catch the true body scent of the bird.

With too much cautioning, many dogs are coaxed into false points on foot scent or deserted roosts before definitely locating the bird. For these reasons, I do not teach my dogs to whoa in preliminary training (Phase I). The temptation to use it in the field at early stages is too great.

Once a pup starts to hold point long enough for you to walk up to him, restrain him in the pointing position and sweet talk him. At the same time you can stroke him gently with your free hand and style him up. Restrain him in a pointing position for about a minute, then flush the bird and let your dog chase.

You can take advantage of that chase to get the dog used to gunfire. Simply fire a 20-gauge shotgun when the dog is 30 to 40 yards away from you chasing the bird. There is no need to start with a cap pistol.

Field lessons should last twenty to thirty minutes. You can make your bird supply last longer by releasing only one quail at a time. By carefully observing the flight of flushed quail, you can mark its new location and get an additional find.

Over a period of two months, fifteen to twenty field trips should bring your pup a long way in his development. His search should be aggressive and he should at least flash point. Judging from my experience only 5 percent of the Pudelpointers won't point after these lessons. I have no estimate for other breeds.

If a dog is either late maturing or lacks sufficient strong pointing instinct, we continue to plant birds for him, but to cut expenses we use wing-clipped quail we can easily recover. We also snap the check cord on his collar and after he has scented the bird restrain him in a pointing position. Then we "flush" the bird by lifting it up and throwing it out of sight. If your dog has not shown any sign of natural pointing by the time he has reached eleven or twelve months of age, I would give up and contact the breeder for a replacement.

A well-bred dog should hunt his heart out, but don't be carried away by his speed alone. Your dog should also show signs of hunting, not just running. Once your dog *searches* boldly and goes on point in a positive and decisive manner, he is ready for the tracking lesson.

Phase III

Tracking is relatively easy to teach and does not require many lessons. Needed is a 50-yard strip of low cover not over 4 inches tall. The only equipment needed is a strong 8- to 10-foot pole, a 2-foot string, and the same check cord used before. This lesson should be given in the cooler hours of the day.

Give the pup a twenty-minute run in the field before commencing with the tracking lesson. While he is getting some of his breath back, tie the wings of the pheasant at the body with the string and attach the other end to the pole. Now "scent mark" the start of the track by dragging the bird over the ground a few times in small circles and leave a few feathers in that spot also. Hold the pole horizontal to one side, keep it just high enough for the pheasant to touch the ground. By walking slowly you can lead the pheasant in a straight line *down wind* for about 50 yards. Place a dead game bird at the end of this track. A quail is fine and not easily visible. The pheasant is left attached to the pole and resting in a location away from the dog.

Snap a check cord on the dog's collar and point out the start of the track to him. At this point it is advisable to use a distinct command such as: "Find!," "Dead Bird!," "Track!," or whatever you like. Some dogs will track as if they've done it all their lives. Others will track a short distance and then try to search with high head. A few will make no attempt to put their heads down.

The speedster who wants to do the tracking with his legs rather than his nose needs lots of calming down. Force his nose to the ground a few times so he can pick up the scent and hopefully get the idea. Walk very slowly in the track's direction, holding the dog fairly short on the check cord and keep calming him in a low voice. Repeating this will cause him to catch on. I've never had a Pudelpointer that did not learn to track very quickly.

If he tracks fairly well and gets to the dead bird, let him mouth it for a moment, then take it away from him and praise him lavishly.

Give your pup a few days rest before repeating the tracking lesson two more times, on slightly different terrain and in a little higher cover.

Let him work the entire track, which can be up to 100 yards this time, on the check cord. If he does a reasonable job of tracking I leave it at that and discontinue those lessons. I feel that tracking, if overdone, can have a detrimental effect on a dog's search as it encourages a low head. Failure to track is often the result of the dog's relying more on speed than his nose. I think a little story illustrates my point very well.

While a young bull and an old bull were grazing on a hillside the young bull looked down on the lower pasture where a herd of heifers were grazing. Turning to the old bull, the youthful stud said, "Hey! Let's *run* down the hill and breed one of those heifers." The old bull looked at him quizzically. "What do you say we *walk* down the hill and breed all of them," he suggested. Speed alone does not always accomplish the most.

PART 3

Dogs and men have a lot in common. One thing they share is hunting ability. Some dogs and some men were born to hunt. Others have acquired a fondness for the sport and by diligent, intelligent training and application have become hunters of equal or superior ability to the "naturals" who may have lacked opportunity, discipline, and direction. At the other extreme, some dogs and some men are duds in the field.

The dog that will come the fastest and be the most fun to work with possesses a strong, atavistic urge to hunt—anything, anytime, anyplace. At one time, all dogs and most men were hunters or they didn't survive. Humans have "progressed" to a point where natural hunters among men are a minority. And, increasingly, large numbers of gun dogs, reflecting our society, are weak in the age-old instincts that would make them hunters. This is often overcome because we have become highly sophisticated about training dogs and can not only curb and channel strong natural instincts to put them to work for our benefit, but may be able to mechanically instill responses in a dog that will make him at least a satisfactory hunter in given situations. That's why books on training are needed and why sportsmen who know how need to share information with others who don't but are willing to learn, whether man or dog is being programmed for the hunting fields.

There is no sure way to pick a natural-born hunting pup. I have had great dogs come from "common" stock and poor dogs out of "superior" ancestors. The dogs I remember, from the dozens I've owned personally rather than those I've trained for others, that I considered really great gun dogs, had a natural quality about them and took to hunting with an avidity that brought your heart to your throat.

Old Tar, my first purebred dog, an English cocker, showed me much about game and hunting and responded to my teen-age training techniques, rudimentary know-how gleaned mostly from reading about dogs. My father died when I was three and hunting was something I discovered on my own, stimulated by the fact that in a small central Wisconsin town in the 1930s and 1940s there wasn't a great deal for boys and young men to do but work, play ball, go down to the creek with a fish pole or onto the wooded ridges with a .22 rifle or shotgun. Had Tar not been as natural and adaptable as he was, I would have failed in my training efforts and lost interest in hunting with and training gun dogs.

If you have been blessed with a natural hunter for a training prospect, take full advantage of the philosophies expressed and the training techniques outlined by the experts in this book. You too can have a great dog. Barring the possibility that you've been saddled with an impossible pup, by getting out and doing what you are advised to do by these highly successful trainers, you can *make* yourself a delightful gun dog measuring up to the standards you personally require.

Most bitch dogs have a stronger, natural hunting instinct than their male counterparts, perhaps because in the wild when they attained womanhood it was their responsibility to provide for their whelps. I also believe bitches catch on quicker, are more precocious, and as a rule train easier than males. They just seem more submissive and less prone to distraction. They are born wanting to please, just as girl children were once conditioned.

Therefore, I think the amateur starting with his first dog is more likely to achieve success if he picks a bitch. With dogs being confined and controlled as they are today, there is certainly less reason to discriminate than in bygone years when a bitch in heat was a neighborhood problem. However, hunting with a female in season can be difficult. They are barred from most trial competition, and are prone to be erratic as estrus approaches, which can complicate training. So when picking a pup or buying a trained dog, don't reject a good prospect just because of her sex.

The experts have pretty much said it all, in all four sections of this book, regarding shock collars. Summed up, they say use good judgment and *don't overdo it*. In fact, you will note throughout a warning not to do anything with a dog too much and too often.

Surprisingly, since it is a harsh form of punishment, you may find that the shock collar works very well with a "soft" dog. I have an English setter that all of a sudden discovered the great, wide interesting world well beyond my reach could be enjoyed with impunity by ignoring my call and whistle. He is soft, intelligent, lovable, and affectionate. But I shocked him.

For four successive mornings, *when I could see him* and knew he was ignoring my shouts, I hit the button, *once*. Once each morning. He now can be taken into the grouse woods and comes to me happily out of virtually any situation when called up.

A major mistake too often made is shocking the dog one time and then deciding to "give it to him" again as a reinforcement measure, either immediately or later during the run or during the day. Every dog has a different tolerance. But the safest, most effective method, to start at least, is no more than one jolt, once a day.

The slingshot is also a valuable training aid. As far as I am concerned, it is a poor man's, short-range shock collar. It and a pocketful of marbles are easy to carry. Most pro retriever trainers I know have become dead-shots with the slingshot. It usually takes only two or three plinkings with a marble to get any but the most bullheaded dog's attention and immediate response to whatever command he chooses to ignore. The marble startles the dog, sometimes really hurts if it hits a rib or leg bone, and the dog instinctively comes to you for sympathy or attention if you've done your groundwork well and he trusts, respects, and loves you.

Always aim for someplace from the rib cage back. It is better to miss than to risk striking a dog's head. Once a dog has been plinked once or twice, a near miss or even the snap of the slingshot's rubber bands (or his seeing it in your hand) is as effective a reminder as a direct hit.

I've silenced a kennel full of dogs, barking because they wanted out where the training action was taking place with one of their number, by threatening to let drive with a marble while shouting "Stop That Noise!" or rattling a marble off the kennel run wall or floor.

If you've read this book carefully you may have noted a somewhat skeptical attitude expressed in regard to the value of starting a pup's training at a very tender age. There is some opinion that if a pup "has it" it makes very little difference how early or how late training commences.

This, of course, conflicts to some degree with the most recent fad in dog training that would have us believe that yard training can, and should, be completed by the time a pup is four to six months old. This approach to dog training follows the thinking of psychologists and social workers who emphasize the effect of environment over heredity in developing a child's personality and ability. At the same time, the canine pupil is assumed to have inherited enough talent so that if he doesn't respond in apple-pie order to early instruction procedures it isn't worth devising and implementing means to overcome these faults or shortcomings.

Which system works best, early conditioning or no-nonsense training and discipline later in life, can be debated—just as it can be questioned whether criminal acts and antisocial behavior by adults can be blamed in all cases on their environmental background and parental example. It even goes deeper than simply assigning everything good or bad a dog does to "heredity" or good or bad bloodlines.

It raises the question of whether we might be doing gun dog breeds a disfavor by starting too early and managing to "make" good dogs out of pups that may not possess top qualities that will survive adversity and a poor start in life, strong qualities that would be transmitted to offspring.

As competent amateur and professional trainers, we may be "making" dogs that shouldn't be made because they have little or no natural ability to pass on to their offspring, for the benefit of the breed and the enjoyment of the sportsmen who hunt with them. So a case might be made for just treating two- to ten-month-old puppies casually, and then later, as they approach maturity, when more positive judgments can be made, trying to determine which dogs have inherited the desired qualities.

Housebreaking a puppy would have seemingly little relationship to training a gun dog. But the experts mention it as an early form of training and reference is made to using a travel crate to aid in housebreaking. Housebreaking means becoming accustomed to being in the home and around people as well as teaching a pup that the parlor rug or the patio tile is an unacceptable place to relieve himself.

The procedure in using a travel crate to teach a pup his manners in the house involves confining him in that crate at times when you cannot supervise or keep an eye on him while he is inside. The essence of teaching a dog not to relieve himself inside is eternal vigilance. You have to anticipate his need to get outside and hustle him out of doors or catch him in the act and scold him for his misdeeds.

A pup should be confined to a crate for short periods of time, at frequent intervals, the best times being right after he's been romping and is tired and has been out to relieve himself. Ignore his protests until he settles down. If you give in when he fusses you've lost, he's won, and he'll never accept confinement. Once he's accepted the crate and will settle down, he can be left for increasing lengths of time. He'll learn he can get out only after good behavior, at your convenience, or when he has to make the outhouse run.

Even tiny pups avoid "dirtying" their sleeping quarters. And pups, when they have to go, are uncomfortable and will whine and fuss and want to get out. So when a pup is restless and starts sniffing and whining a bit, open the crate or scoop him up if he's running loose in the house and take him immediately to whatever spot you've selected for his personal latrine.

Pups usually have to relieve themselves shortly after eating, so figure on taking little walks or letting a pup play outside for a while right after feeding time. They also should be hustled out first thing in the morning when they get restless and whiney. This routine and the crate confinement will condition the pup to indicate to you when he needs to be let out and will permit him considerable freedom in the house. It will also teach him some responsibilities and save a great deal of "watchful-eyeing time" and clean-up on the part of family members.

Getting a pup accustomed to a crate has a zillion benefits. It becomes his home away from home when traveling by auto or air on hunting trips, it's a safe, convenient, clean means of conveying a dog anywhere, and a no-nuisance way to take your dog along on visits to friends and relatives. It is one of the most useful conveniences and training aids any dog owner can have.

One of the most difficult things to do is to tell another person verbally or in writing how to do something you are well versed in. Every trainer does little things he or she isn't conscious of doing. Several times during my interviews I asked questions or commented and the trainer responded, "Oh! I'm glad you noticed that. I meant to say something about that, but forgot."

As you gain experience handling your own dog, you will unconsciously develop "moves" and perspective, even easily observable techniques, which will make the dog uniquely your own. Your dog will adjust and adapt to this body language or telepathy. But if you send your dog to a professional trainer, visit this trainer, observe closely what he does, have him write down the commands he uses for later reference. Ask questions. It will make the transition from a trainer's accomplishment to your personal pride quicker and easier on the dog.

A specific example of "body language" can be observed when getting a dog to retrieve cleanly to hand. A sort of rule of thumb is to turn away from the dog in training as he approaches you if you expect him to bring the object to you promptly and cheerfully. Staring at the dog or moving toward him is interpreted as a threat by the dog. If such apprehension isn't atavistic it certainly is learned, and reinforced, by a handler's attitude when he metes out punishment. A trainer going to a dog to punish him is really concentrating, zeroing in on that dog. Eventually any approach or stare cautions the dog and worries him.

Even after a dog is fully trained to retrieve and is completely reliable, he may be reluctant to come in with a bird and meet the handler head-on. He will circle and come up from behind or from the side. You may also note that it is the rare kennel dog that will leave or enter his kennel gate crossing in front of you. He will try to pass behind you. (House dogs, constantly around people, are different. Most of them would let you fall over them before they'd get up and move out of your path. It's as if they expect you to apologize for disturbing *them*, so confident are they about their position in the pecking order.)

I believe this trait is a combination of age-old instinct and training procedures, since experience with wolves and other wild animals indicates that most predators prefer to approach anything questionable or strange from the side or back. A sharp handler will modify this trait in order to make a showy delivery by having the incoming dog do a half-loop around him as he makes a hand gesture.

Some people would be stunned if they were told the circling dog actually wants to get rid of his burden as soon as he can and he's trying to figure out the easiest way to do it, or has been intimidated by his handler and is reluctant to come in. A field trial judge impressed by the swing around and sit to deliver might better credit the handler with superb showmanship than to give a dog performing in this manner an edge over one approaching directly or obliquely and matter of factly handing over the bird while still standing.

232

In making a retrieve, dogs prefer to approach their handlers from behind or the side as this Labrador is doing during a National Amateur Championship stake.

The terms "trainer" and "handler" are often used interchangeably, probably because most pros and many amateurs train and handle dogs. But they aren't the same, and in today's age of specialization I wouldn't be surprised to see the recognition of separate categories.

Some people are good at both training and handling. Others are fine trainers, but mediocre or poor handlers; and some excellent handlers, of choice or necessity, leave most of the introductory and basic training to others.

Like a dog in competition, a handler must be a showman. He often has to think quickly to show his dog to best advantage or to minimize a fault or convert a possible disaster into a plus performance. Not many people have this flair.

A trainer, on the other hand, will have time to think things over but must be doggedly persistent in getting a dog to do his bidding and be able to analyze a dog's personality, anticipate what it may lead him to do, and devise and carry out the means to get the job done. Good trainers may be more numerous than good handlers. But top trainers are just as rare as top handlers. A few talented men and women are both.

The handler is comparable to the attorney who pleads or prosecutes his case before judge, jury, and the public. The trainer is the behind-the-scenes lawyer who lays the groundwork by a foresighted and meticulous preparation of the brief of argument. This applies to all types and breeds of dogs, not just retrievers.

PART 4

Once a merry little gun dog, the Cocker spaniel has become virtually a nonentity in North American covers. Sportsmen largely abandoned them following World War II after the breed had peaked in popularity as a pet and show specimen and it was difficult to obtain Cockers of field stock. The breed's decline was steady from then on.

The last National Championship field trial for Cockers was held in Missouri in 1960. Cockers may still compete in spaniel trials in Canada, but must run in the same trials as the larger, more popular Springers.

Cocker and Springer spaniels, until about World War I, were often whelped in the same litters. Pups were simply sorted out according to size, the large ones classed as Springers, the smaller as Cockers. As a youth my first "purebred hunting dog" was an English cocker. He was an excellent dog, hunting well on ruffed grouse, woodcock, pheasant, duck, squirrel, and rabbit until he died in his twelfth year. I have seen and hunted over other good Cockers and was fortunate enough to have observed and reported on the last Cocker National Championship for *Outdoor Life* magazine. As a professional trainer, in the early 1970s I had a litter of working Cocker pups turned over to me for evaluation and training. Their natural qualities impressed me greatly and I am convinced of their suitability as woodcock and ruffed grouse dogs in the United States.

While good working Cocker spaniels have much to recommend them, readers should be aware that pups bred from proven field stock are difficult to obtain in the United States. Fifteen years ago there was a small pool of field-bred stock maintained by such enthusiasts as the late Henry Berol and the Peter Garvins in the East. The late Clark Gable owned a fine golden-colored Cocker I saw in the last national event held. But today, acquiring a good Cocker would be mostly a matter of luck in getting a pup or dog of latent ability that happened to inherit the right genetic makeup or importing one from the British Isles.

Early training and development of Springer spaniels, as noted by the experts, has a decided appeal for sportsmen. It means they don't have to waste any time after acquiring a pup. As a practical matter, while far from being "well-broke," when properly introduced to such things as gunfire and cover and given a taste of actual hunting, very frequently Springers can be expected to produce game for the gun from the age of six months on. Some hunters do very little training beyond that, their spaniels learning by doing, and accept some unmannerly performances as long as they can shoot birds. Others, proud to display disciplined and proper dog work, add whatever refinements they think necessary by formal training both in and out of season. The choice is the owner's.

During his brief center-stage appearance in each act (series) of a field trial, the competition spaniel must make the most of his time in impressing a judge with his desire to find game and the speed and accuracy of location, both to flush and fetch. Hence the emphasis on speed, drive, and style that must be displayed along with the niceties of complete obedience if a dog is to show creditably in a trial.

Hunters may accept a great deal less. Some even prefer a careful, almost plodding type spaniel or one that is hesitant or actually points before flushing. But the greater degree of animation a spaniel displays, the more pleasure he is to gun over. Veteran spaniels learn to pace themselves and may trot during the long lulls that occur in the field between one bird and the next. But the good ones step up the tempo upon encountering scent, and even if the trotters do not break into sweeping gallops as they push the bird, the increased tail activity and obvious excitement of the dog are the tip-off for a hunter to move up as close to his dog as he can get and be ready to swing on a hard-flushed bird.

While the hunting spaniel and the trial spaniel may be marching to the beat of different drummers, that doesn't mean the hunting dog must lack the animation, the hustle and bustle of eagerness that sparks a sportsman's interest and provides exciting and better work.

Aside from puppy competition, there are two important stakes offered in Springer spaniel field trial competition, open and amateur. Dogs may be handled by either professional or amateur trainers in open stakes, but only amateurs may blow the whistle over dogs in the amateur stakes.

There are no restrictions regarding who trains the dogs competing in either stake. The amateur is an amateur-handled event, not an amateur *trained* and handled affair. Some competent types go the whole route with their dogs, although frequently training in concert with a professional. But most field trial spaniels get at least some schooling from a pro and their owner–handlers get some practice and instruction under professional guidance before embarking on trial competition.

That amateur competition is extremely keen in Springer trials is well documented by the fact that in recent years amateurs have crowded the pros out of the winning circle in the National Open event and a special National Championship for amateur-handled dogs has been a regular event since 1963.

The successful amateur trainer–handler rides his hobby hard, to virtual exclusion of all other pastimes, and for interested sportsmen there is solid satisfaction in competing in a dog sport allied to hunting in which the dog is asked to do everything a fine hunting dog must do, only better.

"Loose-heeling" is more the order of the day in spaniel work than the "tight-heeling" customarily taught retrievers. The former keeps the dog under control walking in close proximity to the handlers; the latter has the dog virtually glued to the handler's leg as they walk along, very much like the heeling demanded in obedience work. There are advantages and disadvantages to both types, with tight-heeling preferred if a dog accompanies his master off-leash when pedestrian and motor traffic is present (a risky practice) or perhaps when spaniels are to be used as nonslip retrievers for dove and duck or as pickup dogs behind pointers of upland game.

But the main thing is control, and as long as a dog does not wander off or have to be spoken to constantly to keep him close, as a practical matter afield the somewhat casual loose-heeling keeps a dog out from underfoot and seems less likely to inhibit a spaniel's game-seeking desire.

While it's unlikely that 90 percent of the hunters who train their own spaniels overdo it, the experts' warning that trainers should lean toward underdoing rather than attempting to exert too much pressure should be well taken. As in a crap game, it pays to get out while you're ahead.

Overtraining does occur. Every now and then I receive a letter from some *Outdoor Life* reader whose dog was coming along brilliantly but suddenly quit or retrogressed. With the training schedule he follows he can't understand what's happened. He then proceeds to describe a program of training sessions that would gag a maggot.

Whether your puppy is coming slow or fast, use some judgment. The slow dog will simply take longer, cramming is too much for him and he'll learn nothing. And with even the most eager and precocious youngster there is a limit to the training pressure he can withstand before he decides, "Hell, whatever made me think this is fun?" and he sours. With the older dog, brush-up sessions are fine, but make them infrequent and brief or move on to teaching something new. Like veteran athletes, experienced dogs that have learned their trade are often less than enchanted with training sessions.

If your dog does sour, lay him up for a week. Don't do any training and pay him only minimum attention. When you start up with him again, he'll be eager and willing. Then keep your foot off the throttle and make the sessions short and snappy.

Rabbit pens, as noted, are used extensively by British trainers to introduce their spaniels to game and sort out their pups according to the keenness and cleverness they display when left to their own devices in an enclosure containing bunnies. While it seems unlikely that many U.S. sportsmen would find this method of training possible, hunters are missing out if they refuse to consider a Springer as a rabbit dog as well as an upland game bird and waterfowl dog.

Properly trained spaniels, or those allowed to follow their natural inclinations, can be both fur and feather dogs. For the man who likes to hunt a bit of everything and finds himself in a locale where he may encounter several species of game during a day's hunt, a Springer is unbeatable when it comes to versatility. In central Wisconsin, on one memorable day, I took ruffed grouse, woodcock, pheasant, Hungarian partridge, teal, wood duck, jacksnipe, rabbit, and squirrel over one English springer spaniel.

In the United Kingdom, spaniels are expected to produce and retrieve any kind of game encountered. In fact, until a combination of myxomatosis, which wiped out England's rabbit population, and American field trialers clamoring for and paying high prices for English-bred Springers occurred in the 1950s, the Springer had been generally thought of by English sportsmen as a rabbit dog.

Repetition and persistence are keys to obtaining a decently trained hunting dog. Repeat, Repeat, Repeat until the dog gets it. Rome wasn't built in a day and few dogs learn even a single step of their training in one session. Even if a man is hung up on dogs, there are times when this becomes nothing but plain work.

That is the most probable cause for a sportsman sending his dog to a professional for training. As I've told many a client, "There's very little I'm going to do with your dog that you couldn't do yourself or figure out how to do. The general rules for dog training are no deep, dark secret. But you are paying me for doing with your dog what you could be doing if you'd take the time."

If you cannot afford the time or if training is nothing but a chore, send your dog to a professional or buy a trained dog from him if you want to enjoy good hunting. But you can do it yourself. No matter how tedious some repetitive sessions can get, the reward is great when "the light goes on" and your dog grasps what you've been trying to get across to him.

Just as differences in game, climate, cover, and terrain have an effect on styles of hunting, which may dictate variances in training procedures for dogs used in various parts of the United States, it's inevitable that general attitudes toward good dog work and what's wanted of a dog will diverge from country to country. For this reason, I thought it would be valuable to include a rundown on spaniel hunting methods as practiced in Great Britain.

In England, hunting refers to fox hunting, horses, red coats, protocol, and all the trimmings. Shooting refers to the gunning of birds driven over stands by beaters. What we refer to as "hunting" in the United States (following a dog afield and shooting flushed game) is called "rough shooting" in England.

English-trained spaniels must learn to abandon a line of scent either on their own or when ordered to and retain a pattern that thoroughly covers their "beat." There are two reasons for this.

Spaniels may be worked either on rough shoots or as an aid in driven bird shooting. When used as a rough-shooting dog, because there is an abundance of some variety of game on keepered estates, there is no great concern with trying to produce a head of game from each scent line a dog may strike and an abundance of different scents is often difficult to sort out and will distract or suck a dog out of his ground-covering pattern.

When used on "shoot days" spaniels may be utilized in place of or as an assist to human beaters moving large numbers of pheasant or partridge ahead of them until they reach a flushing point where they take wing and fly hard and high over the waiting guns stationed at their stands. When used as beaters the dogs do not retrieve. This is left to pickup dogs, used in the manner of nonslip retrievers, in the vicinity of the guns. The beating dog's job is to more or less herd the birds along, not to drive in and flush or to go kiting off after individual birds. Thus, it is imperative that British spaniels ignore lines, or abandon them when tempted, so that the shoot may proceed in orderly fashion.

In contrast, when a U.S. spaniel strikes a scent line he is encouraged and expected to take it until he produces the bird. If he starts "lining out" and gets out of gun range, he should be taught to stop and wait until the hunter can close the gap. And excited U.S. hunters move up at a pace that would dismay a Britisher and be a cause for consternation about bad form.

In the United States, except for preserve shooting (where stocked game is generally of one species during a hunt), sportsmen seldom encounter either an abundance or variety of game in any given cover. Because the bird a dog has winded may be the only head of game seen for a long period of time, perhaps the only legal bird in a day, the only rule or protocol most hunters adhere to is "get the bird." If hunting with an unbroke dog or one that comes unstuck, even sprinting may be resorted to in order to get close enough for a shot.

Britishers frown on a dog frequently throwing his head in the air and homing in on body scent, leaving a hole or uncovered spot of cover that would have been investigated had the head been kept low and a pattern maintained, while Americans are in favor of a shortcut if it will quickly produce that hard-to-come-by bird.

The manner of flushing is another bone of contention. U.S. hunters (and field trialers because a desired style in hunting is reflected in the competitive events in each country) prize a hard-driving flush and thrill to a dog leaping into the air after the bird, trying his damndest to catch it before dropping in a sitting position and holding until sent to retrieve. (Or, if not properly broke or forgetful of his manners, breaking and chasing. In England the term for breaking is called "running in.") If a bird doesn't get out of there as the dog drives in, U.S. hunters expect and approve of their dogs catching the sticky bird and brag about not having to fire a shot.

British spaniel men do not want their dogs collecting unshot birds. They are out to shoot and the dog's job is to provide shooting, not catch birds. So English trained dogs will work until they literally nose a sluggish bird out of the nest, refraining from grabbing anything that doesn't have blood scent on it. Dogs "pegging" (catching) unshot birds are dropped from further competition in a British trial. This demand can result in "soft flushes," which are anathema to U.S. trialers.

When a bird is shot, the dog that accurately marks the fall or follows the flight line and makes his retrieve without assistance from his handler is most highly prized by Americans. Because of thicker cover and the fact that rabbits and hares are as likely to be shot as flying birds, affording little marking opportunity, Britishers fully expect that they will have to handle a rough-shooting or trials dog on a retrieve and don't penalize for it. Thus, while a proper Englishman may be too polite to express his adverse opinion of what appear to be the wild, unmanageable, overexuberant, virtual outlaws American hunters put up with, he is likely to think it.

A less-inhibited U.S. sportsman may be unable to restrain himself from voicing his distaste for what he sees as a too mechanical, overly dependent dog that fiddles around trying to flush. Yet varied conditions and traditions, or lack of them, dictate that what is lauded by one man as a delicious stew may be rejected by another as inedible slop. The fortunate thing is that in Springer spaniels reasonable people have been able to view both sides of the coin from both sides of the ocean, for their personal and financial betterment, while developing a dog breed most suitable for hunters who can keep only one dog that will satisfy a variety of wants.

Spaniel breeders and trainers in the United States have recognized that Britain has something to offer and for more than twenty years have been importing heavily. As a result a majority of the U.S. trial winners in recent years, if not bred in Britain, have had English imports close up in their pedigrees. While most of our good hunting stock is American bred, top trial dogs have made important contributions to it. The result is that many of the best of our gun dogs are only a generation or two removed from some English estate.

U.S. importers brought over dogs that were intelligent and biddable enough to adapt to U.S. standards during retraining periods or at least produce highly trainable offspring with great natural ability that could be started from scratch to perform the way it's done in the United States.

Furthermore, some Britishers have found the financial rewards great enough to direct their breeding and training operations toward developing "Yankee dogs," catering to overseas demand without regard for what tradition-bound countrymen consider best in a proper English spaniel.

The unfortunate thing is that, because of Great Britain's strict quarantine laws, the traffic in dogs has all been one way. Americans have had no opportunity to demonstrate they can breed and train dogs that can win trials or hunt properly according to British standards. Exporting dogs from England is just a matter of money. Importing them is virtually impossible because of lengthy quarantine time designed to keep Britain free of rabies.

Depending upon his needs and his training approach, the U.S. hunter who trains his own dog can have it either way. There are good reasons for most hunters preferring a hard-flushing, sharp-marking, catch-it-if-I-can spaniel. But if you are organizing a pheasant drive in a South Dakota, Iowa, or Nebraska cornfield, consider how useful a well-controlled dog would be that could herd birds down to the end of the rows where your standers are stationed.

To each his own. There's plenty of room for tolerance and willingness to let each man enjoy his particular cup of tea—and his particular type of dog.

Epilogue

One question frequently asked me as a professional trainer and as hunting dogs editor of *Outdoor Life* magazine involves what a sportsman can expect, at what age, from his gun dog.

There is no pat answer. But I believe an accurate estimate can be made if you compare what would be expected in the line of learning, performance, endurance, and know-how from an infant, a child, a teen-ager, a young adult, a mature adult, and an older adult.

This of course requires a comparison between relative ages of dogs and people and the recognition of individual variances and exceptions. I was never satisfied with the old formula of one year of a dog's life being the equivalent to seven years of a human's life, except as it pertains to what might be called the prime years, three to six in a canine and twenty-five to forty in a human. So much more is expected of a one-year-old dog than of a seven-year-old boy, and so on. So I came up with my own formula that has helped me to gauge expectations and to understand problems a dog may face.

This comparison has been widely published, and as far as I know hasn't been challenged or even quibbled over; it's offered here as an aid in understanding and training your gun dog. You would not expect the same response and performance from your five-year-old grandson, your thirty-year-old son, yourself, or your seventy-five-year-old father. Treat your young, mature, or aging gun dog with the same consideration and respect.

INFANCY

Dog	Man
Birth to 7 weeks	Birth to 1½ years

CHILDHOOD

2 months	2 to 3 years
4 months	5 to 7 years
6 months	9 to 10 years
8 months	11 to 12 years

ADOLESCENCE

10 months	13 to 14 years
1 year	15 to 16 years

MATURITY

2 years	21 years
3 years	25 years
4 years	30 years
5 years	35 years
6 years	40 years
7 years	45 years
8 years	50 years
9 years	55 years
10 years	60 years

OLD AGE

11 years	65 years
12 years	70 years
13 years	80 years
14 years	90 years
15 years	100 plus years

Another frequent question I get from both young and old in correspondence with *Outdoor Life* readers is "How can I get to be a professional dog trainer?"

Many men and women become professional dog trainers by happenstance of birth—their fathers trained dogs either as pros for others or as hunters for their own pleasure. Others start out without the advantage of a dog-training family background but have such a deep and abiding interest in hunting with dogs that they switch jobs and careers, perhaps gradually merging a favorite hobby into a full-time business.

For a start, of course, a person should have successfully trained some of his own dogs, and done well enough so that friends or other hunters might want him to train dogs for them. But there is really only one way to become an experienced dog trainer: serve an apprenticeship under an established professional trainer.

There is no shortcut that's shorter, and there is no easy road to "big money" in the dog-training game. And sometimes for those starting out as kennel help and assistants the discouraging times far outnumber anything approaching great moments. Some trainers will not share "secrets" or are unable to train trainers as well as they can train dogs. Others will be helpful and good teachers. But it will be up to the trainee to keep his eyes open, absorb techniques, and request answers to questions that puzzle him. And every trainer expects his helpers to put in the same long hours he does, do a good job with even menial tasks, and accept low wages.

More than one or two factors, like willingness to work hard, knowledge of dogs, and ability to deal with people, mark a professional. Real pros are ever on the alert for opportunities to utilize their craft to provide income that will tide them over when things don't break right or the purses are slim, when old customers aren't in the market and new ones haven't appeared.

And pros who do not get along with other pros seldom do well or last long in the dog game, despite a natural and understandable rivalry that exists. In the field a pro does his best to beat a rival handler fairly, letting the performance of his dogs and his handling acuity bring him customers rather than boosting his own stock and downgrading the ability and techniques of other trainers in back-of-the-barn and cocktail-hour tête-à-têtes.

As a result, in training and competition honest pros, with or without asking, get help from other pros who may find another man's dog on point, exchange scouting duties with him, take over the handling of a dog that shows up while his handler is off looking for him, and so on. It is a strange and unique occupation, each man a fiercely competitive and independent individual, yet dependent upon the good will of his fellow competitors.

An occasional son of a bitch survives—who connives with an owner to take a winning dog away from the man who trained him, deliberately rides off another handler's dog, fails to share a purse for services rendered by another handler, and is dishonest or nasty in dealing with owners—but for the most part, rough-hewn as they may be, pro dog trainers are basically honorable and responsible gentlemen. Thus, in the dog game as in all sports or ways of life, it is a pleasure to do business with a pro. Aspiring professional dog trainers will do well to bear this in mind.

You have now completed a symposium, round-table discussion, bull session, whatever you wish to call it, with ten of the top gun dog and field trial trainers who make their professional services available to the public. I've enjoyed the role of moderator.

It might be termed a crash course in gun dog psychology, successful trainer philosophy, and proven training techniques. It will do your dog very little good, however, if you are content to be an armchair expert, entertaining half-snozzled business and social peers with your newly acquired expertise in a field in which they are unversed or restrict yourself to counseling hunting buddies who are having trouble training their dogs.

The purpose of this book was to enlighten you so you can do something for your dog, with your dog, to your dog—to ensure that he does his utmost in making you a better hunter. Any man who spends the time, effort, and money to own and train a useful gun dog just automatically becomes a nicer guy and a sportsman several cuts above the average.

Those of us who contributed to this book can hope you will put into practice the information and help we've tried to pass on to you. That will serve as a living and continuing monument to all men who have trained their own dogs and those of others well and enjoyed doing it.

There is much more to be learned of training and hunting with gun dogs than appears in the printed word between the covers of this book. Such knowledge is best acquired by doing.

I only hope the reading of this completed work affects you the way putting it together stimulated me. During the two years it was in the making, the travel, the interviewing, listening to the tapes, reading the copy, and assembling things in a logical and readable order, I frequently found myself seized by an urge to get out and do something with one or more of my dogs—try a different approach, a new idea, a reasonable suggestion—or something long buried and virtually forgotten in the recesses of my mind was joggled. There is something about discussing gun dogs that triggers a desire to try it, see if it works, use it, and enjoy it—and then talk about it over a thirst-quenching beer or an ache-relieving Bourbon at the end of a hunting day while a pair of worn-out dogs snore contentedly at your feet.

So whether "old hand" or explorer of the wonderful realm of hunting with a well-trained gun dog, let's hope this book has grabbed you in the same way. Good luck, and may your hours and days in the hunting field be long and rewarding. But above all, good gun dog work to you.

Index

Studnicki, Steve, 165

T

Temperament, *see* specific dog, Traits
Tracking, 227–28
Trained dog, *see* specific dog
Trainer, 233–34, 243–44
Traits, *see* specific dog
"Two-in-one" dog, *see* specific dog

U

Utility Field NAVHDA test, 222–23

V

Versatiles
  age for training, 69–70, 71, 77, 223,
    230–31, 242–43
  amateur training, 70, 84, 85, 232,
    233, 237
  backing, 84
  biddable dog, 72–73
  and birds, 78–79
  close-working dog, 77–78
  commands, 72–74, 75–77, 82, 83, 84,
    85, 224, 226, 227
  Continental breeds, 222
  covey dog, 78
  faults, 84–85
  field-trial dog, 68, 222, 232
  flushing, 84, 226–27
  force-training, 79–84
  gunfire, 79, 85, 226
  heeling, 74, 75
  holding, 74–75
  house dog, 69, 86
  hunting dog, 225–29
  hunting to the limits, 77

  NAVHDA tests, 222–28
  pointing, 70, 78–79, 225–27
  praise, 79, 80–82, 85, 225, 228
  punishment, 72, 73, 75, 76, 77, 78,
    83, 85–86, 229–30
  puppy, 70, 71, 224, 225
  range, 72, 77–78
  reasons for training, 68–69, 222
  retrieving, 79–84, 232, 233
  singles dog, 78
  started dog, 70, 71
  staunching, 78–79, 84
  tracking, 227–28
  trained dog, 70–71
  training suggestions, 72, 84–85, 237
  traits, 69, 77–79, 85
  in water, 224
  wing and shot, 84
  yard training, 72, 77, 230

W

Wallace, Cliff, 165
Water dogs, *see* specific dog
Weimaraner, 68, 222
Whistle signals, 72–73, 75–76, 128,
    130, 136, 137–38, 139–42, 172,
    179, 186, 194, 196, 201–202, 203,
    204, 205–206, 209, 213
Wilson, Jack, 105
Wing and shot, 25, 28, 54–57, 84,
    138–39
Winterhelt, Sigbot (Bodo), 68, 223
Wolves, 90
Wylie, Jimmy, 215

Y

Yard-training dog, *see* specific dog